The Cronulla Riots

The Inside Story

Carl Scully and Mark Goodwin

Connor Court Publishing

Published in 2024 by Connor Court Publishing Pty Ltd.

Copyright © Carl Scully and Mark Goodwin

All rights reserved. Not to be reproduced without the permission of the Copyright holders.

Connor Court Publishing Pty Ltd.
PO Box 7257
Redland Bay QLD 4165
sales@connorcourt.com
www.connorcourt.com

ISBN: 9781923224360

Cover Design by Maria-Grazia Giordano

Front Cover photo: Gary Ramage / Newspix, used with permission.

Back Cover Photo: 'Muslim lifesavers' by John Veage, photographer, used with permission.

Printed in Australia.

Whilst the full title and name of both writers at the time these events occurred were respectively, Assistant Commissioner Mark Goodwin and Minister for Police Carl Scully, they will be mostly referred to as simply Goodwin and Scully.

Additionally, where appropriate, we use descriptor words such as Caucasian, European, Muslim, and Lebanese, and where appropriate, we have used the slang versions of these such as 'Aussies', 'Skips' or 'Lebs'. No disparagement is intended in the use of these slang terms which were universally used at the time.

CONTENTS

PART 1: BACKGROUND 1
Preface 2
1 Introduction 4
    What were the Cronulla Riots? 5
    Our approach 6
    It was mostly men 7
    It wasn't racism 7
    It was differenceism not racism 8
    Structure of the book 8

2 The Clash of the Suburbs: Cronulla vs Lakemba 10
    Background 10
    Cronulla 11
    Lakemba 12
    What does the Census of 2006 tell us? 13
    The 2006 Census 13

PART 2: POLICING THE RIOT 19
3 The Build up to Riot: 'Skips' v 'Lebs' 20
    The lure of the beach 20
    The arrival of the Arabic 'other' 20
    Violence in the lead-up to riot 22
    The assault on the Lifeguards 22
    Enormous media reaction 23
    Police plan ahead 24
    The 2nd assault 24
    The few days before a riot 25
    The police prepare in advance 25

4 The Fateful Day — 27
- The morning — 27
- The gathering warms up — 28
- Enter Glen Steele: rioter or patriot? — 29
- An afternoon of racist violence — 31
- Further incidents — 32
- Enter the evening news — 33
- The 'revenge attacks' begin — 34

5 The 'Revenge Attacks' — 35
- Why is it just Cronulla? — 35
- Reporting the riot unleashes revenge — 36
- Cronulla explodes — 37
- First signs — 38
- The Maroubra dare — 39
- Riot Police on the move — 41
- The following day – Monday 12th December 2005 — 46
- Battle lines drawn: Maroubra Beach v the Lakemba Mosque — 47
- Evening of 12th December 2005 — 50
- The police response in perspective — 53
- Police operations continue – 13th to 16th December 2005 — 55
- Special sitting of the NSW Parliament — 60
- Police operations Sat 17th – Sun 18th December 2005 — 63
- The personal cost — 65
- Police operations the following six weeks – Operation 'Seta' — 65

6 Police pursue the offenders — 67
- Introduction — 67
- The results — 67
- Allegations police had "Gone soft on Middle Eastern crime" — 69

PART 3: INVESTIGATING THE POLICE   73

7 Investigating the Police   74
   The removal of Supt. Bray   74
   Goodwin gets as much notice as Bray   80
   Goodwin left to explain why he was being investigated   80

8 Challenges from the outset   81
   An assistant commissioner investigating an assistant commissioner   81
   Norm Hazzard appointed by Commissioner Moroney   81
   Strike Force Neil begins   87
   The 'investigation' proceeds   88

9 The 'Investigation': Beginning at the End   89
   'Strike Force' Neil: setting the end at the beginning   89
   'Cronulla Riot' Commander's 1st meeting with Hazzard   90
   The second and last meeting between Goodwin and Hazzard   91
   Creating an existing commanders course   92
   The work of Sydney Region command continued   93

10 Moroney releases a "*Draft*" report   94
   A draft is a draft   94
   The delay queried by the minister   95
   Hazzard in the media   102
   Moroney says 'It's unfinished'   105
   Iemma and Moroney release the 'unfinished' report   106
   A ministerial career comes to an end   108
   A police commander's career comes to an end   109
   The Police Ministry and ALP perspective   111

11 The Strike Force Neil Report — 112
- Risk assessment — 113
- Planning — 118
- Location of the Command Post — 121
- The Sydney Operations Centre — 123
- Command structure — 125
- Police left without command direction — 135
- Major Incident Response Team (MIRT) — 138
- Missed opportunities — 140
- Conclusion — 143

12 Operation Pendennis: CTC a Role Model — 145
- Operation Pendennis — 145
- The Pendennis Report — 148
- Commissioner's commendations for Pendennis but not Cronulla! — 150

PART 4: REFLECTIONS FROM THE FIELD — 151

13 Interviews: MPs, Police and Community Leaders — 152
- Background and the questions — 152
- Methodology and broader findings — 155

14 What Caused the Conflict? — 157
- Theme 1: It wasn't racism — 157
- Theme 2: If not racist, then what? — 161
- Theme 3: East meets West — 170

15 Broader Perspectives — 176
- Theme 4: The media amplified it — 176
- Theme 5: 'That's not a riot' — 180
- Theme 6: Containing the rage of revenge — 182
- Theme 7: Law enforcement — 189

16 Scapegoats of the Riots — 196
    Theme 8: Scapegoats of the riots — 196
    Craig Campbell — 196
    John Richardson — 199
    Lost Learnings — 207
    Ron Mason — 208
    Discussion — 212

PART 5: EXPLAINING THE RIOT — 214

17 Was it Really a Riot? — 215
    What is a riot? — 216
    Compared to Cronulla — 221
    Our own history of riots — 223
    The Los Angeles Riots 1992 — 226
    The Macquarie Fields Riot 2005 — 227
    Back to Cronulla — 228

18 Did the media cause the riots? — 232
    The visual image of the Cronulla Riots — 232
    What is the 'media'? — 235
    The 'media' did it! Really? — 236
    The TV footage — 237
    Mass text messaging — 240
    The Daily Telegraph — 246
    Was Alan Jones to blame? — 248
    Did the Media do it? — 253

19 Was it motivated by racism? — 254
    What is race? — 255
    What is racism? — 256
    What is bigotry? — 257

What is Islamophobia?	257
No races but plenty of racism	258
The myth and reality of racism at Cronulla	259
Reverse racism	262
Racist denialism and forgetfulness	265
The downtrodden Shire	267
A Muslim woman's view	268

20 Why Did it Happen? — 269

Making sense of it all	269
Belonging	270
Firstly, grew where?	271
Secondly, restricting movement for whom?	272
Thirdly, who and what is the 'other'?	273

21 Tribalism and Identity: Belonging and Otherness — 275

What is tribalism?	275
Tribalism and identity	276
Tribalism rules	278

22 Difference-ism not race-ism — 280

Tribalism and difference	280
The superficial approach: disparage, do not analyse	281
Difference-ists not race-ists	282
Intolerant to difference not just intolerant	283
The authoritarian dynamic	284
What was the 'threat' to sameness at Cronulla Beach?	285
Threats to our wish for sameness	286
Multicultural conviviality vs intolerance to difference	288
Labelling the 'racists'	290

23 A Threat emerges: Incivility on the beach   292

    Civility and incivility   292

    Why be rude?   293

    What is respect?   294

    The beach: there to share   296

    The Cronulla local perspective   296

    Bad manners   298

    Enforced togetherness: How we are meant to behave   299

    Our learned and ingrained habits: 'habitus'   299

    Police inattention of the Other: How civil society works   300

    Clashing behavioural codes: conflicting habitus   302

24 Claiming Territory: "It's our Beach!"   304

    Spatialising tribalism   304

    Localism, masculine bonding, and spatial claim   305

    Claiming the beach   307

    The "us" excluding the "them" from the beach and the flag   308

25 Claiming the Aussie Identity: "It's our Flag"   309

    Only 'Aussies' welcome!   309

    The United States   311

    China   312

    Australianness   314

    What is it to be an 'Australian' or 'un-Australian'?   315

    Nationalism versus patriotism   317

26 Why was it Mostly Men?   320

    Statistics   322

    The actual arrest numbers at Cronulla   323

    Aggression and violence at Cronulla   327

    Still mostly men   328

27 Why was it Mostly Lebanese Muslim Men? 329
   The Lebanese concession 329
   Not a Lebanese enclave 330
   The greater preponderance for crime and violence 332
   Transposing the Lebanese village 332
   Drawing on the least qualified 333
   Lebanese Muslim gangs 336

28 Conclusion 338
   Implications of this book 338
   An unexpected outcome 339
   It wasn't just Cronulla: Redefining place 339
   A 'riot' 342
   It wasn't racially inspired 341
   Media influence 342
   Police performance 343
   Recognising those who matter 344
   Recommendations 348

About the Authors 348

PART 1: BACKGROUND

Preface

"It may not have been racially inspired but it was racially hijacked…in order to put a badge on it".[1]

Why write about the Cronulla Riots all these years after the event?

It is now a long time ago, yet whenever 'racism' is on the agenda of Australian media, Cronulla always comes to the fore in debate as the alleged Anglo, Caucasian, white-supremacist enclave of Sydney. A lot has been discussed in that time by scholars, the general media and talkback radio hosts. However, little of that material, subjective comment or even more informed reflection, drew on the thoughts and actions of the two leaders given the unenviable task of quelling the riots and restoring order and peace to the streets of Sydney: NSW Police Minister, Carl Scully and Police Commander, Assistant Commissioner Mark Goodwin. This is primarily their story from their unique perspectives, of what happened and why, and what they needed to do at the time to bring 'the troubles' to an end.

The riots had a big impact on the psyche of the city and demonstrated both the worst of human nature and the best of law enforcement. Despite the extraordinary efforts of the police command, control and operations in restoring peace and calm to the streets, suburbs and beaches of Sydney, the subsequent report of the 'investigation' into that performance unnecessarily contributed to a sudden unplanned end to both the Minister's and Commander's careers. To ensure a proper and accurate account was put on the record in relation to that police performance, and to provide an evidence based contra narrative to disputed issues set out in that report, have all been major motivating factors in writing this book.

---

[1] S. Stanton, Transcript of Interview, February 16, 2021.

Preface

However, on the journey in providing a behind the scenes view of the riots as they unfolded, the authors reflected upon, and then strongly challenged the notion that the riots were driven, if not solely caused, by Caucasian xenophobia. In that sense, the above quotation from Lebanese Christian barrister Stephen Stanton, captures the essence of this explanation of the Cronulla riots. He was amongst the 12 people we interviewed as part of 'Reflections from the Field' set out in Part 4.

Outlining the case against a deeply held view that the riots were solely racially motivated, has been a rewarding experience for both authors, and hopefully provides a more accurate account of the real, as opposed to imagined, reasons for the confronting and at times menacing human behaviour which unfolded during late 2005 / early 2006.

It is hoped that in the end, this interpretation of these events provides to the reader a more satisfying and accurate account of how the riots were policed, why they occurred, and why they came and went so quickly, and thankfully, never to return.

1
Introduction

"...much of what we call racial intolerance is primarily about difference more than race".[2]

So much has been written and said about what happened at Cronulla and beyond during late 2005/early 2006, that a legitimate question to ask is, why more? Why now and what more needs to be said on it?

Our initial response to such questions is to say that almost all of what has been said has been from sideline observers in the press, the media, academics and the community. Almost nothing has been written from the perspective of the actual leaders and decision-makers in responding and dealing with what so unexpectedly unfolded all those years ago, until now.

We provide a perspective on these important events, not from an academic or journalistic point of view, but from a law enforcement leadership perspective by the two people charged with the task of restoring order and peace to the streets of Sydney: The minister for police and the police commander in charge. This alone provides originality and a unique addition to the Cronulla Riots narrative.

When history is written by non-participants, the account must by definition be secondary to the primary source of information, views and perspectives. We certainly do provide opinion and analysis as many commentators have done, but from the viewpoint of being the two leaders at the helm making the decisions, not from the vantage point of the reading room of an academic, the office of a print journalist, or the editorial cutting room floor of a TV

---

[2] K. Stenner. *The Authoritarian Dynamic,* Cambridge University Press, 2005, p. 276.

newsroom announcer.

As a result, we believe we have provided something new, and something of broader historical interest. We are confident that we have also added new information to the record, a new consideration of the causes and contributing factors, and why the events having occurred, have not returned to the suburbs, streets and beaches of Sydney.

This is enough for the book to matter, and for it to be of interest to the general public, current and former police officers, historians, academic, journalistic and social commentators. However, let them be the judges of that.

What were the Cronulla Riots?

For those who were too young, or not living in Sydney at the time, a brief outline of the events misnamed, in our view, as the 'Cronulla riots', is appropriate. By late 2005 there had been years of simmering tensions at Cronulla Beach, between the local surfer and beach going community, with that of visiting young male Lebanese Muslims. These tensions were often around incivility and disrespect of young women, and how locals and visitors alike sometimes found it challenging to interact with one another on and around the beach in a civil and culturally respectful way. There were varying reasons for this cultural clash.

Firstly, the conflict was often at the mildly irritating level when 'visiting' amateur soccer players would ignore the convention of how 'local' families would spread out on the beach and enjoy 'their' space. In this respect, we call the developing tension as literally, 'The Towel versus the Soccer Ball', as different cultural mores on how to use the beach manifested. One set of cultural practices were not wrong, just different compared to the other.

Secondly, far less civil and far more confronting, were the many disrespectful and misogynistic encounters between some Lebanese men congregating in number at the Cronulla Beach car park, as they articulated their sexualised thoughts to local bikini clad women and teenage girls, whenever they happened to walk past them. This would occur as these women walked to and from the beach via the boardwalk, whilst using the outdoor shower at the top of the boardwalk, or just walking along the concrete esplanade along the beach. Not surprisingly, these encounters fuelled resentment among locals.

Thirdly, in amongst this simmering tension, on Sunday the 4th of December 2005, two local volunteer lifeguards stepped up to defend some local women, an altercation pursued, and the lifeguards were assaulted. Normally this assault would have quickly disappeared from the light of day, as yet another scuffle between the competing beach tribes in their struggle for spatial domain. But on this occasion, the attack on the lifeguards was magnified across talk back radio and the general media, as an attack by Lebanese Muslims on the very essence of what it meant to be Australian.

With literally tens of thousands of text messages and saturation media calling for a 'defence of the beach', unsurprisingly, a huge Caucasian demonstration of mostly young men, took place the following Sunday, the 11th of December 2005, in front of the North Cronulla Surf Club. This quickly descended into alcohol fuelled racist rants, and then a very unpleasant attack on two Arabic looking people on a train at Cronulla Railway station. As set out in in Chapter 5, days of 'revenge attacks' across Sydney from mobile convoys of angry young, mostly Lebanese Muslim men, quickly followed.

These were troubling times for Sydney which took over 2,000 police with emergency powers to aggressively restore order to the streets, suburbs and beaches of Sydney. This battle of the beach was widely reported then and in the years which followed, as a racial one driven by anti-Muslim sentiment. As you will see, this rather simplistic explanation, is a notion we contest.

Our approach

The starting point for our chronicle of these historical events was to draw upon the 2006 census and the Bureau of Crime Statistics for the time, which gave a fascinating comparison of the education levels, income, religion, language, place of birth and crime levels for both the southern and southwestern suburbs of Sydney forming the fulcrums of conflict: Sutherland Local Government Area –v- Canterbury/Bankstown Local Government Area, and Lakemba –v- Cronulla.

We also wanted to test the geographical, racialised and public disorder description and assumptions laden in the name 'The Cronulla Race Riots'. This involved a close consideration of where the events occurred, whether or not they were race related and whether they were intense enough to warrant the description as a 'riot'. In our view, these are important considerations

Introduction

as little challenge has been provided over the years to these descriptions.

Additionally, we analysed the role of the media in reporting or contributing to the riots. This is an important issue which we believe has not been given sufficient reflection over the last several years.

Protecting NSW citizens in the face of unrest, is a critical, if unenviable task of both a Minister for Police and the Police Commander charged with restoring order as soon as practicable. This book is a rare insight into the perspectives of the two people who held those positions and responsibilities.

Finally, rather than leave the record and narrative to the whims and views of two long retired public servants, we decided to test those views and perspectives against those of twelve senior community figures through a series of semi-structured face to face interviews. Semi-structured, in that there was a degree of consistency in the questions asked but not so constrained as to hamper what they may have wished to say. This allowed for comparison as well as a free flowing conversation. It was a very valuable process which illuminated perspectives other than our own. Our analysis of those interviews, set out in Part 4, is in a sense, a book within a book.

What follows are the key issues we canvass.

It was mostly men

Given the riot and revenge attacks were a mostly male affair, we thought it would be remiss of us if we didn't examine the possible reasons for why this may have been so. In doing so, we canvass in Chapter 26, various factors which have been explored by experts over a number of years, around such things as genetic inheritance as opposed to environment and upbringing (nature versus nurture), testosterone, alcohol consumption, notions of protecting honour and self-respect, and even a lack of early parental empathetic love.

It wasn't racism

We argue that the notion the Cronulla Riots was a solely racist event is a contestable one. As we 'peel away the onion layers' on the underlying causes of the sociological phenomena known as the 'Cronulla Riots', we come to conclusions which challenge its historical racial epithet.

Many people including well informed scholars, given the sheer volume and noise of an alternative view, will find this initially a challenge to accept, and that is understandable. We ask that the reader park that reaction until considering all that we have said on the matter. A racist tag is an easy one with which to besmirch a community, a place, or a major troubling event, and even harder to set aside, even if in our considered view, that is warranted.

The descriptor of these events of late 2005, have almost ubiquitously designated them as the 'Cronulla Race Riots'. All three of these emblematic depictions of location, cause, and type of event, are contested by our analysis of the facts, theory, and the views of those we interviewed. This may also challenge the preconceived views of some, given the length of time that the events on North Cronulla Beach have been classified as racist, that the tribal contest occurred wholly within Cronulla, and that it was actually a riot.

It was differenceism not racism

Undeniably there were many racist chants, slogans, tattoos and texts during the riot and revenge attacks of Sydney in late 2005. Our contention is that to conclude racist language as the defining point of determining that the whole event was racially motivated and little else, is unjustifiably cursory and superficial.

Being offended by what are demonstrably racialised motifs and messaging, ought not to justify an incurious approach to learning what might have been the real underlying motivation for expressing them, rather than asserting a description solely based on the simple fact of their expression. This will remain a challenge for many, including rather surprisingly, many scholars who chose not to dig a little sociologically deeper on the matter.

Structure of the book

We have split the book into five separate almost stand-alone sections:

Part 1 orients the reader by giving context and details regarding a cultural and statistical comparison of Cronulla and Lakemba.

Introduction

Part 2 covers a detailed description of the lead up, the 'main event' and the revenge attacks which followed.

Part 3 explores the sustainability of some of the findings of the Strike Force Neil investigation report into police performance during the riots, and provides an evidence based contra-narrative on a number of its aspects.

In **Part 4** we embark on perhaps some of the most interesting components of our research and narrative with the interviewing of MPs, senior police and Muslim community leaders at the time, about their own perspectives. This certainly provided some fascinating viewpoints into these events from a much wider lens than just our own. All these individuals provided valuable insights in addition to anything we have tried to provide, or what has been extensively recorded by academics and the media. This has given voice to a small but important group of people who are, or would have been, otherwise forgotten in Cronulla riots commentary.

And finally in **Part 5** we endeavour to provide a sociological explanation for what occurred, and a much deeper analysis and consideration of the events, than any provided to date by academic, media, or social commentators.

In providing an historical and sociological perspective of the so called 'Cronulla Riots', not from the vantage point of academic distance, or closer to home, as the journalistic voyeurs of the media, but as pivotal law enforcement leaders, we believe we have provided something of interest to police, journalists, scholars, and the wider community generally, and to the people of Cronulla and Lakemba in particular.

2

The Clash of the Suburbs: Cronulla vs Lakemba

Background

The unexpected and confronting events which took place around Cronulla and beyond in late 2005, then and now, are almost universally summed up with the nomenclature: 'The Cronulla Riots', or even more disparagingly for that suburb, 'The Cronulla Race Riots'! Like many sobriquets, it is our view, that both are neither wholly satisfactory nor entirely accurate.

We contest the notion that it was just located at Cronulla, that it was a riot on the day at Cronulla, or even that it was underpinned by racism. Challenging these concepts is an important part of our assessment of what really happened at the 'Cronulla Riots', however, in this chapter, we focus on the two suburbs at the centre of it all: Cronulla and Lakemba.

A very narrow view of these events of late 2005, would be to treat them solely as having unfolded on the sands of one of Sydney's iconic beaches, to protect an Anglo Celtic way of life from Lebanese hordes pouring out of the Lakemba Mosque, to claim the beach, and to respond to verbal and physical attack. But it is far more complicated than that!

A Christian Anglo-Celtic Cronulla and a Lebanese Muslim dominated Lakemba, were then and now, seen as being at the heart of a 'clash of cultures' in late 2005/early 2006 played out in violent fashion on our beaches, our streets and suburbs before police were able to fully restore order. It was, of course, always broader than just the two suburbs with Cronulla being but a part of the Anglo-Celtic Sutherland Shire, and Lakemba being but a part of the wider Lebanese diaspora across a large part of southwest Sydney. However, the beach and the Mosque make Cronulla and Lakemba emblematic focal points for analysing what happened to the peace and quiet of democratic and relatively tolerant Australia all those years ago.

Cronulla

Cronulla, is a sleepy surfside suburb on the southern outskirts of Sydney Australia, where an Anglo Celtic culture dominates in a relatively isolated peninsular bound by ocean, rivers and national park. The area is known for its sandy beaches and equally its sandy blonde hair. The name Cronulla comes from the word Kurranulla, meaning ''place of the pink seashells'' in the dialect of the area's Aboriginal inhabitants, the Gweagal, who were a clan of the Tharawal (or Dharawal) tribe of Indigenous Australians. They are the traditional custodians of the southern geographic areas of Sydney.

Cronulla's long-term residents grew up in the 60's, 70's and 80's as carefree kids and never left. Why would they? They believed that they already lived in 'The Shire' or 'Gods Country' as it is locally called among the great Aussie surf culture.

Life was simple and carefree, but residents of the area were, and remain, fiercely protective of their mates and their culture in a tribal like manner. It had been so for decades as visitors coming off the train clashed with locals, as to how the beach should be used and occupied. Young Lebanese men clashing with the Anglo-Celtic locals, was just another version of the cultural clash on Cronulla Beach, which is the only beach in Sydney accessible by train.

The conflict between 'westies' and locals has endured for decades and whilst many at the time were quick to label the troubles in late 2005 as racially inspired, no such label was ever posted about the earlier conflicts between local and visitor Caucasians. We will have more to say on this later.

There is another factor that heavily influences the very strong Anglo Celtic culture of the Cronulla area. Nearby at Kurnell, just down the road on the same peninsular, is the landing place of Captain James Cook, the first European man to ever step foot in Eastern Australia in 1770. A monument of Captain Cook stands at the landing spot, reminding all of the European heritage of this nation.

Surfing and the surf culture took off in Cronulla when Duke Kahanamoku alias 'The Duke' from Hawaii (the world's most famous surfboard rider) visited our shores in 1915 ninety years before the Cronulla Riots. The NSW Amateur Swimming Association had organised The Duke's Australian tour, where he conducted surfboard riding demonstrations, gave an exhibition with his board, and so began the surf culture at Cronulla, at the very beach (North Cronulla) where the troubles unfolded in December 2005.

Lakemba

The contrast between Lakemba with Cronulla is a stark one. Home to the Cadigal Clan of the Eora Aboriginal Nation, there are no beaches and no National Parks, but it may claim a piece of Captain Cook with Cooks River playing a strong part in local and regional history.

A beacon of multi-cultural Australia with a diaspora in modern times from Bangladesh, Pakistan, India, Lebanon, China and Vietnam, Lakemba is now about as far from an Anglo-Celtic outpost, as any suburb in western or southwestern Sydney. However, like Cronulla, in a sense, there were simpler and different times to those we see now.

For much of its history, Lakemba was settled by British and Irish migrants who in time established Anglican, Catholic and Uniting Churches. By the late 1940s and into the 1950s, the suburb absorbed a large influx of Greek and Italian migrants, which began the rich and diverse cultural, linguistic and dietary contribution we have come to know, respect and enjoy as part of multi-cultural Australia. Not surprisingly, the strong Catholic presence resulted in Catholic schools which endure to this day.

This Anglo-Celtic working-class provincial suburb of Sydney was transformed in the early 1970s with the arrival of migrants seeking to escape the Civil War in Lebanon and soon enough followed by those seeking a better life from Asia, the sub-continent and the Middle East generally. The strong Muslim population which this brought, much like the Irish Catholics before them, embarked on creating their own places of worship and education. The Mosque was built in 1977 resulting in Lakemba, as being seen as Lebanon Central, and Islamic schools continue to thrive locally alongside both Catholic and Departmental ones.

This enormous change in the demographics of Lakemba from the early 20th Century to the present day can be seen by the changes in ethnic ancestry of each of its State Members of Parliament. From the creation of the Lakemba electorate in 1927 until 1999 the area was represented by Anglo Celtic MPs, from 1999 until 2015 by two MPs of Italian ancestry and from 2015 by a Muslim MP, who migrated from Lebanon when just a toddler. This alone sums up the diverse changes in the history of Lakemba. This is a stark contrast with the Cronulla State Electorate which since its creation at the 1959 election, has had just four MPs but all of Anglo Celtic stock.

What does the Census of 2006 tell us?

The empowerment and resourcing of the police response to what could be called the 'Battle of the Cultures and the Suburbs' is at the heart of this book, but to fully contextualise that battle and the response, we need to better understand, on an empirical level, what each looked like to the other at the time.

In other words, in the lead up to December 2005, what was the cultural, educational, linguistic, and religious make up of Cronulla and Lakemba? Who and what were these suburbs? What were their differences and their similarities? And how do they look now?

The source for this analysis has been the extensive data available for each suburb following the 2006 and 2016 census, as well as crime data from the NSW Bureau of Crime Statistics for 2005. Predictably, there is an enormous contrast in income, ancestry, and crime levels in each suburb. Lakemba being generally painted as 'Lebanon Central' is surprisingly, not supported by the statistical facts, although it can accurately be labelled as the 'Centre of Muslim Faith' by the sheer number of followers from a variety of Islamic countries.

Here are the numbers.

The 2006 Census

To ensure that the ABS Census data for 2006 is not skewed in any direction by only considering two suburbs, a much broader review was undertaken of the regional context in which those two suburbs were located. In the case of Cronulla, this was the local government area of Sutherland Shire, and in the case of Lakemba, this was the then separate Local Government areas known as the City of Bankstown and the City of Canterbury.

This is what the data for 2006 reveals:

2006	Sutherland No.	Sutherland %	Canterbury-Bankstown No.	Canterbury-Bankstown %
Median Age	37		36	
Population	205,448		300,452	
Aust Citizenship	186,195	90.63	249,884	83.17
Place of birth				
Born overseas	33,980	17	122,056	41
Australian born	160,509	78.13	154,447	51.4
England	7,790	3.8		
New Zealand	3,288	1.6		
Vietnam			19,401	6.46
Lebanon			19,285	6.42
China			12,889	4.29
Age-15-24	27,887	13.6	40,608	13.51
Age 25-54	86,987	42.3	125,508	41.8
Total 15-54	114,874	55.91	166,116	55.29
Religion:				
Catholic	62,891	30.6	86,574	28.82
Anglican	55,310	26.9	29,392	9.79
No religion	26,558	12.9	25,734	8.57
Islam			43,788	14.57

Most of this is unsurprising except for two standouts:

1. That 38.61% of residents of the Canterbury/Bankstown area were Catholic/Anglican and just 14.5% were Muslim. On raw numbers alone, the contrast is extraordinary from what we had expected: 115,906 residents nominated Catholic/Anglican as their religion whereas just 43,788 nominated Islam.

2. That despite a reasonably large cohort of Islamic residents in Canterbury/Bankstown, the number of Lebanese residents in the same area, numbered only around 19,000 out of just over 300,000, or just 6.42%. This is much lower than might have been expected, given the level of attention this community receives from both media and the police. That there were more residents from Vietnam than Lebanon emphasises the point.

A far more diverse community than just Lebanon Muslim Central is revealed by these numbers for southwest Sydney. Sutherland certainly confirmed its place as Caucasian Central.

The Clash of the Suburbs

Let's drill down into the census data of August 2006, for the two main protagonist suburbs of the riots, Cronulla and Lakemba. This is just 8 months after the Cronulla Riots began in December 2005.

2006 Census	Cronulla No.	Cronulla %	Lakemba No.	Lakemba %
Median Age	36		31	
Male/Female	50/50		52/48	
Population	16,754		14,468	
Age-15-24	2,231	13.3	1,902	13.1
Age 25-54	8,083	48.2	6,617	45.7

The two suburbs look similar here on age, gender mix, and population.

Interestingly, if the catchment for troublemakers is in the 15-24 and 25-54 age groups then the suburbs have similar profiles. However, just a little further digging into the data and a chasm begins to appear in the nature and demographics of the two:

2006 Census	Cronulla No.	Cronulla %	Lakemba No.	Lakemba %
Australian Citizenship	13,943	83.2	10,088	69.7
Born Overseas	2,587	15.4	8,232	56.9
Place of birth:				
Bangladesh			1,220	8.4
Lebanon			968	6.7
Vietnam			686	4.7
China			582	4.0
Pakistan			524	3.6
England	670	4.0		
New Zealand	380	2.3		
English only at home	13,926	83.1	2,453	17.0

A fundamentally different set of suburbs now emerges.

Cronulla as an Anglo-Celtic enclave with few born overseas and those few, coming almost entirely from the same Caucasian stock. This contrasts starkly with Lakemba, with its far greater numbers being born overseas and mostly, from the Middle East and Asia.

Once again, the relatively low presence of Lebanese residents in Lakemba, as in the wider Canterbury/Bankstown area, invites a wider discussion as to how so few have resulted in so much attention from so many. And we have done just that at the end of Part 5 'Explaining the Riot' in Chapter 27 called, 'Why was it mostly Lebanese Muslim Men'? By the 2016 census those living in Lakemba and born in Lebanon, declined to just 4% compared to 15% from Bangladesh or 6% from Pakistan. Yet, it is young Lebanese Muslim males who continue to gain extraordinary attention for loud, violent law breaking, as it was also in 2005.

The data in the 2006 census for disparity in income, employment and family structure between Cronulla and Lakemba is unsurprisingly quite large:

2006 Census	Cronulla No.	Cronulla %	Lakemba No.	Lakemba %
Full time job	6,415	67.7	2,906	53.4
Unemployed	283	3.0	665	12.2
Not in workforce	3,627	21.65	4,448	30.74
Personal Income	$727		$304	
Family Income	$1,651		$703	
Number Renting	3,103	37.9	2,336	45.8
Median weekly rent	$250		$175	
Own with mtg	1,816	22.2	1,131	22.2
Median monthly mtg payment	$2,000		$1,285	
No. of families	4,017		3,513	
Couple without children	1,995	49.7	911	25.9
Couple with children	1,292	32.2	1,875	53.4

What stands out here in sharp contrast is that Cronulla compared to Lakemba had families earning double the income, but almost half the number of those families had children. The disparity in income was unsurprisingly supported by a much higher level in Cronulla, of post school qualifications.

The comparison of the two suburbs on levels of crime which were reported in 2005 for both the areas of St George/Sutherland and Canterbury/Bankstown throw up some unsurprising but also some unexpected results. The below figures are drawn from the 2005 NSW Bureau of Crime Statistics[3] as reported for that year make for some interesting reading.

---

[3] Steve Moffatt, Derek Goh and Suzanne Poynton, 'New South Wales Recorded Crime Statistics 2005', *NSW Bureau of Crime Statistics and Research*.

The Clash of the Suburbs

Crime category	St George/ Sutherland No.	St George Sutherland Per 100,000	Canterbury Bankstown No.	Canterbury Bankstown Per 100,000
		Assault:		
Sexual	135	30	100	32
Domestic	984	223	859	276
Common	2,557	580	2,054	661
		Drugs:		
Dealing in narcotics	2	0.05	20	6.4
Dealing cannabis	20	4.5	35	11.3
Dealing cocaine	3	0.7	6	1.9
Possess narcotics	30	6.8	63	20.3
Possess cannabis	595	135	270	87
Possess cocaine	11	2.5	9	2.9
		Robbery:		
Robbery w/o weapon	253	57	394	127
Robbery with weapon no gun	158	36	281	91
Robbery with gun	26	5.9	55	18
Fraud	1,867	424	1,975	636
Break and Enter	2,161	490	1,769	569
		Theft:		
Theft of car	1,548	351	2,269	730
Theft from car	2,604	591	2,494	569
Steal from store	758	172	580	186
Steal from dwelling	748	170	555	179
Steal from person	410	93	317	102
Malicious damage pty	5,059	1,149	3,500	1,127
Break AVO	382	87	223	72
PCA	1,472	334	645	207
Offensive conduct	191	43	34	11
Offensive language	242	55	63	20

In relation to incidents of sexual assault, assault and assault related to domestic violence there were similar levels of incidence during 2005 in both St George/Sutherland and Canterbury/Bankstown.

As for drugs, there is a fascinating disparity between the two regions when it comes to dealing and using. The folks of St George/Sutherland in 2005 had a much greater inclination to possess and use narcotics and cannabis compared to a much stronger preference for trafficking them in Canterbury/Bankstown.

Robbery, fraud, use of guns and theft of or from a motor vehicle, was demonstrably greater in Canterbury/Bankstown. Interestingly, the residents of both regions had a similar penchant for stealing from stores, dwellings, or people but perhaps unexpectedly, a noticeably higher proportion of breaching AVOs in St George/Sutherland.

In summary, based on these reported incidents, the people of St George/Sutherland in 2005 which encompassed Cronulla, were drunker and speedier drivers than their Canterbury/Bankstown counterparts, and more susceptible to smoking pot, behaving poorly, using foul language and breaching Apprehended Violence Orders. However, the residents of Canterbury/Bankstown which encompassed Lakemba, were far more inclined to engage in serious crimes such as robbery, use of guns, fraud and dealing in drugs.

Not surprisingly then, when the Lebanese responded to the slights and provocations of an inebriated Anglo-Celtic Cronulla crowd, they did so with greater violence and impact, than anything the Cronulla protestors, ostensibly defending 'their beach' were able to unleash on their day on the beach.

PART 2: POLICING THE RIOT

3

The Build up to Riot: 'Skips' v 'Lebs'

The lure of the beach

Cronulla beach is the only one of Sydney's many beaches on a train line which provides this beach with unique accessibility for the people of Sydney. It is a beautiful place and well worthy of regular visiting by both locals and day trippers alike.

For years, many locals have resented 'their' beach being used by so many 'outsiders' and these resentments have from time to time degenerated into verbal and physical conflict between the two groups. Tribes anywhere usually use labels to describe what they see or regard as the 'Other,' and at Cronulla over the years it has been no different, with the 'Rockers' doing battle with the 'Surfers' in the 60s, which then morphed in the 70s to 'Westies' or 'Bankies' (from Bankstown), and in time the local 'Skips' versus the visiting 'Lebs'.

The arrival of the Arabic 'other'

The early 2000's saw a relative newcomer emerge at Cronulla beach. This was a whole new cultural, ethnic, and religious contrast between locals and visitors than anything which had occurred in the past. There had always been differences between the local and visiting tribes, but these differences were soon cavernous compared to the past. What is surprising is that it took so long for those new differences to go from male 'preening' on both sides, to verbal altercations, to physical challenge, and finally to riotous behaviour. Gradual and then increasing yet still simmering levels of discontent between the tribes was fuelled by incivility generally, disrespect to local women and cultural clashes as to how the beach should be used and enjoyed by local families or visiting amateur soccer players.

Young men of Arabic Muslim descent from Sydney's western suburbs increasingly came to the beach in packs in their 'hotted' up cars. They dressed not in beachwear, but in designer track suits, with buzz-cut hairstyles, dripping with jewellery. A lot were gang members, a great number of whom were well known to police and had extensive criminal records. They were not at all representative of their humble and respectful wider culture. Most were born in Australia, sons of hard-working immigrant families who had escaped war-torn countries and violence for a brighter and peaceful future in Australia. As with most first and second-generation immigrants, these young men often struggled with identity. Of a weekend they would 'escape' to Cronulla Beach from the much hotter western suburbs of Sydney, where their gangs were constantly under the close watch of, and targeted by, the police from their own local areas.

At this otherwise peaceful family beach carpark they would congregate together in modified cars playing loud Arabic music, sitting on their bonnets. They were mostly not there for the sun, sand, and beach or to surf. They were there to dominate, assert 'their' way, intimidate and impress local "Skippy" girls. Strict cultural upbringing meant that a majority of women from their own families were covered head-to-toe as part of religious belief, but here at the beach, bikini clad girls by the hundreds were on display like a smorgasbord. Their manner was often aggressive, offensive and deliberately intimidating to anyone walking past, as they tried to assert their maleness and dominance. As girls walked by or used the nearby open-air shower at the top of the boardwalk from the beach, gang members would often yell out very offensive things like, *"Have you ever tasted Lebanese Honey"* or *"Have you ever sucked on a Lebanese cucumber"*.

These gangs would frequently walk the nearby streets and Cronulla Mall where there are dozens of cafes and designer shops. They would strut up and down the mall, always in groups, staring down the locals and other visitors. Aggressive verbal exchanges often took place between the locals and these visitors. After these groups departed the beach there would often be piles of rubbish left behind, thrown on the ground near their cars or left on the beach in a further disrespectful act in the local's eyes.

Only a mere few metres from this carpark stood the North Cronulla Surf

Club. On a weekend dozens of Volunteer Lifesavers would congregate there. Sprawled out on the grass between the club and the carpark were all manner of surf rescue boards, inflatable boats, beach buggies etc, with busy Lifesavers coming to and fro. These two cultures were worlds apart but were literally forced together only metres away due to the environmental design of the area. The local 'surfies' hated the 'gangster' activity going on in the nearby carpark and on the beach. Verbal clashes often occurred.

At a micro level, the behaviour of these 'others' enraged the locals and regular beachgoers. But in that era another wider influence was also at play - world affairs. Newspapers and TV news was being pumped into every Sydney household lounge-room on an almost daily basis full of articles on 'Lebanese Gangs' in Western Sydney – Drugs, Guns, Shootings and Pack-Rapes were often the headlines. As well, overseas Terrorism issues involving Arabic Muslim men were seemingly never-ending – 911 in the USA, Bali Bombings, and the London and Madrid rail bombings.

These widely publicised acts of violent extremism combined with local long simmering tribal tensions, provided the powder-keg ingredients for the 'perfect storm', and a clash of cultures was lit.

Violence in the lead-up to riot

In the immediate lead up to the 'Cronulla Riots', which took place on 11th December 2005, a number of violent incidents and clashes involving groups of Middle Eastern and Caucasian young men occurred. Many included confrontations with, and interventions by, police.

During the Labour Day long weekend, 1st to 3rd October 2005, three separate and significant incidents took place requiring police intervention, and others soon followed as tensions simmered, no doubt dozens of other similar but smaller incidents also occurred, thus helping to shape the local mood and public opinion but did not directly involve police.

The assault on the Lifeguards

Communal friction had been building for weeks and exploded on Sunday 4th of December 2005, with an assault upon local volunteer lifeguards, by a group of Middle Eastern young men in the local beach carpark.

The following exchange allegedly took place amongst four 'Skips' and about eight 'Lebs', after a comment about staring each other down in some kind of male preening:

> **Leb**: "I'm allowed to, now fuck off and leave our beach".
>
> **Skip**: "I come down here out of my own spare time, to save you dumb cunts from drowning, now piss off you scum".

A Leb swung a punch, the lifeguards were surrounded, pushing and shoving then escalated into two of the lifeguards being punched, one of whom fell and hit his head causing minor injury. Another was punched in the head as the assailants fled the scene.

Two of the Surf Lifesavers were later treated at Hospital but released. One received bruising and a laceration above his eye requiring gluing and the other was cleared during scans of any fractures to his jaw region.

The response by local police was swift. As they were arriving the men dispersed. An investigation commenced and one of the main assailants, Ali Osman (18 years old), was later arrested on 7/12/05, which drew significant media attention.

Enormous media reaction

It is extraordinary how years of stewing tribal tensions on the beach hardly warranted any media attention whilst all the conflict remained as just misogyny towards local women, kicking soccer balls amongst families lying on the sand, or even the occasional minor scuffle and punch up between Skip surfers and Leb visitors. But the moment an 'Aussie Icon', in the form of a volunteer lifeguard was assaulted, it was then given saturation coverage. The incident was literally blown out of all proportion by media who portrayed this as an assault on the very Aussie way of life and the bashing of our 'Sons of Anzacs', the bronzed zinc-cream wearing lifeguards who volunteer their time to save our lives over summer on our cherished beaches.

To say this was a somewhat disproportionate response would be an understatement. Former local police officers Craig Campbell and Lee Howell, who we interviewed as part of our research were equally dumbfounded about how the tabloids, talk back radio and TV news escalated this to a lot more than it was, or should have been:

> **Campbell**: *"The media played a very big role in hyping it up...It should have been dealt with as a common assault under the Crimes Act and that should have been it".*[4]

Lee Howell was equally dismissive, and also derisory of the idea that the scuffle with the lifeguards was being elevated to a question of what it meant to be an Australian: *"Such hype...over something that was so small".*[5] Some scholars have identified these kind of minor events as "flashpoints",[6] that ignite a much wider riotous conflict. As the media certainly played a part in not just reporting the news, but also in contributing to it, we have assessed the extent of their culpability in a later chapter 18, 'Did the media cause the riots?'

Police plan ahead

Given the enormous coverage given to the 'attack on the lifeguards', the extent of troublesome mass text messaging calling for a defence of the beach, and the likelihood of more serious levels of inter-tribal clashes throughout the summer, the NSW Police over the 6th and 7th of December 2005, prepared and settled its risk assessment, expected police resourcing requirements, and if events spiralled, an escalation plan to rapidly respond. It was called, 'Operation Seta'.

The 2nd assault

Late afternoon on Wednesday 7th December, three Caucasian males were walking along the Esplanade in front of North Cronulla Beach, one of whom allegedly addressed a group of four Middle Eastern men they had chanced upon with: *"Fucken Lebs"*. This caused an angry reaction, one of the Caucasian males was punched, fell and was kicked on the ground. More locals approached and the fight ceased. Police quickly responded, dispersed the crowd but the main assailant had successfully fled the scene.

The media were already in full force around the Cronulla Beach area, a photographer was assaulted by three men of Middle Eastern appearance and were arrested and charged by police. These relatively very minor issues then set off a media and texting firestorm.

---

[4] C. Campbell, Transcript of Interview, 22 November 2020.
[5] L. Howell, Transcript of Interview, 6 February 2021.
[6] G. den Heyer, *Police Response to Riots,* Springer Nature, 2019, pp. 29-31.

The Build up to Riot

The few days before a riot

The tabloid newspapers, the Shock Jock talk back radio announcers, and aggressive text messaging now went into full 'moral panic', about what they regarded as an attack on Australian icons like lifeguards and the beach, and what it meant to be an Aussie. Much of it was pretty unpleasant stuff.

The Australian flag began appearing on balconies and draped around locals, and even on face paint, as a means of expressing patriotism, when perhaps it was doing the opposite, in fanning the flames of inter-tribal exclusion, by the building up of the Caucasian "us" thwarting the visiting Lebanese "them". Our national symbols had never before been used in such a divisive way.

Angry crowds and swarms of media began gathering at North Cronulla Beach in anticipation of more trouble. Activists and White Supremacists began to appear in the area to hijack the situation and began handing out pamphlets supporting various far-right extreme political parties, views and ideals.

For the first time in Australia, text messaging was used as a clarion 'call to arms' from both sides. Here are some examples:

Caucasians	Middle Eastern
"*Aussies... this Sunday every fucking Aussie in the Shire get down to North Cronulla to help support Leb and wog bashing day*"	"*All lebo / wog brothers. Sunday midday. Must be at North Cronulla Park. These skippy aussies want war. Bring ur guns and knives and lets show them how we do it*"
"*Bring your mates and let's show them that this is our beach, and they are never welcome... let's kill these boys*"	"*O fight each Aussie. Yulleh. Lets get hectic and turn gods country into wogs country. Habib will be cookin victory kebabs after. Tell all your cousins*"
"*Who said Gallipoli wouldn't happen again! Rock up 2 Cronulla this Sunday...u can witness Aussies beaten Turks on the beach*"	"*We fear no ozy pigs*"
"*Every fucking aussie. Go to Cronulla Beach Sunday for some Leb and wog bashing Aussie Pride ok*"	"*Get the Aussie dogs*"

The police prepare in advance

These text messages weren't just inflammatory but were being sent in their thousands to encourage acts of violence on Sunday 11th of December 2005, by "us" on "them". Senior police acted accordingly, and on Thursday the

8th of December, the risk assessment of the planned protest was elevated to 'HIGH', and the Sydney Region Commander, Assistant Commissioner Mark Goodwin, took overall strategic command with local Superintendent Robert Redfern having local operational command.

On Friday 9th of December, Premier Morris Iemma, Police Minister Carl Scully, and Police Assistant Commissioner Mark Goodwin, all held major media conferences at Cronulla Beach, warning of a strong police operation that coming Sunday, where anti-social behaviour and violence would not be tolerated.

On the afternoon of Friday 9th December, senior police commanders and police public order experts, including the head of the new Public Order and Riot Squad, conferred and formally agreed upon a 'Concept of Operations'. This document set out in detail the police plan for expected trouble on North Cronulla Beach; the number of personnel needed, tactics to be used, specialist squads to be engaged, resources and equipment required, and the logistics necessary to support it all. Police were well prepared ahead of the event, and if things turned nastier than expected, an 'Escalation Plan' had also been agreed with the ability to quickly ramp up a strong police response. The Commissioner of Police attended at the end of the planning session and was fully briefed.

That day and into Saturday and early Sunday, tens of thousands of aggressive texts continued to be sent by both "Aussies" and "Lebs" calling for battle, Shock Jock radio hosts continued to add their fuel to the fire, and the tabloid newspapers didn't disappoint with their own versions of causing, rather than reporting the news.

The gauntlet was thrown down and the Police were ready to respond. The following Sunday 11th December 2005 was to become enshrined in Australian history. The day of the 'riots', the 'revenge attacks' and the weeks of inter-tribal tensions that ensued, as never before seen in Australia, are explored in the next two chapters.

4

The Fateful Day

The morning

People awoke the morning of 11th December 2005 to a calm balmy summer's day. The weather was fine, and the skies were blue. Little did anyone know the storm-front that was brewing upon the horizon. By mid-morning crowds began to assemble on the North Cronulla beachfront, some wearing patriotic clothing. The mood was initially one of a party, a celebration, almost like an old version of Australia Day.

Meanwhile, at the nearby Cronulla Police Station, a vast array of police were being briefed on their individual and team duties, together with command expectations. This was primarily a public demonstration. And thus, the police strategy was to initially have a large number of riot police in groups walking through the crowd and chatting to people. There was not the early necessity to adopt police lines in tactical riot gear to make it look like police were there waiting for trouble. However, police were well prepared and had planned for any such contingency. An extensive amount of riot specialist personnel and gear was present onsite for immediate deployment should the need arise, or the situation deteriorate.

Police were briefed by Goodwin, that any violence or over-the-top offensive conduct was to be swiftly and immediately dealt with. Offenders were to be arrested and extricated from the crowd. Whilst there is always a degree of discretion in dealing with public disorder incidents, he instructed police that they were not to tolerate any violence or extreme behaviour by gangsters or individuals with agendas in the crowd hijacking the day.

In fact, ample later media footage clearly shows this strategy in action. The footage reveals every act of individual, or crowd aggression filmed being immediately met with judicious but strong use of police force in extracting troublemakers. All media vision shows that police were well in control of every hostile situation and took immediate firm action. The strategy worked extremely well without escalating the situation. The day was primarily a protest. Debate continues to this day as to whether it was just a protest with sporadic examples of drunken poor choices and criminal behaviour within the crowd, or whether it was a 'riot' in the traditional sense of the word.

Policing responses to protests often provide police with a difficult dilemma. There is a need for great restraint and balance. On the one hand, respecting and facilitating people's democratic right to free speech and to protest, whilst on the other hand, maintaining peace and order when things become unduly disruptive. It is always a judgment call, and often a difficult balancing act between these competing aims. The call on how best to achieve that balance is based upon what individual officers at the scene, or their commanders in the field deem appropriate at the time.

It is a fine line to ensure the security of people and public property, whilst not antagonising an otherwise potentially volatile crowd and turning it against the police themselves, who are often seen as the face of Government and, in reality, are normally subject to much abuse and hostility on the ground at some protests. As this was an inter-tribal conflict, police commanders made the correct call that they were unlikely to be the target of angry protestors, although they came prepared for a contrary outcome.

The gathering warms up

Back on the North Cronulla beachfront the big Aussie Utes with jacked up suspension began to arrive in the carpark. These were not Cronulla locals or surfers there to protect their beach culture, they were activists and White Supremacists from outside the area, who'd attended to hijack the day on the back of the huge media build-up. They set up with Eureka Stockade and/or Australian National flags flying from their truck-like utilities and nearby power poles. They cooked up traditional Aussie food on BBQ's mounted onto their utility tray-backs. They handed out bacon and sausage sandwiches to the crowds. It was initially an almost carnival like atmosphere. There was no real direction or purpose. There was no real crowd leader/s. People just congregated there to make a statement to the wider world via the throng of media present that they were 'taking their beach back'. Many seemed to have turned up to watch everyone else watching. Throughout the morning a few played up to the media. Some had chests emblazoned with offensive racist slogans like *"We grew here. You flew here"* or *"Love 'nulla, fuck Allah"*, or perhaps worst of all, *"Ethnic Cleansing Unit"*. But most just stood around eyeballing and 'rubbernecking' at the antics of a few vocal outspoken rednecks, who emerged in the crowd.

By about lunchtime, under the hot summer sun, the flowing alcohol started to take effect. The whole of Sydney's media was there. Reporters and news cameramen by the dozens lingered in hungry anticipation for headline busting copy. But for most of the day they were bored and waited, as the crowd instead stirringly and patriotically sang Waltzing Matilda, Advance Australia Fair and other Australian ballads, and songs.

Enter Glen Steele: rioter or patriot?

A local identity Glen Steele, who was later demonised as an instigator of riotous behaviour, stood on a milk crate with a handheld megaphone and spoke forth. He was accused publicly as a troublemaker who had stirred up many unpleasant emotions and incited the riot. But what really happened?

Glen Steele is a solidly built local Sutherland Shire character, and a well-liked former rugby league footballer and surfer. He was the quintessential solid muscled bronzed bear-chested loud Aussie male up on his milk crate, with his Aussie peak cap and a loud-hailer in hand. That made for a great picture by newspaper journalists, who later inferred he was the crowd agitator and one of the riot instigators. A picture does tell a thousand words, sometimes, but not always!

This is what the media reported at great length: **Steele**: *"This is what our grandfathers fought for to protect this (pointing to the beach) so we can enjoy it. We don't need these Lebanese or other wogs to take it away from us."*

Unhelpfully, as he said these words, he was 'supported' by many in the crowd chanting: *"Fuck off Lebs"*. However, what was blatantly ignored and not reported by any cameraman or the very patient journalists, were the following words, also strongly used by Glen Steele, and clearly heard by police commanders operating out of the first floor of the North Cronulla Surf Club: **Steele**: *"OK people, we're not here to fight the police today, they are white men like us, they are the good guys"*.

Mr Steele then used his megaphone to start chants from the crowd: *"Cops are tops"* and *"Three cheers for the Cops... Hip Hip Horray"*. He then led the crowd singing Waltzing Matilda and the National Anthem. Hardly the stuff of riotous assembly. But alas, none of this was ever reported, it simply didn't fit the agenda. All the former and none of the latter above comments by Steele, got wide coverage, including in the tabloid press. The following day pressure was brought to bear on Goodwin from the NSW Police Senior Executive to immediately charge Mr Steele with incitement to riot, more as a token scalp to appease the by-then hungry media and questioning public. Goodwin's response must have taken the NSW Police senior executive by surprise:

> **Goodwin**: *"If that happens, then I'll be a witness for the defence. There is no way I'm going to charge this guy for inciting the riot, when he was stirring the crowd up to sing, 'cops are tops', and telling them that, 'we're not here to fight the police'. Really? I don't think so".*

Whilst two hundred people would be charged arising out of their conduct, in either riot or revenge, Glenn Steele would not be one of them.

On the morning of the day of the 'riot', the local North Cronulla Surf Lifesaving club had planned to launch a new surf boat, and despite some concerns from the club, the event proceeded smoothly with the support of police already stationed at the ready. It all received strong support from nippers, families, sponsors and club officials, and encouragement and interest from the growing crowd of 'protestors'. This very positive event, literally in the middle of all that happened on that day, yet again received absolutely no media coverage. Why?

Throughout the day the crowd grew to around 5,000, the vast proportion of which were young Caucasian males. The major issue that drove crowd dynamics throughout the afternoon, under the hot summer sun, was the excessive consumption of alcohol. During the afternoon, the Operational Commander, Superintendent Redfern, requested hotels and bottle shops in the local area close off their liquor sales. This was a wise tactical manoeuvre with much foresight. Interestingly, he did not then have the power to demand this, but had he not done so, the situation throughout the afternoon could have, and probably would have, become far worse. To his credit, Redfern had built up a great rapport with the licensed establishments in his local policing area via a 'Liquor Licensing Accord', of which the members met regularly to discuss emerging and local issues in the Liquor and Gaming industry. Whilst these licensed premises had no legal obligation to abide by Supt Redfern's request, and also to their credit, they all willingly complied and shut down liquor sales. The Police Minister would ensure just four days later, with Special Legislation passed, that the power would then be available to police if ever needed.

From about 1pm on the day, crowd dynamics changed. The mood by a relatively small few in the crowd of around 5,000 people, became one of alcohol fuelled aggression, and antagonistic confrontation. Spurred on by a combination of tribalism, alcohol, racism, a false sense of loyalty, bravado and group mentality, a number of people in the larger crowd engaged in violent incidents throughout the afternoon. Put in perspective, these numbers amounted at most to no more than a couple of hundred people, not the entire 5,000 strong crowd. The bulk of the crowd simply watched on, cheered, and rubbernecked at the antics of a select few.

An afternoon of racist violence

The morning and afternoon at North Cronulla Beach that day were so different that they could be regarded as completely separate events. One was more a carnival like party of patriotic BBQs by the many, which by the afternoon became somewhat darker one for the relatively few.

These darker moments on that day, by no more than around 200 almost entirely alcohol fuelled young men, is what became the defining moments of the 'Cronulla Riots' and provided extraordinary and graphic copy to the media and the world, that even in peaceful law-abiding Australia, there is an unpleasant side of human nature.

We have summarised in the table below the events at Cronulla which provided indelible footage:

Time	Description
1.00pm	A man of Middle Eastern appearance chased across Dunningham Park towards the local hotel, where police gave him protection. Many ran too to watch and chanted outside the hotel.
1.45pm	Two Middle Eastern men assaulted in Dunningham Park, punched and kicked, police escorting them to safety, one assailant arrested and charged.

2.30pm	Two Middle Eastern women repeatedly abused, and then punched and kicked by two Caucasian women. Police quickly intervened to protect, and to arrest and charge one of the Caucasian women.
2.40pm	Two young men from Bangladesh in a car, chance upon the crowd in the local surf club car park, bottles thrown, someone jumped on the bonnet, another smashed a window with his fist, they make their escape. Later, one 'rioter' charged by police.

At around 3.00pm that afternoon, a rumour had spread amongst the large crowd that several Lebanese men had arrived at Cronulla Railway Station. Like a swarm of bees, a large pack of angry Caucasian young men, left the Surf Club area, and found two young men of Middle Eastern appearance on the train. They were assaulted in the train carriage. Ugly scenes ensued, and without the intervention of police, these two men could have been killed.

Sergeant Craig Campbell of the local Transit Police, stepped up and with his swinging baton, supported by a few colleagues, saved these men, and cleared the train and the station of thugs. What happened that afternoon on Cronulla Railway station, thanks to saturation TV News coverage, is an event that is seared into our memories and became emblematic of both the best and worst of human nature on that day. A public servant putting himself in harm's way and living up to his oath of office, and the darker side of a marauding alcohol fuelled pack of racists. Sadly, Craig Campbell did not in our view receive adequate recognition for his courage and bravery, a matter we address fully in Part 4 'Reflections from the field'.

Further incidents

Time	Description
3.20pm	Two young Middle Eastern men harassed and one, punched and kicked, cnr Elourera Rd and Mitchell St. A single highway patrolman on intersection duty steps in, uses capsicum spray to subdue assailants. Victim escorted to police vehicle and crowd throws bottles injuring both officer and victim. Police vehicle damaged, 17 Caucasians later charged over this incident.
3.25pm	Police manage to escort three Middle Eastern men safely into a restaurant with many Caucasians banging on the window and breaking the glass.

Time	Description
4.20pm	An ambulance used to ferry six Middle Eastern men to safety, with four mounted police and riot police providing escort. Ambulance officer struck with a beer bottle after windows smashed by bottle throwing. Three Caucasians arrested and charged.
4.30pm	After this escort, police abused, a bottle thrown and smashes near them, offender apprehended and charged. Crowd gathers and further verbal abuse directed at police.

By late afternoon, the anger of the crowd had subsided, alcohol had been turned off, the police substantially retuned to 'barracks' on standby, and people started to head for home. During the day, police presence had been literally everywhere; helicopters in the sky, inflatable boats on the water, mounted police, highway patrol, police dogs, and riot police. As the day finally reached a calm, these forces were quietly withdrawn from view.

Compared to what had happened in the Paris 2005 riots, just a month earlier, this day at Cronulla was a much more placid event, and perhaps hardly met the threshold of what would be normally regarded as a 'riot'. We explore this further in chapter 17: 'Was it really a riot?'.

Enter the evening news

And then came the inevitable 6.00pm evening news. Every TV Newsroom editor had gone through hours of footage, from what had been a mostly peaceful day of demonstration, to present the worst aspects set out above, over just a few minutes of provocative broadcasting. This successfully left a deep impression upon anyone watching, that these awful video images were just samples of what had been going on all day. Truth is, the day had mostly been one of BBQs, boat launches, drinking and talking, racial chants, rubbernecking, milling around in the sun, and with only the occasional acts of unacceptable violent excess. But selective inflammatory footage only showing hostile acts were now strung together and presented for all to witness, thereby somewhat falsely leading viewers to believe this was the behaviour all day and by the whole crowd.

The suburb of Cronulla and the Sutherland Shire itself, were now seen and labelled as White Supremacist enclaves, and the day itself given the maligning nomenclature of the 'Cronulla Race Riot'. It is a label and a name that has proved all but impossible to shift, given the way the day's event was graphically angled and displayed by Walkley Award seeking cinematic cameramen and newspaper photographers alike.

The 'revenge attacks' begin

There are consequences but usually no accountability when the media provocatively presents something to maximise ratings. The whole of Sydney watched with jaws dropped, as the night news footage unfolded. Many young Muslim Lebanese men were so angry with what they had seen both on TV that night and read in the Caucasian text messaging, that they reacted swiftly that very evening, and over the following nights and weeks. These would become known as the 'revenge attacks'. Little except for some grainy commercial CCTV footage has been seen of these far more violent attacks which terrorised Sydney for several days before police were able to restore order.

This has led to a very skewed public, academic and media perception that most of the violence, and all of the racialised behaviour, occurred during the day at Cronulla and not during the evenings which followed. Interestingly, as journalists celebrated at the bar for a job well done, the police day had just begun in earnest. We set out in the following chapter what happened next.

5
The 'Revenge Attacks'

Why is it just Cronulla?

One of the extraordinary things, amongst many in respect of the 'Cronulla Riots', is that the suburb 'Cronulla', gets the full stigmatising nomenclature as the geographical epicentre of all the conflict which occurred in late 2005/ early 2006. We shall see in our discussion below that given that most of the violence and significant property damage occurred a long way from that suburb, the dubious title is a misnomer.

However, successfully shifting this historical inscription to something far more accurate, such as, 'The Sydney Riots', is unlikely given just how ingrained is the term's common parlance. Accordingly, despite the varied and random locations of the revenge attacks, we will continue using the misnomer.

This chapter focuses on the 'Revenge Attacks' which followed into the evening and following day of the 11th and 12th of December 2005, and the enormous risk to public safety that developed as a result.

For the first time we lift the veil on the extreme risk intelligence with which police were confronted, and we have endeavoured to give the reader an account of a Minister for Police and the most senior Police Commander running riot response operations, working closely together, often in multiple conversations over many days, as they both did what needed to be done to bring 'the troubles' to an end as quickly as possible.

This is a detailed chapter for good reason. The single most important part of the 'Cronulla Riots' and in fact of any riot which has occurred in New South Wales, was not the offensive xenophobic actions of the inebriated few on Sunday the 11th of December 2005, but the serious violence and significant property damage and terrorising of suburbs which followed in retaliation.

Without these rampaging, violent and terrifying revenge attacks, we may now just have instead, a distant memory of a drunken protest day in the sun, which got a bit out of hand for a few hundred violent chauvinists.

This is the story of what these 'retaliators' did, the impact they had on the community, and how police were able to abruptly bring it all to a halt. Why the revenge attacks occurred, and why the inebriated few acted as they did, is addressed in Part 5: 'Explaining the Riot'.

Reporting the riot unleashes revenge

On Sunday 11 December, the 6pm evening news on every TV channel broadcast headlines showing angry mobs and scenes of violence sweeping across the streets and public spaces of Cronulla. The extraordinary manipulation of different footage, at different points, at different times of the day, all strung together in quick succession for greatest sensational impact on the evening news, together with excitable newsreader voiceover, gave a searing and indelible image that hours and hours of non-stop racialised violence against Arabic looking people had taken place at Cronulla. Whilst the footage used was real, the story around it and the impression it left was distorted. What is "truth" is always contextual, and never more so when journalists and their editors are spinning something out of a kernel of truth into something much bigger. We assess in greater detail in Chapter 18 'Did the Media cause the Riots?', the extent to which this graphic and visual overselling of the excesses of the day on Sunday 11 December, may have contributed to the violent revenge attacks.

Police had pre-empted a strong reaction from young Lebanese men, the pre-documented 'Escalation Plan' had been activated, and fresh troops had been brought onto duty to deal with the inevitable evening of retaliatory violence and revenge. Goodwin had been Crime Manager at Bankstown for several years and well knew what to expect from angry Lebanese men.

Ugly scenes indeed emerged soon enough that first evening, at Maroubra, Brighton-Le-Sands and then later at Cronulla itself. The violence rapidly spread on multiple fronts throughout Sydney over the ensuing days. By the following weekend Assistant Commissioner Goodwin commanded a police operation involving 2,000 police in 7 separate zones from Wollongong to Newcastle utilising new police powers legislatively bestowed following an urgent recall of the NSW State Parliament. That police operation was known as 'Operation Seta' and continued for the following six weeks over the December-January summer holidays.

Cronulla explodes

The first initiative of senior police was to send a strong Highway Patrol presence to the three bridges that enter the Sutherland Shire to prevent convoys of angry young Middle Eastern men from entering the area. Cronulla is located on a peninsula surrounded by waterways – Georges River to the North, Port Hacking River to the South, Woronora River to the West and Pacific Ocean to the East. Traffic was filtered; car occupants were visually inspected; people were spoken to; licences were checked and reasons for entering the area were determined. Other than conducting random breath testing, at the time there was no specific power to put in these roadblocks, but the risk was just too high. This anomaly was soon fixed with the special police powers enacted to assist police in quelling the riots, which we address later.

Multiple different groups of aggrieved Middle Eastern young men began congregating near the Mosque at Punchbowl and in the immediate areas outside of the Sutherland Shire's geographic peninsular. Groups emerged at Brighton-Le-Sands, Arncliffe, and Maroubra. No person could possibly predict what, where, when, or how they would strike. It became a mobile riot on simultaneous multiple fronts and a situation that had never been encountered in Australia.

The police command post during the day had been appropriately located on the top floor of the North Cronulla Surf Club with commanding views over the expected field of police 'public order' operations. As the expected retaliation was not going to be so geographically concentrated, Goodwin shifted command and control of the police operations to the Police Operations Centre (POC) in Sydney's CBD, which was the best place to manage a riot on the move and in multiple geographic locations.

As part of the Escalation Plan, a number of Local Area Commanders were brought back onto duty that Sunday evening covering commands in southern, eastern and south-western Sydney. Their job was to take charge of any policing issues in their area and to report directly through to Goodwin.

Signs of impending trouble had begun earlier in the day, when two pigs' heads were found on the front doorstep of Arncliffe RSL Club. A group of Middle Eastern young men had been seen earlier by the RSL staff poking the pigs' heads with sticks in the adjoining park. However, after the 6pm evening news, things really ramped up.

Analysts later used the logs and records of Goodwin and other commanders, police radio logs, records of the investigation team 'Strike Force Enoggera' and an array of other official police records, to create a chronology of events that occurred during the 'Revenge Attacks'. These analysts, from Strike Force Neil, which was later set up to investigate command and control of the Cronulla Riots, provide a concise and useful timeline of events for these Revenge Attacks.[7]

We have drawn from this analysis and from Goodwin's own firsthand recollections as well as that of Scully. As the revenge attacks exploded like a series of bombs in a rising crescendo across Sydney that same evening, for convenience, we have broken up this violent riotous 'activity' into three separate time periods: Early, Mid and Late evening.

First signs

Date	Time	Reported Activity
11/12/05	5.20pm	The first reprisal attacks began to appear. St George Hospital staff requested police assistance when a large group of Middle Eastern men assembled at the hospital following injuries received that day by compatriots. Vehicles had been damaged in the vicinity after bottles were thrown.

Early evening

Date	Time	Reported Activity
11/12/05	7.45pm	About 20-30 Middle Eastern men were seen walking along The Promenade, Sans Souci, some of whom were carrying baseball bats. At Arncliffe Park, about 60 Middle Eastern men reported to have assembled.
11/12/05	7.48pm	At Punchbowl Park a group of Middle Eastern men reported as calling other people to meet up.

---

[7] Strike Force Neil Report, pp. 45-50.

Date	Time	Reported Activity
11/12/05	8.00pm	Police gave on site reports of approximately 100 Middle Eastern men at Punchbowl Park some of whom shouted profanities at police, who were heavily outnumbered and did not engage with what was by then a volatile crowd. Many were later observed entering several motor vehicles and dispersing in many different directions.

This then began what was probably our first mobile riot with multiple attacks and acts of violence in numerous places across Sydney. Police soon learned that some vehicles were travelling south on King Georges Road and east on the M5 Motorway. A radio direction was given by police command to all police for 'zero tolerance' of any anti-social behaviour or traffic offences.

Convoys of vehicles had left both Punchbowl Park and Arncliffe Park and were soon on their way to Brighton-le-Sands, Maroubra, and Cronulla. One such vehicle was followed by police towards Wollongong on the Princes Highway, was stopped, and searched but no breaches of the law observed.

Unusually and perhaps for the first time for law enforcement, Police Highway Patrol began monitoring the three road access points into the Sutherland Shire.

Mid evening

Date	Time	Reported Activity
11/12/05	8.27pm	In Bay Street Brighton-le-Sands, 60 Middle Eastern men were observed harassing people. Police attended but quickly asked for back up as the numbers of intimidators was increasing.

The assault on the Australian flag

Date	Time	Reported Activity
11/12/05	8.40pm	The infamous attack on the Brighton-le-Sands RSL flagpole unfolds with a Middle Eastern man climbing the RSL roof, removing the national flag and proceeding to desecrate it physically and culturally as they spat, kicked, urinated and burnt this National symbol. This was a disrespectful and disgraceful attack which will be long remembered. Following an investigation, police later arrested and charged three Middle Eastern males in relation to these offences.

The Maroubra dare

On the 9th of December 2005, just two days before the 'Fateful Day', the *Daily Telegraph* published what was a very irresponsible dare from the leader of the Bra Boys Maroubra Surf Gang effectively accusing young Middle Eastern men of being frightened of them, being cowardly, and simply too afraid, to put themselves anywhere near the incredibly tough and scary Bra Boys. We assess the correlation, or even causality of this 'challenge', with what subsequently happened at Maroubra, in chapter 11, 'Did the media cause the riots?'

Police having set up a gauntlet for 'visitors' on all the Sutherland Shire and Cronulla access points, the roving troublemakers opted to relocate elsewhere, particularly and unsurprisingly to Maroubra.

Date	Time	Reported Activity
11/12/05	8.44pm	A cavalcade of 12 vehicles ladened with Middle Eastern men is reported on their way to Maroubra Beach, 7 of which were later observed on Malabar Road. The occupants were heard yelling out profanities and xenophobic remarks to locals on the street. A parked car caught alight when a 'flaming object' was thrown from one of the vehicles.
		Despite the attempts of police to stop the motorcade only 1 vehicle was interdicted, with police confiscating the keys as the driver was unlicensed. Four youths in this vehicle aged between 15-17 years old were later charged following investigation.
		By now about 100 Middle Eastern men had congregated in and around Maroubra. They were intent on making an unpleasant presence felt and heard. Alarmingly, some of these marauding young men were yielding, and started using baseball bats to frightening effect. Over 50 cars were damaged, and many locals left public places and cowered in fear within their homes, but some were not so lucky!
		The attackers called for the Bra Boys to emerge, but none came forth.

The 'Revenge Attacks'

Date	Time	Reported Activity
11/12/05	8.50pm	'When a man arrived at his home in Maroubra, stepped from his vehicle and was confronted by Middle Eastern men who inquired about his race. When he told them he was Greek, a Middle Eastern man replied, "Then you're alright mate". When the Middle Eastern man left and walked towards a vehicle, he struck the victim's vehicle with a baseball bat. The victim then ran towards his vehicle that had just been damaged, he was struck in the face with a baseball bat and fell to the ground unconscious'.[8]

Riot Police on the move

One of the extraordinary initiatives taken by senior police at this time, and unlike any other riot in our history, riot police were mobilised via general police vehicles and unusually via Highway Patrol. This was not only the first riot on the move, but concomitantly, also the first riot police on the move in response. Unusual events and circumstances called for atypical, nimble, and responsive policing. When Scully, met with senior Paris Police just a few weeks after both the Cronulla and Paris riots, they were already well aware and impressed with our mobile police response. In quick enough time, this initiative worked wonders in restoring peace, rounding up offenders, and allowing people to again feel safe in their homes and in public places.

By this time in the evening of Sunday 11th of December 2005, around 50 riot police had been deployed to Maroubra to deal with the emerging threats to public order, as well as riot police being dispatched to the Botany Bay area of Brighton-le-Sands, Ramsgate and Kyeemagh. This was in response to about 60-70 Middle Eastern men arriving at Cook Park, Brighton-le-Sands in a convoy of 30 motor vehicles. These 'intruders' were intent on causing as much public disturbance as possible.

---

[8] Strike Force Neil, Volume One, p. 46.

Date	Time	Reported Activity
11/12/05	9.00pm	A man and a woman who had gone outside of their Maroubra home to examine the damage done to their vehicles were violently assaulted by Middle Eastern men. The woman was battered on the head by a baseball bat and the man was kicked.

Shortly after these incidents, police put road closures in and around the Maroubra Beach area but by then, the Middle Eastern men who had terrorised this suburb had moved on. They had responded to the call of the Maroubra Bra Boys Surf Gang, and it was the local surfers who ironically cowered in fear and not the loudly and publicly invited 'visitors'. As a precaution police kept the road closures in place until 4.30am the following morning.

Late evening

The riot moves south. Having tormented, violated, and menaced Maroubra, these young and violent Middle Eastern males then focussed the weaponising of their anger on the Southern Suburbs of Sydney.

Cook Park, Kyeemagh

Date	Time	Reported Activity
11/12/05	9.30pm	About 100-150 Middle Eastern men who had gathered in Cook Park, Kyeemagh turned their anger on five police who had started checking motor vehicles. Procuring from a construction site these lawless young men then began raining down, rocks, bottles, and lumps of concrete, upon police doing their job. Police vehicles were damaged, capsicum spray was used to scatter the horde of troublemakers, and numerous arrests were made.

Date	Time	Reported Activity
11/12/05	9.50pm	Again, in Cook Park, the number of Middle Eastern angry young men had grown to around 200 who did not appreciate being filmed by a Channel 9 cameraman. Six of these men then punched and kicked him and took his camera which was dumped in another part of the park.

Woolooware Golf Club

Then the revenge attacks got particularly nasty and violently criminal. A crowd of Middle Eastern males chased a group of four people leaving the Woolooware Golf Club which included two women who managed to escape into local homes for refuge. Unfortunately, one of their male companions was not so lucky. He was thrown to the ground, kicked by two Middle Eastern men and then had a knife planted into his back. His injuries were so serious he was lucky to survive the attack.

Brighton-le-Sands

By this stage of the evening around 200 Middle Eastern males were congregating at Bay Street, Brighton-le-Sands. After the crowd started throwing bottles at police, riot police were deployed, and the crowd dispersed.

Incredibly, as police were setting up a roadblock on Grand Parade and Bay Street, Brighton-le-Sands, one vehicle driven by a Middle Eastern male, swerved towards a police officer stationed at the roadblock. The driver was later arrested.

This suburb then bore the full brunt of Middle Eastern anger, unfortunately almost entirely directed at police trying to keep the peace. One police car had a shopping trolley thrown at it, and others were damaged. Several motorised revenge attackers were driving around, hanging out of the vehicle, and using objects to damage parked cars. Around 50 Middle Eastern rioters were reported armed with 'pieces of timber and steel' near police lines and throwing objects at police.

Of great concern was 'a member of the community hearing a group of about 30 Middle Eastern men in Crawford Road, Brighton-le-Sands about re-grouping at Punchbowl Park', just as a report came through 'that about 25 Middle Eastern men had gathered' at that very place.

Police needed no convincing at this stage, that a long and difficult night for the streets, public places and homes of Sydney still lay ahead.

Cronulla

Date	Time	Reported Activity
11/12/05	11.00pm	A local Cronulla resident attempted to intervene when he observed some Middle Eastern men using baseball bats to vandalise several motor vehicles. For his trouble he was battered numerous times with a baseball bat and luckily was able to take cover in a nearby home.

Re-grouping in Punchbowl

Date	Time	Reported Activity
11/12/05	11.30pm	Several Middle Eastern men were by now using their vehicles to block traffic in and around Punchbowl Park. Police approached these vehicles, and their police car began being attacked. This crowd of troublemakers then dispersed into a convoy of about 30 vehicles which was soon observed travelling towards the Cronulla area.

Cronulla continued to be an area of concern for police until the early hours of the morning of 12th of December 2005.

Cronulla stays targeted

Just after Midnight about 30-40 Middle Eastern men were seen waiting in vehicles near Cronulla High School, one of whom was seen carrying a baseball bat. It was unclear as to when this convoy 'entered the Cronulla area' but was not the only convoy of Middle Eastern males trying, in the early hours of Monday 12th of December to enter Cronulla.

Police, who had been staffing all the access points into the Cronulla area and had been re-deployed earlier in the evening to Brighton-le-Sands, were now recalled to interdict vehicular bound Middle Eastern troublemakers, intent on revenge attacks within the midst of where the earlier Caucasian protest and riot had occurred.

The 'Revenge Attacks'

Date	Time	Reported Activity
12/12/05	12.07am	The Punchbowl convoy slipped across Tom Ugly's Bridge ahead of Highway Patrol re-blocking that approach.
12/12/05	12.19am	The convoy is followed by police near Taren Point Road but near Cronulla, the convoy divides into smaller groups. Despite police setting up roadblocks on numerous Cronulla streets, and several vehicles containing Middle Eastern males being prevented entry, a large number of them and their cargo of angry young Middle Eastern males, had already slipped the net and were loose in Cronulla.
12/12/05	12.30am	Police stop 5 vehicles with Middle Eastern occupants in Elouera Road Cronulla. They were searched and directed to leave the area. At around this time 4 vehicles containing Middle Eastern men in Mitchell Road Cronulla attempted to drag a driver from his vehicle, but he managed to avoid capture.
12/12/05	1.15am	Police issue a 'Move On' direction to the drivers and occupants of 8 vehicles containing Middle Eastern men on Ewos street, Cronulla. This is the last sighting of revenge attackers that evening.

Sydney becalmed

By mid-early morning the next day, Monday the 12th of December 2005, police were able to report that the suburbs earlier under assault were calm and quiet. At 3.02am Assistant Commissioner Goodwin handed command over to Assistant Commissioner Denis Clifford.

The Strike Force Neil Report into senior police management of the Cronulla Riots concluded after this phase as follows:

> *"The situation that police had to manage and respond to on the 11th of December 2005 is unprecedented in Australian policing history...*
>
> *The reprisal attacks on Sunday evening across the Cronulla, Brighton-le-Sands areas which were mostly simultaneous, is unprecedented in public disorder anywhere in Australia...*
>
> *...The attacks were well planned and co-ordinated. The offenders attacked in the dark of night fuelled by racial prejudice and anger, showing no fear of authority and no mercy to their unsuspecting*

> victims...
>
> ...The challenge of commanding a police response to such an event is also unprecedented in the history of policing in Australia".[9]

This is an accurate account of extraordinary police performance, which is quite inconsistent with the tenor of other parts of that report. We explore this side to the riots in Part 3 'Investigating the Police'.

The following day – Monday 12th December 2005

Police plan for more trouble

These revenge attacks across many suburbs were violent and terrorising for a normally very peaceful and law-abiding metropolis. The randomness of the attacks meant anyone anywhere could be targeted and senior police were up early to prepare for the worst.

Goodwin drew on Supt. Mark Hutchings and Insp. Wayne Laycock of the Police Metropolitan Planning Unit to ensure that all the personnel, resources, logistics, equipment, and command structure were quickly put in place for an anticipated evening of further violent criminality.

The police operation was divided into three Sydney zones – Southern Suburbs (including the Brighton-le-Sands and Cronulla areas); Eastern Suburbs (including Maroubra); and the Western Suburbs area around Lakemba. Superintendents were placed in charge of all three areas reporting directly to the Police Operations Centre. Whilst planning and then approving a substantial police presence for the evening, Goodwin had to also be available for briefing political, community and policing leaders, as well as managing the media firestorm that the previous day and evening of riot and revenge had created.

Journalists, cameramen, editors and presenters from across the media occasionally act like a pack, in agreeing upon the story and then collectively presenting it. And that is what happened regarding the story of the first day of 'Cronulla Riots'. The 'pack' simply all but missed the main story, which was not the demonstration during the day which turned nasty, but the violent, property rampaging attacks in revenge which followed. The pack

---

[9] Strike Force Neil Report, p. 49.

were simply 'out to lunch'.

There had been virtually no cameramen on duty overnight. They had all gone home after their daytime scoop. Even the few usual night-time 'stringers' (freelance cameramen who work overnight to sell their footage to the TV networks), barely captured any footage because of the considerable geographic distance between these random acts of violence. This left the general public and the academics with a skewed and erroneous impression of the daytime issues at Cronulla, versus the sheer magnitude and severity of the racist violent night-time attacks throughout wider Sydney. As a result we have been left with a distorted and very one-sided only reporting of racism, which continues to this day.

On the morning of 12th December 2005 there were no reports of public disorder. It was eerily quiet, but Goodwin well knew what to expect under the cover of darkness that night. By late morning there were reports of further SMS text messaging, urging reprisal attacks by 'Arabs' against the 'Aussies'. One example is:

> *"All arabs unite as one we will never back down to anyone the aussies will feel the full force of the arabs as one brothers in arms. Unite now let's show them who's boss destroy everything gather at Cronulla 18/12/2005 midday; spread the message to all arabs meet up at the light house".*

The "light house" refers to Cook Park, Kyeemagh (just south of the Sydney Airport tunnel), where much of the throng of middle eastern young men congregated in cars the prior evening. From there it is an easy drive in convoy over Taren Point Bridge into the Cronulla area to wreak havoc.

Another SMS circulated urging Middle Eastern men to gather at Arncliffe Park that evening.

Throughout the afternoon, reports started to trickle in of sporadic and random instances of Middle Eastern men driving around verbally abusing people from their vehicles in Brighton-le-Sands, Cronulla, and Hurstville areas.

Battle lines drawn: Maroubra Beach v the Lakemba Mosque

The suburb of Maroubra had effectively become 'revenge central', after the predatory convoys had been locked out of Cronulla. Swarming up and down streets, looking for baseball bat victims, people and property were injured, and great fear instilled. The tough guy image of the 'Bra Boys' had taken a dent after daring such a 'visit', and then been unprepared when it happened.

Police began getting intelligence that the Bra Boys were weaponising their suburb, both in defence of Maroubra against an expected repeat attack, and allegedly to raid the Lakemba Mosque that evening.

A battle of Maroubra and the beach versus Lakemba and the Mosque seemed not only plausible in these extraordinary circumstances but now quite likely. The police planned accordingly for what they thought was going to be the start of an even more violent terrorising of a suburb in revenge for itself having been terrorised.

It made awful and troubling sense to both the Minister and the Police Commander, and they talked together and planned accordingly. These were extraordinary times, with Caucasian surfers preparing to defend their icon, the sand of Maroubra Beach, and Lebanese Muslims preparing to defend their icon, the Lakemba Mosque. It could have got a lot uglier than it did, but for the enormous efforts by police in both suburbs, supported by the extraordinary efforts of containment by Muslim community leaders around the Mosque.

Goodwin worked closely with each Local Area Commander to quickly plan and put in place strong police responses for the beach and the mosque: Supt. John Richardson of Campsie Command which covered Lakemba and Supt Phil Rogerson of Maroubra Command. Many years after the event, the extraordinary efforts of Richardson, Rogerson and the brave frontline police who managed this highly volatile situation, remain relatively unknown and unrecognised. They are highly commended by us.

The tough guy Maroubra Beach Bra Boys 'stood down'.

Superintendent Rogerson oversaw a number of police raids and searches in the Maroubra area to seize the stockpile of weapons put aside allegedly by the 'Bra Boys' for violent use later that evening. Police located many improvised weapons including bats, metal poles, crates full of bricks and other crates full of Molotov cocktails (petrol bombs). These weapons had been stockpiled in strategic locations including laneways, parks and on top of shops in the main area of Maroubra. Police from the operation at Maroubra spoke to the leaders of a group of 40 – 50 Caucasian young men

The 'Revenge Attacks'

who had gathered outside the Maroubra Bay Hotel. They were directed to disperse from the area, to which they complied. Without the intervention of these police raids and the strategy removing hundreds of weapons off the streets and directing the dispersal of Caucasian groups, the potential impact of violence that evening would have probably been considerable. Riot Police were in-situ at the ready and other police put in street closures around the Maroubra area, the same as the evening prior. Highly visible police vehicles with flashing lights blocked the roads and police manned those intersections. Helpfully, an Arabic Muslim leader was sent from Lakemba to speak to the Bra Boys and calm down the situation.

When we interviewed local Maroubra MP, Michael Daley about the alleged attack on the Lakemba mosque by the Bra Boys, he was somewhat bemused by it, and advised that not only had that never been entertained, but had it been, they would have had trouble even finding the mosque. Apparently, according to Mr Daley: *"people criticise people from Maroubra for never leaving the area. Well,* [they] *weren't going to leave the area that night".*[10]

Had another convoy of young Lebanese Muslim men attempted a second attack on Maroubra that night, then the police were ready for them, and had ensured that most of the local Maroubra troublemakers and their home-made weapons were off the streets. Thankfully, the plan was not put to the test.

The efforts by both Muslim community leaders and Supt Richardson, in jointly containing the anger in and around the Lakemba Mosque during the evening of Monday 12 December were simply extraordinary. We explore this in greater detail in our account of our interviews with Jihad Dib MP, Dr Jamal Rifi and Supt Richardson in Part 4. In our view, all three ought to have been awarded appropriate commendations by the NSW Police Commissioner, Ken Moroney.

Perhaps 3,000 people had gathered around the Mosque, machine guns stored in car boots, wooden weapons sourced, and an irate crowd ready to violently defend its mosque. Thankfully, due to a combination of no Bra Boys appearing, strong police presence including riot police, leaders talking themselves hoarse and the timely arrival of the 'Call to Prayer', calm took hold and the risk of violent escalation passed. It could have been otherwise.

Whilst Muslim members of the Lakemba community feared an attack upon

---

[10] M. Daley, Transcript of Interview, February 17, 2021.

them and/or their mosque was a possibility, police planned as if it was a probability. This is what the analysts from the Strike Force Neil investigation had to say on reflection:

> *"It is uncertain, despite the intelligence, if an attack on the Lakemba Mosque was ever genuinely intended. Although a significant number of weapons were found in the Maroubra area, their placement would indicate they were going to be used to defend the Maroubra Beach area against attacks similar to those that occurred on the night of 11th December".*[11]

How had Sydney come to this, is an important question, and one we endeavour to answer in Part 5, 'Explaining the Riot'.

Mobile random revenge attacks continue – evening of 12th December 2005

The Lakemba Mosque

Date	Time	Reported Activity
12/12/05	6.00pm	A large gathering of roughly 1,500-2,000 people gathered at the Lakemba Mosque allegedly to protect it from what they regarded as a quite likely Caucasian attack. A media photographer did require police protection, but the crowd was relatively quiet with only a few troublemakers. More police were called to assist.

Back at Maroubra

Date	Time	Reported Activity
12/12/05	6.00pm	Police attended Arthur Byrne Reserve Maroubra and found several Caucasian men 'armed with pieces of wood' and several vehicles containing baseball bats. One vehicle on being searched revealed 15 one-metre-long steel rods. These and other 'improvised weapons' found in the park were confiscated by police. A photographer from a newspaper was spat on.

---

[11] Strike Force Neil Report, Volume One, p. 51.

The 'Revenge Attacks'

Arncliffe Park

Date	Time	Reported Activity
12/12/05	6.35pm	A group of Middle Eastern men shattered a car driver's window and punched the woman driver and her passenger requiring both to be treated at hospital.
12/12/05	7.00pm	Around 150 Middle Eastern men had gathered in Wollongong Road outside the Arncliffe RSL Club. Police attended and had a brick thrown at their car, but the crowd dispersed after police spoke with senior community leaders.

Brighton-le-Sands

Date	Time	Reported Activity
12/12/05	7.00pm	12 Middle Eastern men had been harassing motorists and pedestrians for over 20 minutes with 2 of the men yielding baseball bats. These troublemakers dispersed upon the arrival of police.

Back at Lakemba Mosque

Date	Time	Reported Activity
12/12/05	8.44pm	A large crowd was becoming agitated despite the best becalming efforts of community leaders and 'crowd control marshals'. An arrest was made for 'Offensive Behaviour' and 'Intimidate Officer'.

By 9.25pm the Mosque area was calm with the crowd dwindling.

Cronulla under attack

The late evening was a difficult one for the residents of Cronulla and police endeavouring to protect them as convoys of vehicles, one of which was nearly 40 in number, made their way for reprisal attacks. Five police vehicles were shifted from the Lakemba Mosque to take positions on the three approaches at Captain Cook, Tom Ugly's and Woronora Bridges. Some vehicles of Middle Easterners were successfully stopped by police, but a number escaped the net.

Date	Time	Reported Activity
12/12/05	10.00pm	A cowardly attack by 10-15 Middle Eastern men upon one individual Cronulla man who was set upon with an iron bar, fists, and a bottle, after he sought to move his car to avoid it being damaged. He required treatment for injuries which included facial lacerations.
12/12/05	10.15pm	A male motorcyclist was lucky to have avoided considerable harm when inadvertently chancing upon the Middle Eastern convoy at The Boulevarde and Taren Point Road. Many left their vehicles to pursue him, one successfully struck him in the back with a thrown object, but the victim managed to ride off and escape.

Around this time police observed about 150 Middle Eastern men between Croydon Street and St Andrews Place, Cronulla smashing windows. A bottle was thrown at one police officer who pursued the offender and made an arrest. Police now had two dog teams on site.

Cronulla terrorised

Over a three-hour period from 10.30pm to 1.30am an unparalleled level of random violence was committed by young Middle Eastern men against unsuspecting Cronulla locals for no reason than they were not of Arabic appearance. They were to these unwelcome 'visitors' a "them" and not part of their "us".

These violent attacks were opportunistic, were random and effectively terrorised a whole suburb. The weapons of choice included metal bars, baseball bats and even firearms. The attacks occurred upon locals outside their homes, walking on the streets or occupying their vehicles. There were reports of property damage to private and commercial premises, and vehicles, and of attempts to run police down at roadblocks and assaults on Transit Officers at Caringbah Railway Station.

Even one of 6 ambulances called to treat the injured itself came under attack.

The 'Revenge Attacks'

Brighton-le-Sands cops it again

Date	Time	Reported Activity
12/12/05	11.00pm	The traffic lights near the Novotel Hotel became the focal point for about 100 Middle Eastern men who began assaulting motorists when stopped at the red light. An ambulance called to the scene also came under attack. Not surprisingly, police were called out in number including riot trained police and the Dog Squad. Police vehicles and shop windows were showered with a variety of objects including council rubbish bins. Police pursued them and the offenders dispersed. Weaponising anything they could get their hands on, these Middle Eastern 'visitors' then used rocks, fire extinguishers, fence palings and baseball bats to reign down damage to vehicles in various streets of Brighton-le-Sands.
12/12/05	11.30pm	In yet another case of group cowardice a crowd of Middle Eastern men assaulted a lone man as he departed his place of employment at the Novotel Hotel, Brighton-le-Sands.

The police response in perspective

Whilst it would be days, if not weeks, before police, the NSW Government, and the community, could comfortably feel that the trouble had subsided, the terror had passed and the public spaces were once again safe places, it was these two days and nights which reflect the most worrisome period for both police and community. It was new turf, and no-one really knew during those two days how or when it would all end.

The Strike Force Neil analyst summation of the policing challenges during the second night in our view accurately sums up the task facing police over both the 11th and 12th of December 2005: [12]

> "During this night, the co-ordination and mobility of the assailants made the task of commanding such an operation extremely difficult.

---

[12] Strike Force Neil, Volume One, pp. 53-54.

> *Commanders in the field acted swiftly when intelligence was received. However, it was evident that the speed and mobility of the assailants made it difficult to contain them. For example, at **Cronulla,** by the time the resources from the Mosque at Lakemba could be released the convoy of vehicles had entered the Sutherland Shire.*
>
> *Valiant attempts were made by police to stop the offenders in Cronulla but only a few that individual police could manage, were arrested. These officers put themselves at great risk in taking action, without concern for their personal safety.*
>
> *The same situation applied to police at Brighton-le-Sands who reduced the level of violence by personal commitment and courage in a volatile situation.*
>
> *At **Maroubra**, the Forward Commander (Superintendent Rogerson) and staff took swift and decisive action against what was emerging as a violent situation. A significant number of weapons were confiscated from the streets and road closures were effective in reducing the mobility and intent of any would-be assailants.*
>
> *At **Campsie,** during the debrief session that followed the incident at the Lakemba Mosque, a great deal of credit was given to the Forward Commander (Superintendent Richardson) for his community consultative tactics which had a direct impact on the efficient management of some 4000 people. It was also mentioned that this influenced an increased level of officer safety at the scene.*
>
> *It was generally acknowledged that the community consultation at Campsie, Cronulla, Maroubra, and Arncliffe which took place between Local Area Commanders and community leaders was an invaluable operational tactic. It had the effect of reducing the potential level of the violence down to what eventually took place".*

However, after these two very tough days of the 11th and 12th of December 2005, police were concerned that this was the beginning of a very worrisome summer. Police commanders and operational police in the field, planned and acted, as if the worst was still to befall us all.

We will now canvass some of the details of this policing for the rest of the 2005/2006 summer.

Police operations continue – 13th to 16th December 2005

Over the ensuing days senior police commanders, continued to command complex police operations in these same three zones (Cronulla/Brighton-le-Sands; Lakemba & surrounds; and Maroubra/Eastern-Suburbs). Huge numbers of police resources were deployed and moved around based upon intelligence being received. Sporadic acts and random mobile swarms of Middle Eastern men in vehicles continued, but this time were quickly shut down and their violent intent stymied before they could act.

The phenomenon of packs of violent young men massed in vehicular convoys, as highly mobile rioters carrying out indiscriminate attacks, had never been experienced by police in Australia. The numbers of vehicles, speed, mobility, and randomness of these plundering 'mobs' made it extremely difficult to police. Goodwin determined that the police response also needed to be on the move. Rather than a riot being contained with static police lines, there would be multiple rapid response police vehicles, containing riot trained police, responding in number to swarming rioter vehicles.

Numerous high impacting teams were assembled and positioned in strategic locations throughout Southern, Eastern and Western Sydney ready to pounce immediately against any of these convoys of revenge attackers. Each of the numerous police convoys consisted of thirty Riot Police, ten Highway Patrol officers, in ten V8 vehicles. Each car contained three Riot Police plus their gear and the vehicle was driven by trained pursuit drivers.

This was replicated across numerous groups, each containing forty police in ten police pursuit vehicles all in convoy. It enabled both rapid and fearsome en masse deployment of riot squad personnel. Police themselves became an agile, rapid response and highly mobile assault force in the eyes of Revenge Attackers. Once the teams were formed, they were briefed by Goodwin on expectations and strategically placed in the Lakemba, Cronulla, Maroubra, and other areas dictated by emerging intelligence. In addition, large numbers of other riot police, highway patrol, dog squads and other general & specialist police resources were also deployed into these areas for riot control, roadblocks and to prevent revenge attacks.

Goodwin named these new groups 'Rapid Response Riot Police'. They had the immediate desired impact. Whenever intelligence was received of a mobile group of Middle Eastern men in cars congregating, forming up, or on the move, they were swarmed upon by these fearsome groups of highly trained police. Whilst the Riot Police dealt with any offensive intimidating behaviour and searched cars and suspects for weapons drugs or any other illegal paraphernalia, the Highway Patrol Police would hand out numerous traffic tickets for violations, inspect motor vehicles and issue defect notices if warranted, thereby taking these vehicles off the road. The strategy was extremely successful. It effectively shut down these revenge attacks and public disorder over the ensuing days.

World renowned Commissioner William Bratton of the Los Angeles Police Department (LAPD) (also the former Commissioner of NYPD during the "Zero Tolerance" policing approach and the 9/11 bombings in New York), rang fascinated by this new approach. The strategy had received publicity across global policing jurisdictions.

Extreme Risk Intelligence emerges – Covert and Overt Police Operations

Despite what might appear to the contrary, with the more recent violent contest between rival Middle Eastern families, and the continued criminal activities of Outlaw Motorcycle Gangs, Southwest Sydney is a much calmer and more law-abiding place now than it ever was in the late 1990s and early 2000s. The police station at Lakemba was attacked in 1998 by a hail of bullets and around the same time, the campaign office of Tony Stewart, the MP for Bankstown was firebombed. Serious commercial drug running, kneecapping drug lord competitors, murders, gun possession, and violent gang rapes, were all part of this violently criminalised part of Sydney. Thankfully, well before December 2005, these viciously aggressive individuals, with scant, if any regard for the law and civil society, had been locked up.

Task Force Gain, which would later become The Middle Eastern Organised Crime Squad, had been set up following a spate of suspected Middle Eastern violent and drug related crimes. About twenty of the most violent individuals caught in this police net were by December 2005 welcome additions to Her Majesty's Prison Service and would not have been the sort of individuals the Bra Boys, the general community, or the police, would have wanted to be joining in on any Arabic revenge attacks. During our interviews in Part 4, 'Reflections from the field', Dr Jamal Rifi, and Supt. John Richardson both strongly supported the notion that without the work of Task Force Gain the revenge attacks would have been much more violent and terrorising of Sydney.

The broad intelligence gathered over a long period by Task Force Gain detectives, by physical and electronic surveillance, was invaluable to Goodwin and his team of police commanders.

At the same time, Goodwin had been meeting with his federal intelligence counterparts. In addition, there were several informants from within the Middle Eastern community who came forward and gave police valuable intelligence of what was being planned. This then enabled Goodwin and his senior colleagues to deploy police to shut down groups and issues before or as they occurred. Police were now on the front-foot and deployed strategically and proactively based on this intelligence.

Dangerous threats emerge

Reliable Intelligence had been received during this period from several sources that Middle Eastern men were planning an attack on the 'Northies' Hotel at North Cronulla the following weekend. The plans included a drive-by shooting utilising machine guns and also to throw a live hand-grenade into the beer garden of the hotel from a mobile vehicle and speed away before the blast. This will surprise and shock a great deal of people, particularly residents of Cronulla and the Sutherland Shire, who will not have been previously aware of this, until now. The extent of intelligence police had to deal with was horrendous and the sheer magnitude of high-to-extreme-risk police operations behind the scenes has never previously been known or reported. This is why police and their commanders virtually did not sleep for weeks and there was an emergency special sitting of NSW Parliament (outlined below) granting police extraordinary tough new legislation.

Police knew that Middle Eastern gangs were attempting to obtain a hand-grenade on the 'black market' and, on Friday 16th December 2005, just prior to the weekend, in a secretive clandestine police undercover sting, a hand-grenade was covertly purchased, thus taking it off the market before these Middle Eastern men could get their hands on it. The grenade was rendered safe by the bomb squad and then handed over to Army Bomb Disposal officers. Another targeted search warrant closed down another potential hand-grenade source, who was arrested for illegal guns.

Police also cordoned off and tightly locked-down the whole Cronulla area with road-blocks ahead of the proposed attack, utilising the new special emergency legislative powers. All vehicles and people entering the area were stopped and searched. Valid reasons for being in the area were obtained. These were highly intrusive draconian and tough measures, but as people will now appreciate, they were absolutely needed in the extreme-risk situation and circumstances existing at that time.

The potentially lethal hand-grenade and drive-by-shooting attack was averted by police through both strong covert and overt police operations.

Reliable intelligence was also received of an extremely violent attack being planned upon Miranda Westfield's that Thursday night 15th December 2005. The evening was a Thursday late-night shopping in the lead up to Christmas. There would literally be thousands of people within this huge shopping centre going about their last-minute Christmas shopping, completely oblivious to the extreme threat they were under.

The plan being hatched was for about fifty cars full of Middle Eastern men to pull up at the front of the Miranda Westfield's shopping centre. Drivers were to stay with the cars and the other occupants, totalling about 150-200 Middle Eastern males, would alight and rampage through the entire multi-storey shopping centre smashing all the shops and violently assaulting as many people as possible (both men and women) with baseball bats, iron bars, knives, guns and other weapons. The intelligence being received regarding the intent of this act was to *"Rip the Christ out of Christmas"*.

A massive police operation was then put in place at Westfield Miranda that Thursday evening. It prevented and thwarted this mass assault taking place. Likewise, police were deployed in large numbers to other Westfield Shopping Centres at Hurstville, East Gardens and even Parramatta, where it was feared the attackers may divert if they could not get into the one at Miranda. Groups forming in the Lakemba area were shut down that evening by the 'Rapid Response Riot Police' mobile teams that had been initiated, before they could even amass and get on the move in convoy. This operation was a complete success and, again, no violence occurred.

Police reported during Thursday night shopping on the 15th of December 2005, that complaints had come in from Castle Towers Shopping Mall at

The 'Revenge Attacks'

Castle Hill, that about 20-30 Middle Eastern males had congregated outside the entrance to the shopping centre and were harassing and abusing shoppers and families visiting the centre.

In a fascinating example of bullies sometimes needing to be themselves so intimidated by a show of stronger force that they concede the 'battleground', five Highway Police vehicles turned up carrying fifteen fully equipped riot police, who quickly exiting the vehicles, commenced a slow trot in formation, towards the Shopping Centre entrance, with batons drawn and shields lifted. It must have been a sight to behold as the troublemakers quickly 'ran like the wind'!

These Westfield Thursday night operations continued for weeks, even after Christmas into January 2006, because intelligence continued to be received indicating planned revenge attacks upon them were still afoot.

Westfield's management, who had been made aware of police intelligence and were highly consulted over these police operations, commended the police handling of these difficult weeks. Likewise, police were acknowledged as were their senior commanders, by the Sutherland Shire community in particular.

Intelligence was also received that every shop between Wollongong to Newcastle had sold out of baseball bats and golf clubs. Whilst these are both popular sports, many of the thousands of bats and clubs sold that week, were definitely not intended for Christmas presents. Also, shopping centres were reporting that hundreds of handles from shopping trolleys had been removed and stolen. These iron bar handles surrounded with plastic make an ideal sized weapon.

A mass of intelligence was also being received of violent revenge attacks being planned by both Middle Eastern and Caucasian groups stretching from Wollongong to Sydney to Newcastle the following weekend – Sat 17th to Sun 18th December 2005. The situation was dire and deemed to be an 'Extreme Risk'.

Scully recalls these troubling few days of December 2005:

> *"I was concerned that the Commissioner was allocating insufficient police personnel to respond and to protect the community, as I believed had been the case in the early part of the Macquarie Fields Riot. I was unimpressed that after the initial trouble at Cronulla on the 11th*

of December, Moroney intended to only provide 600 police for the following weekend. I told him bluntly: 'Ken, you'll need hundreds more police than that to do the job properly. If you don't think the cops are up to the job then I'll have to ask the Premier to call for troops to assist'.

That threat of troops seemed to do the trick, as quickly enough 2,000 police and every possible specialist command was put on the job from Newcastle to Wollongong and every suburb, beach, and main roadway in between. This worked! Dissent was stifled, troublemakers rounded up, text messaging inciters charged, and peace restored to Sydney. But why did I have to threaten armed soldiers on the street, before our much-commended Police Commissioner realised the urgency of the hour?

On a far more pleasant note, I do fondly recall the regular conversations and briefings I had before, during and after the Cronulla riot, with Goodwin, and directly with many of his Local Area Commanders, often on an hourly basis, as we all shared our thoughts on events, the available intelligence and the appropriate policing responses. These regular and detailed engagements with my field commanders, left me feeling confident that operational police were being well led, that they knew what they were doing, and all that could be reasonably expected to be done by police, was being effectively done."

Special sitting of the NSW Parliament – Thursday 15th December 2005

After the first day and night 'riots' of Sunday 11 December 2005, all senior police commanders realised they needed special legislative powers to deal with the unfolding crisis: roadblocks, seizing vehicles and phones, and closing liquor outlets. Police had been winging it to a large degree, but Goodwin now requested that the power to do these things was put beyond doubt. Within four days of the initial events, Parliament enacted the necessary additions to police powers.

Barrister Stephen Stanton referred to the resulting legislation as a *"legislative reprisal"* which he regarded as both *"necessitous"* and *"timely"*, without which *"Men like Goodwin, would've had war, not riots on their hands"*.[13]

---

[13] S. Stanton, Transcript of Interview, February 16, 2021.

The 'Revenge Attacks'

We discuss his perspective further in Part 3 'Reflections from the Field'. Goodwin reflects upon that time and recalls,

> "I am forever grateful to the Government for the expediency of their actions and unprecedented recall of Parliament, which urgently gave me the legislation needed to restore public order.
>
> Without doubt, it gave us the authority and mandate we needed to get the job done. It was a real morale booster to the front-line police, who faced off with the worst of Australian society that weekend, with a level of assurance like never before that they were being backed by their Leaders and Government.
>
> The people of NSW really have no idea of the frightening level of intelligence police possessed and the extreme risk they faced. The magnitude of planned violence, together with the threat of mass casualties and death were unprecedented. What would have been the worst weekend of violence ever unleashed in Australia was thwarted via the judicious use by police of these new powers. For that I am forever indebted, as are the people of New South Wales".

Discussions unfolded rapidly over Monday the 12th and Tuesday the 13th of December 2005, between the Premier, the Attorney-General (AG) and the Minister for Police, and their senior Departmental officers, on the steps needed to be put quickly in place, to give police the powers needed to rapidly restore order to the streets of Sydney.

A special meeting of cabinet to discuss and approve the necessary urgent supporting legislation was held at 2.30pm on the 13th of December 2005. All but two of the 21 ministers attended. In just over an hour, the cabinet unanimously approved these legislative riot busting initiatives. Absent was the usual multi-page written and pre-circulated cabinet minute from the Minister for Police, arguing the case for change. There was no time for such Westminster niceties. Instead, a discussion took place, a decision was made, it was recorded, and the Parliamentary Counsel's Office, swiftly put it all into the proper form of a Bill for presentation to the parliament just two days later. This was about as swift as it gets.

The riot occurred, the violent revenge attacks took place, the police advised, the Government acted, and the parliament approved. It was an impressive process.

At the special sitting on the 15 December 2005, The *Law Enforcement Legislation Amendment (Public Safety) Act 2005* was passed with bipartisan support and allowed police to:

- Establish roadblocks
- Stop and search persons or vehicles
- Prevent persons or vehicles from entering or leaving an area
- Seize vehicles or mobile phones
- Demand disclosure of identity
- Close licensed premises and establish alcohol-free-zones.

Each and every one of these powers was urgently needed by police to ensure that what they had been doing to crush riotous behaviour, was undoubtedly permissible under the law, as well as giving a clear message to Caucasian and Middle Eastern troublemakers that both the police and the government meant business. They very soon got the message.

This is what Scully said to the NSW Parliament during the 2nd reading debate:

> "*Our vibrant and diverse culture is something we should celebrate, and we will not sit idly by and let these criminals destroy it. These are onerous and what some would call draconian measures. They are emergency measures in emergency times. We do not lightly empower the police with significant powers of search, seizure, and confiscation...*
>
> *We have seen mobs pursuing people for no reason other than that they do not look like them. We have seen people assaulted in restaurants because they are not Caucasians. This disgusts us all.*
>
> *We have seen in response to the mob rule in Cronulla what can only be called the use of mobile assault vehicles, which descended on suburbs and caused havoc.*
>
> *The community expects the government to respond, and we have responded*".

The 'Revenge Attacks'

Seizing cars, weapons and phones

> "Riot roadblocks will be used to prevent ring-ins and would be accomplices from entering or leaving a lockdown area. Not only will police stop people in their tracks; they will take away any tools that people may use to feed this unrest. Police will search people, seize their weapons, impound their vehicles, and remove their means of communication. That is, at a roadblock, police will be able to conduct a search and not only seize offensive implements but confiscate the car, mobile phones, and communication devices".

Impact on civil liberties

> "I say to those members of the community who are concerned about the bill's impact on civil liberties, that these are tough times, and it is always difficult to strike the correct balance between civil liberties and the need to protect and reassure the community. I think we have got the balance right in terms of how these powers will be used and the seniority of the officers who will be authorised to enforce them".

Police operations Sat 17th – Sun 18th December 2005

Armed with this new Public Order Legislation, Assistant Commissioner Goodwin put a plan forward to the NSW Police Commissioner for the following weekend (and beyond). It involved placing the NSW Police into what was referred to as 'Olympic mode'. Five years before, in the Year 2000, Sydney had hosted the Olympic Games. The security planning and operations for the Olympics had been conducted by the NSW Police Force. The police officers within Goodwin's 'Metropolitan Planning Unit' had been at the forefront of such planning and therefore had the blueprint for freeing up huge amounts of NSW Police resources and diverting them into one single police special operation. And so once again, NSW Police put into effect the Olympic Plan, to ensure the security of our community, but this time, it was rioters not athletes, who were the focus of attention.

The 80 Local Area Commands were joined temporarily with hundreds of police being transferred into Sydney from regional areas to join into the thousands utilised in Sydney, Wollongong, and Newcastle.

Just one weekend after the start of the 'riots', two thousand police in seven zones were deployed in the largest police operation of its kind ever in Australia. Superintendents were placed in command of each of these zones, at all times reporting to the high-tech Police Operations Centre with Goodwin commanding the overall operation. These police zones included Wollongong; Sydney's Southern Beaches, Eastern Beaches, Western Suburbs and Northern Beaches; Central Coast; and Newcastle. After Scully advised the Commissioner he'd consider using the country's military to restore order, *"If you're not up to it"*, the entire NSW Police Force and all its specialist commands, was put at the disposal of Goodwin.

Supt Ron Mason, one of NSW Police most experienced riot control commanders was of the view: *"I think [it] worked...I had 1,000 [police] at Cronulla".*[14]

The interview we conducted with Ron Mason, which we discuss in greater detail as part of Part 4, 'Reflections from the Field', resulted in a fascinating perspective of a NSW Police public order expert coming to light.

During planning, Goodwin consulted closely with the NSW Police Association, particularly regarding industrial rights, entitlements, award agreements, meals, accommodation, welfare, and safety issues. In a spirit of total cooperation, all issues were agreed upon in advance. This level of cooperation ensured police satisfaction, high morale, and made for the smooth running of a successful police operation. The Police Union were highly appreciative of this, later expressing praise for this cooperative approach.

The police operation that weekend was massive and very intrusive. In a unique experience for NSW, entire areas and suburbs from Wollongong to Newcastle were strategically placed into 'lockdown' based upon police intelligence. Any person or vehicle entering those 'declared areas' were stopped, identification and details inspected, reasons established for entering the area, with vehicles/people searched. The public of New South Wales had never experienced such intrusive police powers and operations. But it was necessary.

Literally thousands of weapons were taken off the streets at roadblocks and in targeted searches. Weapons seized included guns, knives, home-made petrol bombs, improvised explosive devices, Molotov cocktails,

---

[14] R. Mason, Transcript of Interview, March 9, 2021.

metal poles, baseball bats, golf clubs, crates of bricks rocks and lumps of concrete, wooden bats with nails protruding, shopping trolley handles etc. People were charged where appropriate with possession of items that were prohibited. Goodwin vividly recalls one such improvised weapon and the damage it would have caused - a billiard table leg that had hundreds of nails protruding from it.

The operation was an enormous success. There were very few acts of violence. The messages and notion of public order, decency and civility were well and truly delivered and restored over the weekend of the 17th and 18th of December 2005. The magnitude of police operations that weekend efficiently and effectively ceased the violence. Thousands of weapons were taken off the streets. Arrests were made where appropriate. Public order and confidence in New South Wales was restored.

The personal cost

Many people across Sydney were fearful and worried during these terrifying few days. Some had endured significant threats and even injury. Others cowered in their homes as their property, streets and public places were terrorised. It was a worrying time for many of us, at community, policing, or political levels.

Let us not forget the personal cost to police too. It was a tough and enduring time for police who put in blood, sweat and almost tears, across many sleepless nights, to get this great city of ours under control. For a huge swathe of our police finest, leave was cancelled, and their normal policing jobs put on hold, as they focussed upon and joined a law enforcement swarm designed and destined to attack and defeat a level of civil disorder the likes of which none of them had previously seen.

Police operations the following six weeks – Operation 'Seta'

Massive police operations in the before mentioned seven zones continued for the following six weeks through to early February 2006. It was exhausting to the front-line police, planners, and commanders alike. Many police and logistics personnel had little sleep for weeks as they mustered every piece of ingenuity to keep the staff and resources flowing to these continual huge police operations.

Order had been restored, but police continued to receive and deal with extreme risk intelligence situations. And then came Christmas Day, New Year's Eve and Australia Day, all of which were extreme risk police operations, given the still simmering racial tension and violence that had occurred. On every occasion, intelligence was received indicating the planning of revenge attacks and disruption to these traditionally celebrated days. And on every occasion, emerging issues and situations were thwarted by police operations.

Over these six weeks large numbers of police resources were continually and strategically moved around in all these areas to address the extremely difficult and dynamic environment. Given the size, scope, complexity and never-before-seen intrusive 'lockdown' powers unleashed throughout the operation, which caused major public disruption in beach side suburbs over Christmas and throughout January's peak summertime, the public were generally very cooperative, receptive, and thankful to police.

6

Police Pursue the Offenders

Introduction

It is standard police practice following a major incident to establish a strike force of committed officers to investigate, find and prosecute offenders. The events surrounding the Cronulla riot and revenge of late 2005 were no different.

Given the TV and print coverage of the day of the riots providing quite confronting footage, it was unsurprising that a Strike Force was established that very first evening of 11th December, then after the reprisal attacks of 11th and 12th December, the State Crime Command took control of the Investigation and on 13th December Strike Force Enogerra commenced, initially consisting of 28 detectives headed by Superintendent Dennis Bray. It was tasked with finding enough evidence to prosecute offenders on the day of the riot or in subsequent revenge.

The work of the task force was an outstanding success in terms of gathering evidence, rounding up suspects, prosecuting individuals and getting a slew of convictions for both the rioters and those acting in revenge.

On 20 January 2006, the Strike Force was increased in size to 100 investigators under the Command of Detective Superintendent Ken McKay for reasons outlined later. The investigation team worked tirelessly under immense scrutiny with unprecedented public interest and media attention with respect to their inquiries and arrests.

The results

A succinct breakdown of criminal prosecutions stemming from Strike Force Enoggera's investigations is as follows:

> "By 19 July 2006, police had laid 285 charges against 104 people, 51 having

been arrested as a result of the original Cronulla riot and 53 arrested from the retaliation riots: These persons were charged with, amongst other things: malicious damage, possession or use of a prohibited weapon, assaulting police, rioting, resisting arrest, threatening violence and affray".[15]

By the time their work was done, approximately 200 had been brought before the courts in roughly equal number between initial rioters and follow up revenge attackers. Only one was a woman. Below is a small selection of the types of cases brought before the NSW Courts. To list them all is not feasible in this book.

A selection of cases

Name	Charge	Description
Ali Osman, 18	Assault	The attack on the lifeguard on 4/12/05, 300 hrs community service.
Yahya Jamal Serhan, 22	Affray and assault GBH	Brutal knife attack outside Woolooware Golf Club. Victim kicked, punched and stabbed 5 times, 9 months gaol.
Marcus Kapitza, 28	Affray	Wore a singlet with words, "Mohammed was a camel raping faggot". He banged on the train carriage yelling: "Fuck off Lebs" and considered a "keen participant in these disgraceful events", 12 months gaol.
Juvenile Offender, 16	Theft	Stole and burnt Australian flag at Brighton Le Sands RSL Club, 7 months detention. Sent by club to Kokoda Track and apologises.
Juvenile Offender, 16	Assault	Photographed attempting to assault train passenger, 46 days in detention. Asserted acting in self-defence.
Brett Andrew King, 25	Using device to incite riot.	Sent 2 text messages 42 times encouraging people to meet at Cronulla Beach on 18/12/05.
Jeffrey Ismail, 27	Using device to menace.	Police intercept phone calls on 12/12/05 organising convoy to Cronulla, and gang retribution at Lakemba Mosque against Bra Boys. Pleads guilty, 12 months gaol.

In the case of Ali Osman, the words used by The Local Sutherland Court

---

[15] A. Clennell, 'Police tough on both sides of Cronulla riots', *Sydney Morning Herard*, 19 July 2006, referring to media statement by then Police Minister Carl Scully.

Magistrate, Jacqueline Trad, herself of Lebanese heritage, could be applied universally to the 199 males and 1 female brought before the courts following the Cronulla Riots:

> **Trad:** *"By your conduct you have turned your back on your family, your culture and your real country (Australia) – all for the sake of some juvenile, impulsive and misplaced allegiance. Over the last 100 years or so, the ancestors of many citizens – mine included – came to this country seeking refuge from hatred, intolerance, violence or simply the opportunity to improve their families' prospects".[16]*

Allegations police had "Gone soft on Middle Eastern crime"

Strike Force Enoggera rounded up Caucasians from the daytime issues at Cronulla quite quickly. Simply, they were easier targets. They had punched ethnic people or engaged in riotous conduct in broad daylight in front of dozens of TV cameras and news reporter's cameras. They were on every TV Screen and Newspaper in Sydney, throughout wider Australia and even made international news. They were more easily identifiable. Very clear professional video and still camera footage existed of their behaviour.

In comparison, the Middle Eastern 'revenge attacks' were well organised, clandestine raids, committed under the cover of darkness and without the benefit of an abundance of media shots from several different angles. Identification of these offenders became quite problematic and a lot more difficult.

As a result, an early imbalance emerged in the numbers of arrests by Strike Force Enoggera of Caucasians -v- Middle Eastern youth. This led to hysterical media and political sniping about police only locking up the 'Sons of Anzacs'. Bizarre accusations were given wide coverage by the media that the relatively new Premier, Morris Iemma, had told police to go soft on Middle Eastern crime because he was the local member for Lakemba and had used the Middle Eastern vote to gain selection.

A sample of media headlines on allegedly 'going soft':

---

[16] *The Age,* September 30, 2006.

The Cronulla Riots

Headline	Quote
'ALP soft on ethnic criminals'	"*Liberal Leader...said...political indebtedness...discouraged* [police] *vigorous pursuit of ethnic wrongdoers.*"[17]
'Iemma calls Debnam a liar'	" [He was] *...unable* [to] *provide any evidence...*[but]*there have been zero arrests*" [of revenge attackers] *...but no foundation to the... "absurd claim"*.[18]
'Lock up 1000 gang members'	"*Not enough Middle Eastern people in gaol...* [police] *should lock up 200 Middle Eastern people responsible for revenge attacks...The government has been soft on Middle Eastern crime*".[19]

It defies both political gravity and policing reality, that a Premier or government would instruct the police to go soft on offenders for any reason, let alone on the basis of how they may collectively vote. The claims were made by the opposition leader without a shred of evidence and blindly repeated by all media outlets. The published denials by the Premier would no doubt have provided a technical compliance with journalistic codes of ethical and balanced reporting. But it did make for great copy and memorable headlines.

In this environment of police and its Commissioner being accused of a political fix in the work of Strike Force Enoggera, the Commissioner had to speak: "*A visibly furious Moroney staunchly defended police in their efforts to arrest...revenge attackers...*[and] *said it was personally and professionally 'offensive' ...to suggest police had been ordered...to go soft on Middle Eastern Hoodlums*".[20]

The headline promoting the story pretty much captured the mood: '*Don't call my officers soft-Moroney lashes out at race critics*'.

However, and very unfortunately for the police investigators and the wider community, the Police Commissioner then went off script on a matter he had not been briefed on and claimed that the reason for a lack of Middle Eastern revenge attack arrests was due to a lack of camera footage. The following words uttered free style by no less than a Commissioner for Police, would have significant repercussions for not only Strike Force

---

[17] *The Australian,* January 18, 2006.
[18] *The Daily Telegraph,* January 18, 2006.
[19] *The Sydney Morning Herald,* January 18, 2006.
[20] *The Daily Telegraph,* January 14, 2006.

Enoggera detectives trying to do their best to gather prosecutable evidence regarding all offenders, but also for the laudable work done by senior police who had commanded through that difficult summer of 2005/2006.

> **Moroney**: *"Unlike the events that occurred in Cronulla where there was visual evidence in the form of photographs and video recordings etcetera, these other attacks late at night were under the cover of darkness".[21]*

Yes, they were "under the cover of darkness" but it was inexact to imply that meant there was no "visual evidence" as plenty had, unbeknownst to the Commissioner, been provided confidentially to the Strikeforce. There was footage of revenge attacks! In fact, CCTV cameras in various businesses around Cronulla and other areas had captured footage of some of these revenge attacks occurring. And the police investigation task force had been supplied this footage, but it had not yet been released to the public for legitimate investigative reasons.

Firstly, some of the footage of Middle Eastern revenge attacks was unclear and grainy, as these incidents had occurred at night. Very experienced Detectives on the investigation were all too familiar with the many problems which can be later experienced during Court prosecutions proceedings regarding identification evidence. They had been dealing with enhancement specialists to try to get these images suitable for public release and, more importantly, to a point where they would be suitable for identification purposes to the very high standard required in criminal prosecutions and proofs of evidence.

Secondly, a well-known 'code of silence' existed among Middle Eastern crime gangs prevalent at the time. Extreme fear existed of becoming involved in identifying offenders to police, and therefore becoming a witness against any of these people. Quite appropriately, it was the intention of the detectives working tirelessly on the case, to have physical and electronic surveillance in place on suspects prior to public release of the footage. The reaction of suspects and offenders seeing themselves in extensive media coverage would then be monitored legally, and potentially could have formed the backbone of briefs of evidence in otherwise extremely difficult prosecutions at Court. The plan was smart and being carried out by very experienced investigators who knew what they were doing.

---

[21] *The Daily Telegraph,* January 14, 2006.

When Cronulla business operators, who had already given their grainy night-time CCTV footage of revenge attacks undertaken 'under cover of darkness', to police weeks prior, heard the 'news', that there was no such footage, they were understandably unimpressed, and soon enough began forwarding their copy to news outlets. No wonder conspiracy theories of cover ups and 'going soft on Middle Eastern crime' had got traction.

One Cronulla business operator gave their CCTV images to a very interested current affairs program, which showed a violent gang assault by a large number of Middle Eastern males upon a single Caucasian male actually taking place at Cronulla during the 'revenge attacks'. This had already been supplied to investigating detectives but not publicly released yet for the legitimate investigative reasons mentioned above.

The Police investigator's hands were forced by this 'revelation', meaning they had to reveal to the media that there was in fact even more video footage of the revenge attacks. Critical media then appeared:

Headline	Story
'Video of revenge riot appears- a month late'	"...Ken Moroney discovered month-old footage of... revenge attackers."[22]
'Cronulla Cop-Out- Why police have made no arrests over this bashing'	"Premier...hauled Moroney into his office to explain why no arrests over the footage. 'I have been deeply disturbed by this footage...Govt...expects swift action'".[23]
'Focus on crime of all colours'	"Serious cracks are appearing at the upper echelons of NSW Police management which raise serious questions about the ability of the force to round up all – and we mean all – the players in the race violence which marred the city last month."[24]

At the time, Police Minister Carl Scully was on a ministerial study trip and was in the middle of a briefing from counter-terrorism police in Egypt regarding the 1997 violent attack at Luxor which killed 62 people including 58 tourists, when he got a call from the Premier, Morris Iemma: **Iemma:** "We need you home. The cops have run amok since you left".

---

[22] *The Sydney Morning Herald*, January 20, 2006.
[23] *The Daily Telegraph*, January 20, 2006.
[24] *The Daily Telegraph*, January 20, 2006.

PART 3:
INVESTIGATING THE POLICE

7

Investigating the Police

The removal of Supt. Bray

As mentioned, Detective Superintendent Dennis Bray had been appointed to head up Strike Force Enoggera just days after the initial demonstration at Cronulla on 11 December 2005. He was an exemplary detective with a long career of extraordinary police performance. He was highly respected and a very sound appointment.

After the media campaign on the alleged lack of revenge attack CCTV footage, Moroney removed Bray from head of the investigation task force.

An example of newspaper headlines which followed his removal:

> **'Riots Claim First Scalp'**
>
> 'Task Force chief axed as key video man identified.'
>
> "The Cronulla riot strike force chief was yesterday stood down as police faced new embarrassment over the bungled investigation. ....The revelation came as police split ranks over the removal of Detective Superintendent Dennis Bray, who was axed for failing to inform Commissioner Ken Moroney of the CCTV footage.....Mr Moroney expressed his 'concern, disappointment and absolute annoyance' at not being told a video existed. He said as a result he had replaced Supt Bray with Superintendent Ken McKay."[25]

What is extraordinary in all this, is that Moroney was publicly chiding the head of his investigation team for not telling him something he had not be asked to brief him upon.

Soon enough the droll humour of journalists began:

---

[25] *The Daily Telegraph*, January 21, 2006.

"Have you heard the latest on the Cronulla Riots? – I'm waiting for it to come out on video".

Bray did defend himself:

> "[telling] *a media conference on Thursday the delay* [in releasing footage] *was due to failed attempts to enhance the CCTV footage. This is part truth – but not the main reason. Supt Bray was in a difficult position: he could not reveal the whole story as it would endanger the hunt for Steve B's attackers. For what is coyly termed "operational reasons" the footage was to be released, but not yet. Every police officer knows what "operational reasons" really means: key methodology used in gaining enough evidence to lay charges. To reveal what they are doing publicly would be irresponsible and tip off criminals on ways to avoid detection... Pursuing those in night-time CCTV footage was a harder slog and less likely to yield quick results. It would be done, but the work had to be prioritised".*[26]

Bray's team quickly threatened to walk off the job. If only Moroney had made a phone call to Bray, reflected for a moment or two, and then said this instead:

> "*The gathering of evidence by the Taskforce is focussed and well resourced. In due course, I am confident that as many offenders as possible, whether Caucasian or Middle Eastern, will be identified and prosecuted. I can't say anymore at this stage except to ask the community for patience as we seek justice on their behalf.*"

What a difference such a measured approach would have had at the time.

However, one journalist did get it right in terms of the impact the untimely release of CCTV footage would have then had on quiet discreet evidence gathering:

> "*...now the footage has been released, the attackers will know to get rid of the clothes they were wearing that night or leave the country the source said. Bray's critics 'all think they're experts, including Moroney, but you never declare everything you've got straight away . . . If you were going to install listening devices or send in informants, you do that before* [releasing the footage]. *You shake the tree and you have to*

---

[26] *The Daily Telegraph*, January 21, 2006.

> be there to see what falls down.' It is a measure of Bray's character that on Friday every member of his taskforce stood beside Police Association president Bob Pritchard to demand his reinstatement".[27]

The detectives on Bray's team were very upset about the treatment given to their commander. On their behalf the Police Association threatened industrial action and issued a strongly worded statement stating that the detectives on Strike Force Enoggera "*have absolute confidence in the leadership of... Supt Bray*" as their commander, called for his "*immediate reinstatement*" and asserted that the release of the video footage "*will compromise their investigation*".[28]

The detectives at Strike Force Enoggera held a stop-work meeting and all stood behind their union boss in an act of solidarity and defiance at the way they had been treated, during a press conference held by NSW Police Association president, Bob Prichard.

The media again went into overdrive:

'Rank and file fury at riot chief sacking'

> "*Tensions within the NSW Police intensified yesterday when Commissioner Ken Moroney's troops rebelled over his decision to sack the detective leading the investigation into the Cronulla riots. The direct attack on Mr Moroney's authority is a slap in the face, with the officers calling his handling of the affair "disgusting".*
>
> *However, initially the Commissioner dug his defensive heels in and continued what was really an unsustainable defence of his attack on the investigation:*
>
> *Yesterday he [Moroney] was unrepentant And said: 'Clearly, I believe that this morning, when I took the level of action that was appropriate (to remove Supt Bray), I still believe that to be the case,...[the] video I believe could have been released (and) might have assisted in the identification of any or all people responsible for attacks on innocent parties'.*"[29]

---

[27] *Sun Herald,* January 22, 2006.
[28] NSW Police Association Circular No.5/20, January 2006, 'Task Force Enoggera Update'.
[29] *The Daily Telegraph,* January 21, 2006.

However, the detectives directly working on the investigation refused to accept this claim of the Commissioner:

> "...detectives in Enoggera claim the commissioner has now compromised their investigation: 'It's clear the placing of the video on television and putting it out to the public completely compromised a number of investigations,' Mr Pritchard said. 'If the tape had been worthwhile putting out there earlier, they would have done that. They are experienced police and know how to investigate crime and we should support them'."[30]

The negative media coverage of all this was unrelenting. A typical example:

'Sacking sparks police revolt'

> "...Moroney, faced open rebellion last night after he sacked the chief investigator of the Cronulla riots for not disclosing controversial video evidence... The Police Association has not ruled out industrial action over the affair".[31]

Moroney then admitted publicly that he had not spoken to Supt Bray before his press conference:

> "The appearance of new video evidence is embarrassing for Mr Moroney....[who] blamed Mr Bray for his slip-up, even though he admitted not talking to him before making his comments. He said he had relied on the advice of others'".

It was never made clear who these "others" were and what high level experience they had in leading investigations.

However, Moroney was the leader and should have asked: "*hang on, has anyone spoken to Supt Bray about this*"?

The Police Association continued its attack:

> "The Police Association president, Bob Pritchard, said members of Mr Bray's taskforce were "completely disgusted" by Mr Moroney's handling of the matter and the "public humiliation" of their boss, in whom they had "complete and utter faith". He said the taskforce had decided not to release the footage because it would tip off the

---

[30] *The Daily Telegraph,* January 21, 2006.
[31] *The Sydney Morning Herald,* January 21, 2006.

attackers". ³²

The Sunday Telegraph summed up very well the difficult predicament that the Commissioner had placed himself in:

'Walkout threatened over sacking'

"Police have demanded embattled Commissioner Ken Moroney publicly apologise for criticising the Cronulla riot taskforce or risk a walkout of his own officers...The union has threatened industrial action as early as this week if its demands are not met. Mr Moroney has agreed to meet with the 28-member taskforce at Botany tomorrow afternoon."³³

Not surprisingly, Supt Bray was reinstated, although as Deputy, and a further 72 detectives added to the Strikeforce for good measure, up from the initial 28, and now with Detective Supt Ken McKay at the helm.

As it turned out:

"Police [had] "well over 100 hours" of CCTV footage of the vicious reprisals that swept through three suburbs in the wake of the Cronulla riots, it emerged yesterday. Only four days after police said they were yet to identify anyone from the revenge attacks from one CCTV video, they admitted there is several days' worth of footage... as Commissioner Ken Moroney performed an embarrassing backflip... seen as a backdown to appease strike force officers".³⁴

The Premier didn't make life any easier for the Commissioner:

"New South Wales Premier Morris Iemma has distanced himself from the decision to sack the head of Strike Force Enoggera, which is investigating the Cronulla riots.... 'It's a decision on his part', he said." ³⁵

"Police should not have to second guess judgements or take into account negative public reaction when they make operational decisions".³⁶

Moroney then suddenly and unexpectedly announced a 'Strike Force'

---

[32] *The Sydney Morning Herald*, January 21, 2006.
[33] *Sunday Telegraph*, January 22, 2006.
[34] *The Daily Telegraph*, January 24, 2006.
[35] ABC News, January 23, 2006.
[36] AAP News Centre, January 23, 2006.

investigation into command and control of the Cronulla Riots. Unexpected, as up to that point, the performance of police and its leadership during the riots had been lauded as exemplary.

The media reacted as the general public did; if an investigation was needed then there must have been something wrong with that performance. The investigation was announced not as a review, or the usual internal debrief for improvement, but as a full scale 'Strike Force' supported by detectives with terms of reference. What concerned Goodwin and police commanders was that a "Strike Force", normally only reserved for serious gang activity, drug syndicates, organised crime and violence, was now being used to scrutinise police themselves, when not a single complaint, to their knowledge, had been lodged publicly or privately about their conduct or performance.

Unlike the senior police management of the Redfern and Macquarie Fields Riots, about which on both occasions, the NSW Police Association expressed its displeasure, the Union on this occasion, was completely satisfied and strongly backed Goodwin's command response and decision making. Goodwin had heavily consulted and involved them throughout planning, which they greatly appreciated and acknowledged.

Goodwin had been given a Community Leadership Award within the Cronulla/Sutherland Shire and had received great recognition from other quarters including Local Politicians, the Mayor of Sutherland Shire, Westfield Management, Surf Life Saving Association, the Police Minister Carl Scully and Premier Morris Iemma. World renowned Commissioner William Bratton of the LAPD (also former Commissioner of NYPD during the "Zero Tolerance" policing approach and the 9/11 bombings in New York) had rung and given accolades for one of the strategies that had been initiated, which had become known as 'Rapid Response Riot Police' where mobile Highway Patrol vehicles delivered well equipped riot police as needed at a moment's notice. The strategy had received publicity in the USA and was of great interest to policing jurisdictions overseas. As mentioned earlier, even the French authorities were fascinated by this approach to a new phenomenon, a riot on the move.

We submit there was simply no known reasons existing at that time to justify the announcement of such a high-level 'Strike Force' investigation. There was no serious or multiple complaints (or any known complaints at all for that matter); no adverse media (police were being highly praised for bringing the streets of Sydney back under control); no Union pressure (they were highly complementary and appreciative of their involvement); no political pressure (both sides of parliament and all local members were extremely happy, particularly with the close consultation and how police had judiciously used their new powers). The only issue on the table of which we were aware at that time was Moroney's own personal reputation in the media. Whilst it is certainly within the prerogative of a Police Commissioner to inquire into operational aspects of their organisation, it is not known why Moroney abruptly and without explanation announced a 'Strike Force' investigation into the police who quelled the riots.

Goodwin gets as much notice as Bray

At the time Moroney announced this 'Strike Force' investigation, Goodwin was finally taking a few well-earned days off at a caravan park on the South Coast after running the massive 'Beach Safe' operations throughout the rest of December 2005 and January 2006. Moroney never rang or consulted Goodwin, he just launched and announced this inquiry to the media and took off on leave. The way Goodwin found out was through random people in the caravan park, who came up to him waving newspapers asking if he knew that Moroney had announced an inquiry into his handling of the Cronulla Riots.

Goodwin left to explain why he was being investigated

After the announcement, Moroney then went on leave. The Commissioner's personal media advisor then demanded that Goodwin do all the upcoming media requests and current affairs programs, which would require him to explain why he now needed to be investigated. Goodwin was called into Police Headquarters with other commanders including Superintendents Rob Redfern (Miranda Local Area Commander), John Richardson (Campsie Local Area Commander), Mark Hutchings (Region Operations Manager) and subjected to a highly charged, emotive 3-4 hour meeting. It was made very clear that Goodwin was expected to front the media.

8

Challenges from the Outset

An assistant commissioner investigating an assistant commissioner

Commissioner Moroney got it right on the Macquarie Fields Riots review when he appointed Deputy Commissioner Dave Madden to head it up. Supt. John Sweeney, as the then Macquarie Fields Local Area Commander, was in the firing line and it was appropriate, that someone of a superior rank would be assessing his performance.

However, in appointing Assistant Commissioner Norm Hazzard to head up a 'Strike Force' into the Command of the Cronulla Riots, when the then fellow Assistant Commissioner Mark Goodwin was under review, the Commissioner ensured no such similar courtesy was extended.

In the words of Moroney himself during a meeting to consider a draft of Madden's report: *"I'm not having Sweeney blamed for this. He didn't let us down, the system did"*.

The Macquarie Fields draft report was duly amended during several consultative meetings to ensure no organisational blame was attributed to the commander. No such courtesy was offered to Goodwin.

Norm Hazzard appointed by Commissioner Moroney

Norm Hazzard, as Assistant Commissioner in charge of the Counter-Terrorism Command (CTC) had been trying to extend the role of the CTC into managing the Regional General Duties policing function with respect to major events and public order management.

This would have effectively recreated main line front and centre field police and their commanders as a specialist resource for the CTC. Conversely, and quite appropriately, at that time the CTC was a specialist resource drawn on by Regional Commanders like Goodwin to assist as required, just like he would draw on, as required, the forensics, marine, aerial, technical or communications specialist commands, to just name a few.

The Climate Change Conference

We must diverge slightly here for context, the reason for which will become abundantly clear. Matters came to a head in December 2005, literally a few days before the start of the Cronulla Riots. Hazzard asserted within NSW Police that his CTC command should run the entire police planning and response to the World Climate Control Conference to be held in Sydney in January 2006. The CTC's actual job was to provide dignitary protection to a select few internationally protected persons, special weapons police (if required), plus intelligence and risk assessments to frontline police, whose commanders had the job of securing and protecting the whole entire event and all its participants. It was not the role of the CTC to start putting barricades up, enforcing road closures and traffic diversions, rerouting public transport, securing and/or fencing venue perimeters, searching venues, ensure rostering of hundreds of uniform police on duty, checking the mounted police, dogs and helicopters were on hand, or that the region's riot trained police were prepped and ready if/when needed for protests that were inevitable at this event. At that point in time in NSW Police history, all that was the job, and always had been the job, of the Regional Commander of General duties police. In this case, one Mark Goodwin.

Between 10-12th January 2006 (just a month after the Cronulla Riots) Sydney hosted this International Climate Control Conference, which involved the attendance of Foreign Ministers from China, India, Japan and South Korea, as well as the Secretary of State of the USA. In total, 18 Ministers from 5 foreign countries were to attend.

There were 7+ venues requiring the Sydney central metropolitan police region to supply senior police as 'Precinct Commanders' which included Government House, Intercontinental Hotel, Four Seasons Hotel, Shangri-La Hotel, Admiralty House and Sydney Airport. It was expected that the conference would attract significant protest activity at one or multiple venues and would thus be a complex and challenging operation.

The security operation required a vast number of frontline police who were day-to-day under the Sydney region command. As well as Venue Security, Perimeter Teams, Search Teams, Static Guards, Public Order/Riot police and Traffic Operations, the police operation would also require a range of specialist resources such as Dignitary Protection, State Protection Group (special weapons), Bomb/Rescue Squad, Dog Squad, Counter-Terrorism Intelligence, Police Air Wing, Electronic Surveillance, VIP cyclists, Mounted Unit (Riot Trained Horses), Transport Unit (prison vans), Marine Unit, Media Unit etc. These are all extremely proficient separate specialist units within the NSW Police, who all come together to assist in these types of operations. However, these units are relatively small specialist units which are not equipped to plan the entire police response or take command of a whole major event.

Goodwin undertook the detailed planning for police operations during the Climate Conference in accordance with the existing Command and Control protocols within NSW Police at the time. As required, he implemented what is known as the 'Major Incident Response Team' (including specialists in planning, logistics, operations, investigation, intelligence and public information). And this was all 'business as usual' for the planning and operation of around 300 events per year within the Sydney Region Command. These included New Year's Eve, the Gay Mardis Gras, City to Surf 'fun run', Anzac and Australia Day celebrations, numerous sporting events, and countless special events, VIP visits, demonstrations and protest marches in the heart of the Sydney CBD. About 90% of the police engaged on these operations worked directly under the command of the Geographic Regional Commander every other day. Specialist Units accounted for about 10% of the staff that come in to assist on those operations.

None of these issues or areas of risk, and the planning and resourcing of an effective response to them, could have been done by a stand-alone specialist police unit. As with other specialist units, the CTC were there to provide extremely valuable assistance within their niche area of expertise, not to take over the planning and command of the entire NSW Police operation in response to major events. It was an unsustainable overreach in our view.

This is the same as other specialised police units. To do otherwise would be akin to the Traffic Commander, the Water Police Commander, the Dog Squad Commander or the Air-Wing Commander demanding they take over an entire police operation.

The Counter-Terrorism Command

Quite appropriately the Counter-Terrorism Command had been established in NSW Police to ensure we had a first-rate Specialist Command to gather intelligence, assess risks, investigate and respond to terrorism threats based on local and global intelligence networks and advise both government and senior police of current and future threat levels.

The Command did great work in placating the fears of the public with the rise of global terrorism, and in keeping police and governmental decision makers well apprised of risks, threat levels and necessary police responses. It was never intended by government that such a Specialist Command would metamorphosise from an intelligence gathering, investigation and risk assessment unit, to one responsible for mainstream general duties policing functions.

On 10th November 2005 Chief Superintendent Jenkins, who directly reported to Norm Hazzard at that time, submitted a report to Commissioner Moroney regarding the forthcoming World Climate Control Conference. In that report Jenkins states:

> *"Assistant Commissioner Hazzard, Counter Terrorism, and Assistant Commissioner Goodwin, Inner Metropolitan Region, have discussed this event and have determined that the most appropriate Police Commander for this event is the Assistant Commissioner Counter Terrorism."*[37]

Then, not long after the delivery of this 'report', on 17th November 2005, an Acting Staff Officer under Norm Hazzard from the Counter Terrorist Command, began acting as if CTC was now in command of the event and began organising the first planning meeting via email on behalf of Hazzard, requesting Goodwin to be at Hazzard's office on 23rd November 2005 at the Counter Terrorist Command.[38]

Goodwin disputed this command challenge, so the meeting was moved back to the Police Operations Centre on 30th November 2005, from where such events were always planned and commanded. This was just 11 days prior ro the Cronulla Riots.[39]

---

[37] Report of Supt. Jenkins CTCC to Commissioner 11/11/05 - File Number NSWP/D/2005/187437
[38] Email from/to A/Staff Officer Anthony Kershler CTCC & A/C Goodwin - 17/11/2005.
[39] Electronic Diary of A/C Goodwin - 30/11/2005.

Goodwin appeals to the Deputy Commissioner

Goodwin formally wrote to Deputy Commissioner Scipione asking for an adjudication on the issue.[40]

Before Scipione had made a ruling, Goodwin was held up attending the next police planning session on 6 December 2005, and had asked Supt Mark Hutchings, Region Operations Manager, to chair the meeting until his arrival, only to have Hazzard insist on chairing it himself. Upon Goodwin's arrival, a discussion occurred between Hazzard and Goodwin as to which command should or shouldn't be leading the planning and delivery. Goodwin then directed the meeting to close until such time as the Deputy Commissioner ruled on the issue. The Cronulla Riots occurred just 5 days later on 11 December 2005.[41]

Scipione ruled in favour of Goodwin, who later went on to plan and command the policing response to this Climate Control Conference. Just a mere few weeks later, Commissioner Moroney appointed Hazzard to be in charge of a Strike Force investigating Goodwin and other frontline commanders, with the first Term of Reference being Command and Control of a Public Order Event (the Cronulla Riots).

Operation SETA concludes as Strike Force Neil begins

By the end of the 2005/2006 Summer the massive Operation Seta under the command of Goodwin had restored peace and order to the streets, suburbs and beaches of Sydney, as outlined in the previous section.

The Commissioner having announced the 'Strike Force' investigation into police performance at Cronulla, went on leave and appointed Deputy Commissioner Andrew Scipione as Acting Commissioner during his absence.

One of Scipione's first tasks was to summon all the Cronulla Riots commanders to Police HQ to inform them of the 'Terms of Reference' of the new Strike Force.

These were the terms of reference:

---

[40] Email from A/C Goodwin to Deputy Commissioner Scipione 2/12/2005.
[41] Electronic Diary of A/C Goodwin - 6/02/2005.

1. **Command and Control**

   What Command and Control arrangements were put in place to deal with the incident/s and whether the planning and preparation for those arrangements was appropriate in the circumstances.

2. **Operational Response Capability**

   Identify critical issues with the initial response by police on 11 December 2005 and the tactics and strategies employed and equally the response, tactics and strategies used on 12 and 13 December 2005.

3. **Education and Training**

   What education and training implications arise from the policing response to the events of 11-13 December, 2005.

4. **Equipment**

   To determine the availability of equipment, the effectiveness of procedures for its deployment and whether the equipment was adequate for the prevailing circumstances.

Goodwin immediately protested to 'Acting' Commissioner Scipione about the sudden establishment of a 'Strike Force' (normally reserved for the investigation of major or organised crime), when he had already organised the usual debrief process, which was always thoroughly conducted after every such operation. Goodwin also protested to Scipione about the manner this 'Strike Force' was announced in the media by Commissioner Moroney without any prior warning, the appointment of Norm Hazzard, as well as the Terms of Reference. However, Scipione simply replied, "*It's Ken's inquiry. I'll pass it on*" and left the room. Goodwin was then left to endure an unpleasant meeting with Moroney's personal media advisor, who demanded that he now do all media interviews.

Scipione did pass on Goodwin's concerns about the appointment of Hazzard in a phone call to Scully who recalls the conversation as follows:

> *"Andrew Scipione called me early one evening just after the appointment of Norm Hazzard to advise that Mark Goodwin was very upset by the appointment as the two of them had had recent adverse history.*
>
> *Calls to me from Scipione were common place but this was an unusual call, as it was the only time Scipione would at least impliedly criticise the Commissioner. I was troubled by the call and dwelled upon what I*

ought to do with what I had been told. I decided to keep a close watch on the results of the investigation to ensure Goodwin had been given a fair hearing. That was a big mistake. On reflection, I think Scipione was giving me a warning, but I failed to heed it with dire professional consequences for both Goodwin and me.

I held Hazzard in high regard, but I was also well aware of how easy it was for an 'investigation' to put someone in a poor light notwithstanding that a good job may have been done".

Strike Force Neil begins

'Strike Force Neil' set itself up behind keypad locked secure doors at a location in Hurstville. Goodwin initially heard nothing from any of its members ultimately requesting a face-to-face meeting with Moroney upon his return from leave.

Goodwin meets with Moroney

On 20th February 2006 (Moroney's first day back at work) Moroney agreed to a meeting at his Commissioner's office with Goodwin. Deputy Commissioner Scipione was also present. Goodwin strongly protested to Moroney about him launching to the media an investigation 'Strike Force' effectively into his performance whilst Moroney himself was under the media spotlight. Also, that after the recent adjudication against Norm Hazzard's wishes regarding command and control of the Climate Control Conference, he had been appointed to head the investigation and had not yet even spoken to Goodwin or his senior commanders at all.[42]

As a result, Commissioner Moroney booked a meeting for the following day, to be attended by both Assistant Commissioners Hazzard and Goodwin, as well as Scipione and Moroney's Chief of Staff, Bernie Aust.

At the meeting, Moroney began with some statements that it had *"been tough for everyone"* and that he *"did not want scalps"*. Moroney then stated that, with an election coming up, he saw the review not in a negative way, but as an *"opportunity"*. He noted that he would like to see funding for a Command College he had long planned as a legacy. (Note: the Strike Force

---

[42] Electronic Diary of A/C Goodwin - 20/02/2006.

term of reference on 'Education and Training').[43]

Then Hazzard suggested to Moroney that he try to get a "Command Vehicle" that had not been previously funded. (Note: the Strike Force term of reference 'Equipment').

After the meeting, Goodwin held private concerns that to make these 'agreed' things happen, the report would critise the command of the Cronulla Riots and then recommend to the Government these expensive 'fixes'.

Goodwin's one regret, in hindsight, was that he did not immediately go to the Police Minister Carl Scully and raise his concerns. He often ponders what a different outcome may have ensured if he had gone straight to Scully in confidence at that point.

The 'investigation' proceeds

This 'Strike Force' investigation into the police performance during the Cronulla riots was now underway. By this stage the media was fully focussed on reporting and analysing this new development, and had quickly lost interest in Moroney regarding revenge attacker CCTV footage, or his removal and reinstatement of Supt. Denis Bray.

How that investigation into police performance unfolded is the subject of the next chapter.

---

[43] Electronic Diary of A/C Goodwin - 21/02/2006.

9

The 'Investigation': Beginning at the End

'Strike Force' Neil: setting the end at the beginning

From the minutes of the first two meetings of the Strike Force team held on the 17th and the 21st of February 2006, it is apparent, that despite Moroney's assurances to the contrary, it was definitely going to be an "investigation".

> *"NH spoke about formulating an investigation plan... one whole day set-aside... to formulate* [it]*".*[44]

> *"NH spoke at considerable length about the inadequacies of training about POM ('Public Order Management') and major disaster integration between emergency services, etc."*

According to their own minutes, Norm Hazzard (NH) was expressing a view at the very first meeting of Strike Force personnel, that training in 'Public Order Management' was inadequate, and 'Emergency Management' integration was inadequate (both under the domain of uniform frontline Region and Local Area Commanders).

In fact, inadequacies in training had been uncovered in the review of police performance during the earlier Macquarie Fields riot just 10 months before Cronulla. In that review a number of recommendations had been made. A brand new Public Order Commanders Course had already been prepared and implemented, and a large number of frontline operational commanders had already completed the course (including Superintendent Redfern, who was the Operational Commander at Cronulla on the day). Additionally, a brand new Senior Emergency Management Course had recently been signed off by Goodwin, as organisational head of emergency management, and two

---

[44] Minutes of Stike Force Neil staff meeting, February 17, 2006.

courses had already been run at Charles Sturt University in Bathurst.

And what it seemed as an obvious attempt to re-litigate the desire of the Counter-Terrorism Command to take over the management by General Duties Regional Command of public order events:

> *"NH (Norm Hazzard) noted that the S/F (Strike Force) needs to advance the proposal of central co-ordination of POM (public order management). At the moment it is fragmented region-by-region with different levels of commitment, response capability, activation SOP's, etc. S/F to propose centralised POM notification and activation via PORS for every such incident in the State."*

> *"NH noted there are concerns about the qualifications of lecturers in POM at present. There must be considerable input from CT (counter-terrorism) personnel, who have up-to-date and best-practice tactics and strategies to teach constables to superintendents."*

> *"The current system of ad hoc responses in individual LAC's or regions is not acceptable. It will be a recommendation that such centralised response to POM incidents be in accordance with NSW police rather than local or region SOPs."*

The recommendations, it seemed, were already being recorded at this very first meeting about how frontline Local and Regional Commanders will undertake their core business in Public Order Management (POM) in the future, prior to Commanders of the Cronulla Riots even being interviewed.

.

'Cronulla Riot' Commander's 1st meeting with Hazzard

On 28th February 2006, Hazzard held a meeting with Goodwin and only some of the affected police commanders. Goodwin's Staff Officer, Inspector Martin Hayston, took comprehensive notes of that meeting.[45]

At that meeting, Hazzard outlined the Terms of Reference and talked about the review 'process'. There was no meaningful depth of conversation or detailed interviews about what actually happened at Cronulla. Inspector Hayston's notes of the meeting also record Hazzard stating he was *"starting from a baseline"* with *"no preconceived ideas"*.

---

[45] Handwritten notes of Inspector Hayston (A/C Goodwin's Staff Officer) 28/2/2006.

The 'Investigation'

The meeting concluded with Hazzard informing the Cronulla Riot commanders that he would be briefing the 'CoP' (Commissioner of Police – i.e. Moroney) every two weeks, so that by the end of his report in August, everything is already in place. Goodwin was never invited to any of those meetings to discuss any progress of the review.

The second and last meeting between Goodwin and Hazzard

A meeting was arranged by Hazzard with Goodwin on the 14th of March 2006. One memorable moment, whilst waiting for Hazzard to arrive, was when the second in charge of the Strike Force told Goodwin that it was going to be a great learning experience for him, because he had never planned, or commanded a public order management event.

Hazzard turned up 90 minutes late for a 2 hour meeting. Next to nothing was discussed during this 30 minutes about what actually happened during the Cronulla Riots or the Revenge Attacks. Goodwin had assumed and expected to be interviewed via a documented and formally recorded question and answer style 'record-of-interview' and for Hazzard to canvass with him a myriad of things to set the scene and clarify the picture of what actually occurred pre, during and post the incident at Cronulla, especially in regard to Command and Control. However, there was just general discussion during that 30 minutes, with very limited discussion at all about the actual Cronulla Riots and Revenge Attacks.

Comprehensive notes being taken at the time by Goodwin's staff officer, Inspector Martin Hayston, show there was some discussion about the newly formed Public Order and Riot Squad (which had been announced prior to the Cronulla Riots anyway, but had not yet been staffed) and coordination of existing Region riot police, with Hazzard suggesting a Counter-Terrorism model. There was discussion regarding use of Negotiators in public order situations (also under Counter-Terrorism Command).[46]

During the meeting Goodwin informed Hazzard that his Staff Officer, Inspector Hayston, was typing up his command logs of the 'Cronulla Riots' from his hand-written notes, so that Hazzard and his Strike Force staff could read the notes, then all the material would be delivered to the Strike Force. Goodwin had not been asked for this material, but was having this done

---

[46] Handwritten notes of Inspector Hayston (A/C Goodwin's Staff Officer) 14/3/2005.

on his own initiative as a cooperative and transparent gesture. Goodwin briefly discussed some of the crowd dynamics on the day at Cronulla and that it was actually more like an Australia Day with Aussie Flags, people singing Waltzing Matilda etc. Briefly discussed was the Abberton boys from Maroubra and their role.

Hazzard suggested they should use the State Coordination Centre (SOC) for these incidents. Goodwin was the organisational head of Emergency Management at the time. It was (and remains) his view that the SOC is not set-up or intended for strictly police operations, nor is it equipped like the Police Operations Centre (POC), which Goodwin actually used during the 'Revenge Attacks'. The SOC is a separate High-Tech room used for Emergency Management (i.e.: Rail Disasters, Extreme Weather Events, Plane Crashes, Major Disease Outbreak, Building Collapses etc). It is used by the heads of Emergency Management during a crisis (i.e. Transport, Health, Welfare, Engineering, Public Information, Utilities, Environment, etc). In Goodwin's view, it would have been totally inappropriate for commanding the initial day of mostly stationary protest at North Cronulla Surf Club, nor was it appropriate for commanding the strictly police operations during the 'Revenge Attacks', for which the purpose-built Police Operation Centre was used.

This half hour chat was the only consultation between Hazzard and Goodwin on police performance during the Cronulla Riots with no specific questions about Command and Control arrangements, logistics, equipment, resources, risk assessment, command post, communication, intelligence, or training, all of which were later canvassed in the Strike Force Neil report when it was publicly released.

Creating an existing Commanders Course

The only time Goodwin ever saw Hazzard or any other member of Strike Force Neil again before the release of their report was when Hazzard conducted a two-day command education forum at Goulburn on 8-9th May 2006.

Hazzard had commenced, with Moroney's imprimatur, a side-project on Command Training, the idea being that all such Commanders would go through four modules: ICCS *(integrated command & control system)*;

Emergency Management; Public Order; and Counter Terrorism.

Goodwin attended only at the commencement of this forum, as the head of Emergency Management for NSW Police. He informed Hazzard, and other forum participants, of the already existing new Public Order Management Commander's Course, which had (by then) been running for over a year. He also informed the group of the already existing new Senior Emergency Management Course, which had already been launched with two courses already run by the NSW Police Academy at Charles Sturt University, Bathurst.[47]

There was no further discussion or interview of Goodwin at this forum regarding specifics of the Cronulla Riots operation. In fact, he did not hear anything at all from any member of Strike Force Neil from that date onwards prior to their report being publicly released five months later in October 2006.

The work of Sydney Region command continued

It is important to note that during these same ensuing months in early 2006, whilst Strike Force Neil conducted its investigation, a number of significant events took place in Sydney under the police command of Assistant Commissioner Goodwin. These included the World Climate Control Conference (mentioned above), the visit of Condoleezza Rice (US Secretary of State), and the visit of HM Queen Elizabeth II. All these events drew large media attention and senior police were given internal and external praise for their response and management. It was the command and control of these events, which Hazzard just a few weeks before his appointment, had wanted taken from Goodwin's Sydney Region Command and vested in his own Counter-Terrorism Command.

---

[47] Electronic Diary of A/C Goodwin - 8/03/2006.

10

Moroney Releases a "*Draft*" Report

"The first draft of anything is shit"
Ernest Hemingway

A draft is a draft

In late October 2006, a torrent of scrutiny was whipped up by journalists, radio shock jocks, and tabloid newspapers about the Cronulla Riots report being allegedly completed and hidden from view. After an almost 'Watergate' style cover up story unfolding in the media, a not yet completed draft report was released to the community.

Some chose to accurately report that it was unfinished, a draft, but others just acted as if the released material was the last word on police performance during the Cronulla Riots. It was not and never should have been given that status.

For anyone involved in writing anything; reports, advices, articles or opinions, and of course, journalistic scribbling and unvarnished opining, would well know that a final polished, fair and accurate document may take a number of iterations before being considered complete, with the last looking very different from the first. Many a journalist would shudder if their first draft was always grabbed and released as their best and final product. But this is exactly what happened with the yet to be completed early iterative exercise which became known as the 'Strike Force Neil Report'.

As one writer summed up the process of writing:

> "Every creative medium has its own version of the editing process... authors...screenwriters...musicians...to take a crappy first draft-a middling effort-and to hone it into something usable...How does the creator respond? With petulance and anger? With open-mindedness and interest?... What are the chances that your prototype is perfect first time?
>
> ...we must be rational and fair about our own work...what are the chances that I'm right and everyone else...is wrong. We'll be better off at least considering why other people have concerns...every project needs to go through this process...
>
> Nobody creates flawless first drafts. And nobody creates better second drafts without the intervention of someone else."[48]

It is little wonder then that when a report was released in a draft state, it contained a number of disputed issues.

The delay queried by the minister

Scully had expected the investigation to take just a few weeks, but a month-long holiday overseas in April 2006 by the lead investigator didn't exactly expedite things. With no clear end in sight by June 2006, Scully asked the Commissioner to bring Mr Hazzard to their next weekly meeting for an update.

Astonishingly, this was core of the update and conversation which ensued:

> **Hazzard:** "The investigation has been concluded and the report is now at the printers".
>
> **Scully:** "Ken, you have got to be kidding. You have sat back and allowed Norm to take months and months to prepare a report and then without reading it, you let it go to the printers".
>
> **Moroney:** "Norm, are you sure it has gone to the printer".

Hazzard then made a phone call, the printing of a report presumably no-one else in the room knew the contents of, was then put on hold. In that same meeting, Scully asked Hazzard directly about consultation with Goodwin:

---

[48] R. Holiday, 'Meditations on Strategy and Life', ryanholiday.net.

Scully: *"Has Mark Goodwin been consulted on the contents of the report"?*

Hazzard: *"He has been given every opportunity to put his case and has done so".*

Scully: *"Yes, but has he been shown your draft report and been given the opportunity to respond"?*

Hazzard: *"No".*

Several months went by when leaks about its alleged contents began to appear in the media. With the *Sutherland Shire Leader* on 28 September 2006 providing the following banner headline:

'Where is the Police Report on the Cronulla Riots?'

Murray Trembath was the paper's lead journalist, and very well-connected throughout the Sutherland Shire. It is unlikely that *The Leader* would have run a story like that without something, or someone fuelling it. Clearly, Trembath had been told, at least, that the report was in its final stages.

The Leader story was quickly followed by the much broader coverage of a *Sun Herald* article on 1 October 2006:

'Riot Report Suppressed – Debnam MP blasts scandalous delay'

"The straight-talking Mr Hazzard is believed to have found there were operational mistakes in handling the riot and its aftermath, and he criticises under-resourcing, man-power levels, training, co-ordination and communications."

Despite Hazzard admitting to the Police Minister in June 2006 that Goodwin had not seen his report, nor been given the opportunity to respond, four months later by October 2006 when these media articles appeared, neither Hazzard nor any other member of Strike Force Neil had communicated at all with Goodwin and still had not shown him the now 'draft' report.

Rather naively in hindsight, the Minister missed the fact, that the much better approach, would have been to let the report go public with an addendum from Goodwin to ensure his perspectives were on the record.

This would have allowed the Minister to avoid the ridiculous impression painted by journalists of a 'cover up' as well as ensuring Goodwin's views were formally on the record. Both Scully and Goodwin missed the warning signs. Seeking genuine consultation with affected commanders only hastened the demise of both minister and commander.

On the same day as the abovementioned *Sun Herald* 'leak' article, Sunday 1 October 2006, at 1.24pm Goodwin sent a somewhat terse email to Deputy Commissioner Scipione complaining of a lack of consultation:

> *"As you know, there is much unrest over the conduct of this review under a shroud of non-consultation, and by a group with limited exposure to the command of demonstrations or public order incidents.*
>
> *Without any internal mechanism to consult and comment, Commanders are ....frustrated and fed-up with the news of this report's release looming, journalists seeming to know what's in it, yet the people who put their hearts and souls into running this operation ....have either never been consulted, or were spoken to briefly over six or more months ago with limited issues canvassed, and not spoken to at all since. Most especially, nobody has had the chance to comment on any findings."*

Scipione replied at 2.28pm stating that the report was in preliminary draft form and subject to review by the Commissioner whilst he was overseas for three weeks. Scipione then went on to state:

> *"I have advocated for the report to be considered by those officers who had a significant role to play in the subject events. I am confident that this will happen, and the Commanders will be afforded the opportunity to comment on the report."*

Despite Scipione's assurance, that never happened. Scipione continued:

> *"I note your concerns and will ensure that the Cop (Commissioner of Police) is aware of the Commander's position.*
>
> *In conclusion let me assure you that I was impressed with the skills and abilities that were demonstrated by the strategic, operational and tactical commanders during the course of SETA.* [The Cronulla Riots Operation SETA] *It was a credit not only to the organisation but also to the individuals involved. The final outcome/results speak for themselves."*

Then on the same day, just over two hours later the Commissioner also emailed Goodwin:

> "*Firstly, allow me to congratulate you and your people for some good, ongoing work in the Region over this weekend. From NARLA, to Beachsafe 2, to a number of high-profile arrests, your people are doing first class work. ....good teams have to have good leaders, and to you and your leadership team I send my congratulations and regards.*
>
> *Secondly, any discussion on leadership is a good lead-in to the issues you have raised with Andrew.*
>
> *You will (hopefully) recall that during and after SETA, many compliments were paid to the overall team for their fine work associated with the events of 11/12/05 and post that immediate period. Those compliments remain and are as true today as they ever were. You should be assured that you, your leadership team and your overall command personnel (and indeed those drawn from other Commands) did a first-class job. Nothing, no report, nobody can remove that fact. Always remain of that view".*

Ironically, this account by the Commissioner to the Cronulla Riots Commander was an accurate and succinct account of exactly how the public and the media had reported on police performance throughout those difficult weeks. It is why we have argued there was no valid and justifiable reason to announce a 'Strike Force' investigation in the first place. However, rather ominously by asserting that nothing in any report can change that fact, the Commissioner had confrontingly confirmed that this is exactly what was about to happen when the report went public.

Incredibly, in the circumstances, Moroney offered belated recognition:

> *"As a side, but nevertheless related issue, I would still like to press on with the formal awards and recognition process. JKA [former Commissioner John Keith Avery] once reminded me that '...recognition delayed, is recognition denied'."*

Offering up belated recognition (which in-the-end never happened anyway) was hardly going to staunch the media attacks about to be unleashed when the damning report was released.

> *"I am concerned at the political opportunism that is currently doing the rounds relevant to SETA and Cronulla. That opportunism takes the form of media and it is, lamentably, part of the current political machinations in which we presently find ourselves. We need to remain*

aloof from the politics of it all and like good cops, and like good leaders of good cops, remain focussed. If we are diverted by ill-informed comments, then we will take our eyes off the main game – crime, social disruption and the like."

Moroney then finally got to the point:

"Now, turning to today's articles. I have a report from Norm that I regard as a DRAFT. I have indicated to Norm that I will take it with me overseas and read same. When I return, I will meet with him and discuss my comments and observations of the DRAFT report. I will seek that any areas of concern be clarified and further commented on.

If there are issues relevant to, say, systems, processes, training, equipment and the like that we need to improve on (and there is rationale to support those conclusions) then we will probably do that. Norm has reached some conclusions and those conclusions – one or all, need to be tested. We need to remember that conclusions need to be based on fact, and that the recommendations arising from those conclusions are based on logic.

I have seen the draft recommendations and primarily they turn on the very principles that I refer to above, training, equipment etc. Initially, they don't cause me a concern, but I need to qualify that statement by saying that I need to read the report in its totality before finalising my mind on that aspect".

Interestingly, Moroney felt the need here to state what ought not to have needed articulating, that conclusions *"need to be tested"* and *"based on fact"*...and *"recommendations arising from those conclusions...based on logic"*.

The original complaints by Goodwin regarding a lack of consultation and the nature of the investigation were ignored by the Commissioner but he did finish off with this:

"Finally, more than most I do understand the pressures that you are feeling. I have sat where you are sitting, and more than any other RC (Region Commander) position, this is the one with the most focus and pressure of all. For that reason, let me reiterate what I have said before, I have every confidence in your capacity and in your leadership. We cannot and will not be diverted from our task by media,

or by politicians. We must lead for the sake of our people, and the community we serve.

Regards,

Ken."

Despite saying he would talk to Hazzard about the "*draft*" report, once he had read it, he made no commitment to allow Goodwin a process of being properly consulted, which was the core of Goodwin's complaint to him. But, after receiving a direct communication from the Commissioner, Goodwin assumed some kind of genuine consultative process would be put in place before the release of the report. That did not happen.

One regret the Minister had from this time was shunning a request by Moroney that Goodwin be allowed to read (but not keep) a copy of the draft report in a closed room, make notes and provide his comments directly to Hazzard. Scully recalls receiving a phone call at home on a weekend just prior to the departure of Moroney for his overseas trip. It was probably the same afternoon Moroney sent off this email to Goodwin, but no mention was made by the Commissioner regarding the email exchange he had had or was about to have with Goodwin. Scully recalls his thinking at the time:

> "I was very concerned about the lack of consultation with Goodwin. I believed that the findings, as reported that day in the Sun Herald, had been deliberately leaked to avoid the sort of iterative process we had gone through during at least three or more meetings on the draft Macquarie Fields riot report.
>
> In that context, I was concerned the whole report might get leaked, then Goodwin would cop the blame. Did I make the right call? Maybe not! But in that surreal fast paced and distrusting environment, one I think in the circumstances, was not an unreasonable decision to make".

The Cabinet visits Cronulla

On Monday 16th of October 2006 the NSW Cabinet held its weekly meeting in the Sutherland Shire, just a suburb away from where the Cronulla Riots had occurred.

Goodwin briefed the cabinet on steps to secure our beaches over the 2006/2007 summer. Afterwards, Goodwin took the opportunity to privately complain to Scully about a lack of consultation, that he believed the process was a denial of procedural fairness, and that neither he nor his staff had had an opportunity to comment on what was proposed to be said about them.

The usual press conference held after every regional cabinet meeting followed with a Channel 9 question on the progress of the investigation batted away by Scully with: *"The Commissioner is working through some documents and I expect the process should be completed soon"*. However, the portent of things to quickly unfold was the presentation of their 'story' in their 6pm TV news bulletin, with a close up of Scully's face whilst he was talking, to try and present him as giving an almost dissembling answer. When asked by Scully for an explanation as to why they had done this, their main political journalist responded by saying that this was *"payback for giving the Sun Tele an exclusive on police plans for the coming summer"*.

Questions in Parliament begin

When parliament resumed on Tuesday 17th October 2006, Scully had just nine days left in his ministerial career. Despite repeatedly stating that the report was a draft and therefore not a report, the media decided that Scully was presiding over a cover up and should be sacked for it. The demise of a minister turned on a few words, not a tawdry misuse of public funds, not a rorted tender process, not forgetting a bottle of Grange as gift, nor sleeping with a backbench MP for whom discreet favours were done, or any infidelity, and certainly not doing favours in any tender processes. In fact, nothing had been done or said by Scully, which went anywhere near to what historically had been the usual cause of ending a minister's career. In amongst the midst of reasons for a ministerial demise over the last few decades, the lack of sufficient emphasis on the word 'draft' is probably the least serious of any in living memory.

When the Leader of the Opposition, Peter Debnam asked Scully on the 17th October 2006: *"why he is trying...to delay and bury the report"*, Scully responded:

> *"...these myths about a report...[the Commissioner's] ... advice was that the report had not yet been completed...that Norm Hazzard had still to interview some operational police before he could finalise it... the report processes have not been completed".*

A safer answer would have been: *"A draft has been prepared and the Commissioner has asked for further consultation after which the report will be concluded and released".*

Hazzard in the media

It soon became very apparent that Norm Hazzard did not welcome requests or suggestions that further consultation was required when Scully went on Channel 9 TV News on the 18th of October 2006. In doing so, he provided the turning point from which Scully's political career could not recover. This is all Scully said in that interview:

> "...there had been an oversight in the preparation of the report. It's not appropriate to finalise a report when the senior command involved in the Cronulla riot operations hadn't been properly interviewed or consulted. There is a bit of a deficiency in the report process that is now being rectified... obviously if it came to conclusions, he must give those officers the opportunity of putting their views before he finalises his opinions and recommendations".

This narrative was quite consistent with what Scully had been saying for some days in and outside Parliament, that the affected commanders needed to be consulted prior to the conclusion of the report. In fact, that same night from the USA, Commissioner Moroney issued the following statement:

> "I've asked Mr Hazzard to conduct further consultation with senior commanders. I will be meeting with him next week... until that interview process is completed, the report is not finalised".

Remarkably, despite these widely reported personal assurances to the media by the Commissioner of Police himself, and all the extensive media banter that followed, no further consultation by Hazzard or any other member of Strike Force Neil ever took place with Goodwin. However, unbeknownst to the Minister, Hazzard was angry after watching the Channel 9 interview with the minister and then placed on record, a defence to what he believed had been a slight on his reputation. *The Sydney Morning Herald* next morning, 19th October 2006 ran the front-page banner headline proclaiming: **'Riot's Report Author's Fury over Scully'**

And it very quickly went downhill from there.

> "Norm Hazzard, 41-year veteran of the force hit back at claims by the minister that the report was deficient... 'I totally refute what the Minister for Police has said in relation to his comments depicted on television tonight. I am appalled he would make such a statement without verifying his information. There is nothing in the report that

verifies or justifies his comment'".[49]

Here was a retired Assistant Commissioner of Police effectively accusing the Minister for Police of misinforming the public, stating things which could not be backed up, and making stuff up on the run *"without verifying his information"*. And if that was not enough, Hazzard then laid to complete rest any notion that the report was yet to be concluded with his sweeping, *'there is nothing in the report that verifies or justifies his comment'*. In other words, there was no 'draft report'. It was a completed report, and not a document in an iterative stage requiring fact checking, polishing, or consultation with those affected. It was now as good as officially announced by its author as finished, and certainly not a 'draft' in need of improvement from consultation and further iterative improvement. And the rest of the media and its journalists acted accordingly, and in a pack.

Scully was perplexed, devastated and non-plussed to say the least, on learning of this career ending personal attack from such a well-respected and distinguished retired police officer. The media were never going to listen to any alternative view. Scully called Hazzard on the morning of 19th October 2006 and was left almost speechless with the following conversation:

Scully: *"Norm, why have you said what you have said in today's SMH"?*

Hazzard: *"Last night I watched what you said on Channel 9 and replayed it 5 times. I was not happy with your use of the word 'deficient', or that there had been an oversight in our work".*

Scully: *"Norm, for some days now both the Commissioner and I have been saying that the report had not been finalised and would not be finalised until further consultation had occurred with affected commanders".*

Hazzard: *"Yes, I have been following that and I did not have a problem with what has been said".*

Scully: *"Then what was the problem resulting in this morning's pretty awful story"?*

Hazzard: *"By saying the report process was deficient, and there had been an oversight in its preparation, you implied that something wrong*

---

[49] *Sydney Morning Herald,* October 19, 2006.

had been done and that's what upset me".

Scully: *"Norm, the word deficient simply means something missing, it doesn't mean something untoward or inappropriate. It just means something else needed to be added, in this case, further consultation, how could that possibly offend you, or be interpreted as an attack on you for the job you have done. I have just said what Moroney himself has said"?*

Hazzard: *"Yes, I can see that. I don't have a problem with that interpretation".*

Scully: *"Equally, if something which even the Commissioner believes ought to have been done and now needs to be done, that is, further consultation with affected commanders, then calling that an oversight, is not an attack on you or your work, but simply another way of saying something else needed to be done before the report can be concluded. How could you be offended by that"?*

Hazzard: *"Yes, I can see that".*

Scully well knew the impact which Hazzard's media statement would have on both the Premier's continued confidence in him remaining as a minister, and the broader media, who hardly needed encouragement in ramping up a public excoriation of an elected official. Scully was just about flattened by Hazzard almost nonchalantly admitting that he wasn't really offended after only a short explanation. However, Hazzard never took any steps then, or since, to correct the record or step back from his own response. If he had done so that same day, the rug from under a ministerial career may not have been so easily pulled by the Premier just a few days later.

If Scully had taken a few short minutes to call Hazzard after he had done the Channel 9 interview the career ending commentary of Hazzard might have been avoided. As it was, the unexpected, if not unprecedented media statement on the Minister just souped up the press gallery into a higher level of indignation against what they regarded as misleading conduct in claiming the report was incomplete, a draft and unfinished, when now according to Hazzard, it was none of those things. *The Sydney Morning Herald* with this story in hand hardly needed any encouragement and continued:

"The furore over the unreleased report on police handling of the Cronulla riots deepened last night as its author contradicted the Police

Minister's version of events.

Mr Scully, who has insisted to Parliament all week that a report by Mr Hazzard into the riots and their aftermath was not complete, was forced to admit last night that it had been given to Commissioner Ken Moroney's office about a month ago.

Mr Scully justified his statements to Parliament by saying Mr Hazzard had not interviewed or consulted enough officers in his report, so it was not complete".

Moroney says 'It's unfinished'

The contrast on the morning of 19 October 2006 between the two front pages of Sydney's competing daily newspapers, *The Daily Telegraph* and the *Sydney Morning Herald* is simply breathtaking.

Just as Scully was giving his interview on Channel 9 on 18 October 2006 so devastatingly challenged the next day by Hazzard in the SMH, Moroney had issued a statement to the *Daily Telegraph* which followed up the next day, also the 19th October 2006, with the following front-page headline:

'Cronulla riot report rejected by Moroney'

The DT article stated:

"Police have botched an internal review into the Cronulla race riots with Commissioner Ken Moroney to reject a draft report because senior commanders were not interviewed.

Mr Moroney last night confirmed he was not satisfied with the report, which criticises senior police management and the lack of equipment given to front-line officers to deal with rioters. In a statement last night, Mr Moroney confirmed he was given a draft of the report before he went on an overseas study trip three weeks ago.

'I am not satisfied the report process has been finalised.' Mr Moroney said. 'I've asked the report's author [former assistant commissioner Norm Hazzard] to conduct further consultation with senior commanders'."

Even at this stage, and despite the raging headline news for days, neither

Moroney nor Hazzard made any attempt whatsoever to contact or speak to Goodwin or provide any mechanism whatsoever for consultation by Strike Force Neil over its now controversial 'draft' report's contents, findings or recommendations prior to its public release via the media.

Also, on the 19th October 2006, in direct contrast to whatever Hazzard had tried to put on the record in that day's SMH, Scully told the parliament:

> "The Commissioner advised me in a conversation he had with Norm Hazzard before he went overseas, both of them were of the view that it was a draft document, that he would peruse it while he was overseas and, on his return, he would discuss it at length with Norm Hazzard. Commissioner Moroney advised me that he has made a number of annotations and comments on the draft, he always intended that affected officers would have the opportunity to put their views to Norm Hazzard, the commissioner would consider those views and Norm Hazzard would have an opportunity to discuss them at length with the commissioner. The report would then be concluded".

Despite Commissioner Moroney effectively confirming the minister's version of the process to that point, it was to little avail. The Hazzard/SMH version stood, and by then Premier Morris Iemma and his team of advisors, had had enough of the issue and wanted the report released even if it was premature to do so.

Eamonn Fitzpatrick, the Premier's senior media advisor, even said to Scully at the time: *"I've spoken to David Penberthy from the Telegraph and if you give them the report, he'll make sure you get a good run"*. Scully rejected the overture as, *"It's not ready for release"* but that newspaper was able to obtain a copy anyway and gave the Minister a roasting as only a tabloid can.

Iemma and Moroney release the 'unfinished' report

Despite Scully's attempts to ensure a fair consultative process had been followed in respect of affected commanders, the Premier it seemed had had enough of what he regarded as unnecessarily distracting media. The catastrophising which only seasoned journalists love and excel in, especially when calling for a ministerial scalp, was too much for a relatively new Premier. He demanded it be released and cared little for the consequences.

Moroney obliged him, and authorised the release of an edited version of the report whilst in the USA.

The media interpreted this public release as not only confirming the report's contents and that it was a concluded report, but also that this had corroborated Hazzard's commentary in the SMH about Scully, and that the minister had clearly misled parliament by claiming that the document was an incomplete draft as opposed to a finished report, for which he should be now sacked.

Looking back with the passage of many years, it is extraordinary to both of us that so many dots could have been so nonchalantly joined by both the press gallery and the Premier and his senior staff, as to warrant a ministerial removal in such scantily justified circumstances.

The *Illawarra Mercury* summed it all up best on 20th October 2006:

> *"Political pressure yesterday forced the release of a sensitive, half-finished report showing NSW police misjudged racial tension in the lead-up to Sydney's Cronulla riot...Ken Moroney...ordered that an edited version of the draft report be made public in a bid to end speculation of a cover-up".*

The *Daily Telegraph* on the same day: *"Moroney was forced yesterday...to release a half-finished report because of public pressure".*

But, the media did not let up in its claims that Scully had misled the House, despite all universally reporting that what had been released was 'half-finished' and a 'draft', in full alignment with what Scully had being saying inside and outside Parliament, that further consultation was required before it could be concluded. An unfinished report can be no more than at best a draft of what eventually will be a final settled document. Journalists collectively claiming at the time that the minister had 'misled the house' because he had insufficiently emphasised that the document was a draft of a report and not yet a completed report, does not make it 'misleading the house', no matter how much they collectively excoriate on the issue. Insisting that affected commanders be consulted is hardly the stuff of either conspiracy or cover-up.

If there had been then or even now, a means of testing the claim and holding journalists to account, the claim would not have been upheld. Unfortunately, the scribes of the media rarely get held to account when disparaging politicians with sweeping unsustainable assertions.

Simon Benson, then a senior reporter with the *Daily Telegraph*, wrote in the following manner on Scully's contribution to the whole affair:

> "He has brought his government into the trough with him. Misleading Parliament is a very serious matter. While Scully is an honest man, he does get a bit cute with the truth...His bending of the truth over the report into Cronulla has unnecessarily tarred the government with "liar, liar," brush. So yesterday, under orders from the Premier, Scully was forced to apologise to Parliament for misleading it over whether he had seen the controversial report".

This 'story' was an incorrect account of what happened and why. He had not been issued with any orders to apologise and had not misled the house.

A ministerial career comes to an end

By the time the Cronulla riot draft 'report' was released, Iemma had come to a private view that Scully needed to retire at the next election, if not be removed sooner. Not for the media beat up of *"misleading the House"* which could not be sustained, but for *"causing so much negative media"* which he believed, could have been avoided and therefore in his view, warranted a political scalp.

On that basis, during the 16 years of Carr/Iemma Government, or even the 11 years of Wran/Unsworth Government, barely a minister in all those years would not have been sacked and probably on more than a few occasions.

When Scully denied in the Legislative Assembly when asked, that he had called the ABC TV Newsroom, and which was then quickly followed by ABC Radio issuing a statement stating that he had called the ABC Radio Newsroom about the draft report, the press gallery assumed that this was another example of misleading the house, and then went into fulminating collective melt down calling for his removal, without bothering to consider that the answer given was in fact a correct one. The Premier decided that *"enough is enough"* and requested Scully's resignation.

After nearly 12 years in the cabinet room, not emphasising the word 'draft' enough, and a nuance between a conversation with the ABC TV newsroom as opposed to its radio news room, is all it took for a media 'storm in a tea cup' to unfold, combined with Iemma's inability to grasp the difference between difficult media based on little, and bad coverage based on something of substance.

Iemma even added at the time, that the Government could not allow *"the air swirling around the minister to continue"*, whatever that meant. The former Premier Bob Carr called Scully to say: *"You should have never been dismissed for that. The most I might have done was counselled you to be more careful with your words, but probably not even that"*. The former Treasurer, Mike Egan, hardly a friend of Scully even called: *"This was just in the 'oops' category and soon enough the media would have moved on to another target"*. Precisely!

As Iemma himself said to Scully just after the latter's demise: *"If it had been 5 months after an election rather than 5 months before one, I probably wouldn't have worried about it"*.

A police commander's career comes to an end

An excoriation in the press of Goodwin quickly followed the release of the Strike Force Neil report.

Immediately upon the report's release police command of the Cronulla riots was subjected to a tsunami of frenzied media which criticised virtually every component of the operation for weeks (and continues to do so to this day), quoting from the report. Commanders were subjected to an onslaught of blame and stinging media headline criticism. Some examples of just a few:

> *"Cronulla Race Riot Response Flawed"*
> *"Betrayed Frontline Police left in Mortal Danger"*
> *"Poor Planning"*
> *"Flawed Risk Assessment"*
> *"Risk Plan in Lead-Up to Riot Inadequate"*
> *"No-one in Command"*
> *"Race Tension Misjudged"*
> *"Riot Response Inadequate"*
> *"Police Leaders Let Public Down"*

Substantial headline TV news was also broadcast showing Goodwin in full police uniform, his face frozen like a 'mug shot', with 'findings' (not allegations) scrolled out underneath regarding issues he'd never even been spoken to about during the 'investigation'. In the days and weeks following, Goodwin was confronted by media at his private home in front of his family, confronted by neighbours, friends, associates and even people he did not know with an opinion, usually an adverse one based on a negative media report which in turn was based on the report's account. That continues to this day causing Goodwin considerable anguish.

Goodwin became the media target, the brunt of local jokes and someone to blame. It totally ruined his reputation, his career, his health, his self-esteem and his trust in other humans.

Despite being made fully aware in writing of disputed issues and alleged inaccuracies in the report by both Goodwin and Supt. Redfern, just a few days after its release, Moroney then joined Premier Iemma, newly minted Police Minister John Watkins and Deputy Commissioner Scipione, in a news conference where he told the gathered media, that he fully accepted Hazzard's report, findings and recommendations and released the remainder of the report without any change whatsoever. Not even a whiff of doubt on Moroney's part. Moroney added *"that it was time for everyone to move on"*.

At that point, the prevailing situation and cumulative manner in which Goodwin had been treated meant it was untenable for him to remain in that toxic environment. It was his last day of active service with the NSW Police. A career as a dedicated police officer ended as that 'wash it under the carpet' press conference concluded.

Hazzard responds

Once the report was *"fully accepted"* publicly by the Commissioner, Hazzard took the opportunity to state the following:

> *"In a statement to the Herald, Mr Hazzard said the Commissioner and police executive had accepted his report 'in totality' after receiving Mr Goodwin's and Mr Redfern's submissions, proving it was accurate".*[50]

Goodwin – the person most affected by the report's contents – remained dignified and silent in the media throughout all these multiple public exchanges, believing instead the correct and ethical way for a senior police commander to deal with such issues was internally within the NSW Police.

---

[50] *Sydney Morning Herald*, October 28-29, 2006, p.5.

In hindsight this was the wrong choice, but one Goodwin does not regret.

Goodwin's Complaints Unanswered:

Between October 2006 and April 2007 Goodwin wrote to and met with Commissioner Moroney, Deputy Commissioner Scipione and other Senior NSW Police Executive members on numerous occasions, during which he raised a number of serious issues and complaints in respect of the conduct of Strike Force Neil and the manner of release of its report. Senior Counsel acting on behalf of Goodwin also officially wrote to the NSW Police Commissioner (by then Andrew Scipione) with similar allegations. The Police Act, as it was then, made it clear that a number of these allegations required those complaints to be recorded, registered and investigated. To this date Goodwin has never received a response or been given any outcome or resolution to those matters.

The Police Ministry and ALP perspective

After his demise, not for any wrong doing, but for being the cause of too much negative media, Scully received two separate comments to that effect as follows:

> **Mark Arbib,** then General Secretary NSW ALP: *"Why did you get between the cops. It was their fight and one you didn't need to get involved in. You should have just let them fight it out amongst themselves".*

> **Les Tree,** then Director-General of the Ministry of Police: *"Why did you get involved over a guy like Goodwin. You didn't need to".*

Scully's response to them was to say that that is precisely what most senior politicians might have done, but that he was simply appalled at the way Goodwin had been criticised, without proper consultation, after doing such a great job at Cronulla. He told them he would do it again, although in a way which would avoid the catastrophising journey that the media love to go on.

However, a draft report, containing a number of disputed issues, had been publicly released causing a tsunami of career diminishing media, with the NSW Police Senior Executive failing to carry out high level testing of the findings and claims for reliability and creditworthiness. Given all this, we submit the document in its current form should never have seen the light of day, but having done so, it is now time for a light to be shone upon it, disputed parts analysed, and alternate opinions and contra-narrative heard.

11

The Strike Force Neil Report

The Strike Force Neil report is available on the NSW Parliamentary website. It is important, fair, just and equitable for us to emphasise that not all parts of the report are disputed. In fact, the bulk of the report is innocuous, uncontroversial and is accepted. We also accept that healthy organisational debrief and debate on issues is key for organisational development. In fact, debriefs that are transparent, consultative and productive are highly encouraged. We acknowledge the difficulties in carrying out this, or any, review. There was some excellent work done. The timeline documented by analysts on Strike Force Neil provides a good historical reference. The bulk of the report's content is not in dispute. Commanders would always welcome constructive feedback and improvements in training and equipment.

It is also important to note, in expressing alternate views, opinions and a contra-narrative on some key issues set out in the report, we are in no way being critical of any individual or group, nor their opinions to which they're fully entitled. We submit it is always a healthier and better end outcome when everyone is heard on a subject and alternate points of view are ultimately expressed and considered.

Whilst we believe that different conclusions and findings should have been arrived at after the completion of the review by Strike Force Neil into police performance, we understand that those conclusions may have been arrived at for good reasons which we of course, respect and accept, and encourage as part of a transparent and open sharing of ideas.

In the end, it is that kind of process which makes organisations stronger and better at what they do.

Some of the chosen wording in the Strike Force Neil report caused a significant and widespread negative media reaction to police performance leading up to and during the Cronulla Riots. There were many issues disputed at the time, and which remain so to this day. Below we outline some of those issues, express an alternate-opinion and/or present a wider perspective. Unfortunately these views were not aired at the time due to the manner in which the report was publicly released via the media. To gain a full appreciation, any interested party would need to read the full Strike Force Neil report. However, it is in 4 volumes and this is obviously not possible, nor feasible, for many, and nor have we canvassed every aspect of it in this book. As stated, a great deal of the matters raised in the report are uncontroversial and accepted. We merely concentrate here on matters we believe warrant further explanation or alternative opinion.

Risk assessment

Statements in the report that generated the most negative and career diminishing media for police commanders revolve around the aspect of risk rating prior to the event.

The report stated that:

> *"The review concluded that the risk assessment to indicate the level of response was flawed. Subsequently the planning for the event was not adequate ... The end result of the formula was that the overall risk assessment for riot was reduced to medium."*[51]

Senior police planners and commanders were shocked to see this 'finding' all over the media, given its contrast with what we allege actually happened in the days leading up to 11 December 2005.

Documents provided to the investigation, show the risk assessment was indeed initially set at Medium, but was then elevated to High ahead of the riots. Detailed police planning took place for a High risk event after Commanders agreed the risk should be raised from its initial Medium to High on the evening of 8 December, 2005 three days prior to the event. It is unclear why the report emphasised the contrary:

> *"The suggested treatment options were then in line with a risk assessment of 'Medium' when it could be argued that based on this risk assessment for racially motivated violence and riot, the risk rating*

---

[51] Stike Force Neil Report, Volume One, pp. 9, 62.

should have been 'High'. The treatment options for 'High' would have reflected that planning should have been relative to dealing with a significant event". [52]

Unsurprisingly, the media drew heavily on these findings and ran many career damaging headline stories including:

"Flawed Risk Assessment"
"Risk Plan in Lead-Up to Riot Inadequate"
"Race Tension Misjudged"
"Poor Planning"
"Cronulla Race Riot Response Flawed"
"Riot Response Inadequate"
"Police Leaders Let Public Down"

The timeline on escalating risk to 'High'

Senior police working behind the scenes from the 4th to the 9th of December 2006, spent a considerable amount of time and effort assessing the risk rating for possible adverse law enforcement outcomes at Cronulla being troublesome during the unfolding Summer. It initially was set at Medium but then was reassessed at High. It is important to examine the timeline.

The attack on the lifeguard: 4th December 2005

The first assault of a Surf Life Saver occurred at Cronulla Beach. This incident was a local matter, well attended to by local police and has never been the subject of criticism. However, the media began creating a 'moral panic' about an attack on an Australian icon. Goodwin as Regional Commander was informed of the initial incident by way of the usual 'Situation Report' and was satisfied with the action local police were taking.

Initial risk assessment set at 'Medium': 6th December 2005

Given the heightened media and local community mood, the Miranda Local Area Command conducted a risk assessment and commenced planning for a Summer pro-active police operation. This was registered and named as 'Operation SETA'. Its mission was to reduce the incidence of anti-social behaviour and intimidation in the Cronulla Beach area. A 'Community Tensions Risk Assessment' for the Cronulla area, as it was then configured,

---

[52] Stike Force Neil Report, Volume One, p. 63.

would normally have designated the risk as 'Low' but given these emerging tensions, it was raised to 'Medium' at that time, requiring a higher level of police planning and 'Treatment Options'. The first set of Operational Orders were drafted on 6/12/05, with an amendment added on 7/12/05. These orders included an 'Escalation Plan', if needed, which would draw upon resources from neighbouring police commands and specialist commands as required.

The second fist fight: 7th December 2005

This 'event' is outlined in detail in Chapter 3, 'Build up to riot', and formed an important part of both police escalating the risk assessment and the media continuing to engage in 'moral panic'. Video footage, camera stills, and journalistic commentary around this second event, added to the narrative of Australia being under attack.

Assistant Commissioner Goodwin was briefed on this second assault incident within 15 minutes of its occurrence, and recognising the potential risk of further inflation, he immediately put in place a team of riot trained police at Cronulla, with extensive supporting equipment and vehicles if needed. The Police helicopter began aerial surveillance and filming, and he placed the Highway Patrol Command on standby. Additionally, the Police Operations Centre and a Major Incident Response Team were put on standby under the command of NSW Police most experienced public order expert, Supt. Ron Mason.

An Operational Plan was put together later that night, with significant additional resources supplementing the Local Area Command's response, with considerable input from Goodwin, Local Area Commander Rob Redfern, and Region Operations Manager Supt. Hutchings. A formal 'Concept of Operations' was prepared and forwarded via e-mail to Deputy Commissioner Scipione. It would be normal practice for him to, in-turn, notify and forward the e-mail to Commissioner Moroney, then discuss the proposed plans and operations via telephone with him.

On the evening of 7th December 2005 Goodwin asked the Cronulla area Police Command to spend the next day reviewing their risk rating.

Risk rating elevated to 'High': 8th December 2005

Cronulla Police reviewed their 'Community Tensions Risk Assessment'. It is important to examine how such risk assessments operate. The risk assessment was conducted utilising the latest template available in

NSW Police at that time, which had been developed after the Redfern and Macquarie Fields riots of 2004 and 2005, and in accordance with recommendations that were adopted after debriefs of those operations. The local police at Cronulla carried out a thorough risk assessment utilising the template's standard Australian & New Zealand system of 'Likelihood' and 'Consequence' ratings. It was based upon all known intelligence at the time.

Various individual parts of the risk assessment were either 'Very Low', 'Low', 'Medium' or 'High' risk. For instance, things like the risk of 'Siege / Hostage situation' or 'Arson / Explosion' were considered a 'Low' or 'Very Low' risk of occurring. But other individual parts of the risk assessment came out as 'High Risk', most notably the risk of 'Large Scale Affray and Riot' and 'Politically / Racially Motivated Violence'. This meant the overall risk rating, utilising this standard template in use by NSW Police at that time, which effectively involved an averaging of all the separate risk categories, was 'Medium'.

However, after the 2nd assault at Cronulla on the 7th of December 2005, and the relentless and exaggerated media coverage of the two assaults, combined with the highly inflammatory text messages that by then had begun circulating ahead of the 'reclaim the beach' day set for Sunday 11 December 2005, a decision was made by police planners and commanders on the 8th of December 2005, to elevate the risk rating to 'High'.

The use of such technology (mass SMS messaging to organise a protest) was a new phenomenon that had not been previously encountered in Australia and was not a specific part at the time of the NSW Police 'Community Tensions Risk Assessment' template. And nor was the impact that massive media attention may have on the rated risk level surrounding racial tension. These never before experienced issues were missing from the existing risk template (at that time) and therefore skewed it's outcome, which was sensibly found wanting, unsatisfactory and was therefore set aside. Local and regional police, including Rob Redfern and Goodwin, well recognised the deficiency in a technical application of this template, acted accordingly in determining that the real risk should be rated as 'High', and agreed that planning and treatment options against that level of risk should now be put in place.

So, after extensive discussions by phone, including into the evening of 8th December 2005, both Superintendent Redfern and Assistant Commissioner

Goodwin agreed the template was inadequate and the risk rating should be increased to 'High Risk'. In addition, all of the local and region police involved in discussions and operational planning also agreed the risk template was inadequate, as it did not consider these emerging issues.

This risk rating decision was officially put in place by an email from Redfern to Goodwin at exactly 8.45am on Friday the 9th of December 2005.

> *"I have no doubt that the current risk is 'high'... If I am ever asked, I will indicate that this risk is 'high'. However, we have been asked to conduct the risk assessment utilising the current risk assessment tool. In my view that tool does "not" allow the concerns or issues in this case to be adequately captured. When one looks at the criterion it is difficult to capture these factors to display a realistic risk rating ... my professional view is that the risk is 'High'".*

This critical change to 'High Risk' was never mentioned in the Strike Force Neil report, which states it was left at Medium.

Nearly 15 years after the release of the Strike Force Neil report, Mark Goodwin and Robert Redfern randomly met up and Redfern for the first time revealed to Goodwin, that:

> *"During Hazzard's investigation, I personally told him that the risk rating had been raised to High. Plus, I personally handed to Hazzard a copy of my email to you informing you the risk was High".*

It is not known why the report did not reflect this information. Had the investigation report simply criticised the adequacy of the existing 'Community Tensions Risk Assessment' template in use at that time, noting it was overridden by commanders, there would have been no issue, and probably no media frenzy about it. Ironically, the deficient 'Community Tensions Risks Assessment' template was revised and improved by Goodwin and his senior commanders after the Cronulla Riots and well ahead of the release of the report. The Strike Force Neil report also made no mention of this. The issue of Risk Assessment was never canvassed with Goodwin in any manner prior to the report's public release.

Planning

The report stated: *"...planning for the event was not adequate [as]...the overall risk assessment for riot was reduced to medium'.*

As mentioned, this assertion is disputed as the risk assessment had been elevated to High three days before the riots which occurred on the 11th of December 2005.

In our view, Goodwin's command was well documented, planned and prepared for the Cronulla Riots based on the increased rating of the risk as 'High'. Again, Goodwin was never asked about Planning by any Strike Force Neil member, nor was any proposed findings regarding it discussed with him prior to the report's public release.

On 9 December 2005, as an immediate and direct consequence of the risk rating being raised from 'Medium' to 'High', Goodwin took over Strategic Command of the Cronulla situation. Medium risk local operations are simply not planned at a Regional level by an Assistant Commissioner. The increase to 'High Risk' is the direct reason Goodwin personally took over planning and strategic command of the Cronulla situation on 9 December, 2005. And from that time on, Supt. Rob Redfern was designated the Operational Commander. (These individual roles are explained in more detail below).

On 9 December, 2005, the same day the risk rating was increased to 'High', Goodwin called for and chaired a significant planning meeting at Cronulla Police Station with relevant operational police. That meeting was attended by public order and specialist experts who reviewed the existing operational plans, made recommendations and approved a substantial increase in police resources required against the new risk rating of 'High'. This meeting also considered a new upgraded concept of operations and tactical plans.

In addition, the NSW Premier and Minister for Police were briefed that same day at Cronulla Police Station on the increased 'High Risk' rating, as well as the latest police intelligence and the upgraded police preparations ahead of the event. Scully recalls the briefing:

> *"I remember being told by Goodwin that morning their risk rating had been raised to High Risk overnight and that he had personally taken over planning and strategic command of the situation as a result. Redfern would remain as the operational commander. I was extremely impressed with the seriousness with which both Goodwin and Redfern were approaching the threat of public disorder, the amount of planning they were undertaking and the kind and level of police resources they*

intended to have in place. Both the Premier and I were confident that Goodwin knew what he was doing and had a potentially difficult matter well in hand".

Goodwin joined the Minister and the Premier on Cronulla Beach for a press conference and emphasised a warning to youth intent on attending Cronulla that weekend of the massively increased police operation. The interviews were headline TV, Newspaper and Radio news for the next 24-48hrs. It is ludicrous to suggest the State's Premier, Police Minister and Police Assistant Commissioner would be all holding headline press conferences over some insignificant local 'soiree' at the beach that police were still allegedly considering as a 'medium' risk event. And it simply wasn't the case.

Commissioner and Deputy Commissioner get briefed by Goodwin

Of some significance and relevance, is that Commissioner Moroney himself personally attended the end of the above planning meeting at Cronulla Police Station on 9 December 2005 where he received a detailed briefing from Goodwin, Superintendents Redfern, Cullen (newly appointed head of Public Order & Riot Squad), Hutchings (Region Operations Manager) and other public order and specialist experts present. Moroney was fully briefed on the increased police resources and new upgraded operational and tactical plans being applied as a direct result of the increased risk to High. Moroney expressed his complete satisfaction with those new and upgraded plans. He was complimentary of all the work senior police had done.

Again, a Commissioner of Police does not personally attend a planning session for a local issue that police are still treating as 'Medium Risk', and it simply wasn't the case. This is not mentioned in the report, nor that earlier that same day Goodwin attended Police Headquarters and gave both Commissioner Moroney and Deputy Commissioner Scipione a comprehensive personal briefing about the increased risk to High and that he was taking over planning and strategic command as a result. He also informed both that he intended holding a high level planning meeting later that same afternoon at Cronulla Police Station to substantially increase the police response and resources. And that is how Moroney knew to attend that meeting, which he did without notice, to satisfy himself that all was in hand.

An 'Escalation Plan' concluded

During that same planning meeting on 9 December 2005, Goodwin also put in place an escalation plan to ensure that, if events 'escalated', then all additional personnel, equipment and logistics which would be needed could be quickly recalled to duty and put into place.

When the revenge attacks began during the evening of 11 December 2005, the Escalation Plan was quickly put into effect with dramatic impact.

The notes of this exhaustive planning work carried out on 9 December, 2005 (and subsequent command logs) clearly show the vastly increased deployment of Uniformed Police, Riot Police, State Protection Group, Marine Command, Air-Wing, Mounted Police with Riot Trained Horses, Prison Van, Traffic & Highway Patrol, Police Dogs and handlers etc, that were all added to the original plans, directly because the risk rating had been raised from Medium to High. All of this detail was provided to Strike Force Neil.

The Battle Plan

Like the military, police forces do not commit their troops to an expected engagement without proper planning and consideration of an 'Order of Battle'. Whilst coppers regularly on duty respond to calls for assistance, they do not just turn up to what has been deemed a "High Risk" event.

Like soldiers, police troops require and are given ahead of time, detailed plans on how police operations will be commanded, resourced, and implemented, and how the unexpected will be covered. Hence the detailed planning, approval and delivery of a 'Concept of Operations' and its concomitant 'Escalation Plan'.

At 7.40pm on 9th December 2005, Superintendent Hutchings (Goodwin's Region Operations Manager) returned to the Sydney Police Operations Centre, where the specialised Planning and Logistics Team under his direct command were housed, and finalised the new plan as directed during the meeting at Cronulla.

Supt. Hutchings documented a new 'Concept of Operations', which clearly articulated the much increased general and specialist resources applied to this operation based upon the new High Risk rating. The new plan was sent via e-mail to Deputy Commissioner Scipione and others, at exactly 23.29hrs (11.29pm) on 9th December 2005.

Location of the Command Post

The choice of Command Post location during the daytime events at Cronulla was criticised in the report, and a panacea for this failing being suggested by the acquisition of a command truck:

> "Taking into consideration the varying opinions, the problems could have been overcome if an appropriate mobile command post was in the fleet of specialist vehicles within the NSW Police".[53]

Goodwin, as overall police commander, agreed with other public order experts in their choice of what he thought was an ideal location for the Police Command Post: on the top two floors of the North Cronulla Surf Lifesaving Club, with a full 180 degree elevated panoramic view of where the proposed demonstration was to be held.

It is not the role of a review body to determine what they might or would have done in the circumstances with respect to locating a Command Post, but to determine if **any** properly trained and skilled public order commander, could have come to the same decision. Not that some commanders may have *"varying"* opinions, or some may have chosen a different location, but that **none** could have come to the same view. It leaves the command post location decision as neither right nor wrong, but just one of the many calls a commander is required to make 'in the heat of battle'.

At least the report did include: *"The commanders at Cronulla are of the opinion that the Command Post was in the best location"*, but then failed to set out their detailed reasons for thinking that. However, it is not known who these unidentified *'commanders at Cronulla'* were. Goodwin, as the overall commander for the Cronulla Riots, was not once asked about the Command Post location, nor the reasons for its choice, nor any alternatives that were considered (like Cronulla Police Station, which was considered too small, had no height/view advantage over the scene and was too distant for staging, hot- debriefs, redeployments etc). Goodwin knew nothing of the surf club Command Post even being an alleged issue, until the 'draft' report was suddenly publicly released.

Why the Surf Club was considered the best location?

Having a height advantage from the 2nd floor of the local surf club, with

---

[53] Strike Force Neil Report, p. 68.

views over the entire field of operation and half the rest of Cronulla, gave a rarely available strategic advantage for Public Order Management. It is unlikely, in our view, that any other experienced public order commander, would have outright rejected this location for command, and opted instead to cramp themselves into the back of a truck parked down the road looking at 2nd hand grainy video feeds.

Additionally, and not unimportantly, the Command Post had toilets, kitchen, fridges, tables, chairs, briefing area, operational commander area (Rob Redfern), strategic commander area (Goodwin), and media liaison area. Over 150 police could be fed there on a different floor, so as not to interrupt the Command centre (and they were), as well as being 'hot debriefed' and re-deployed as necessary by Tactical Commanders. This simply couldn't be done out of a truck?

During the afternoon of 11 December 2005, it became a deliberate Command tactic to try to de-escalate the day by cautiously and gradually removing police vehicles, police personnel, and helicopter (which went to a stand-by location nearby). About 150 police were slowly but intentionally pulled off the streets to make it look like everything was all over and it was time to go home. The strategy worked very well and most people simply did leave and go home.

Those 150 police were housed within a holding area on a separate floor in the surf club and were all fed. Crucially, they could easily be 'hot debriefed' by police command and were ready to be immediately re-briefed and re-deployed en-mass to deal with revellers if they decided not to leave as was planned and tensions began to heighten again.

Most especially on the height advantage aspect, Public Order Operations and Demonstrations are not like Siege/Hostage situations, Covert Operations, Specialist Weapons raids, or indeed Counter Terrorist Investigations. Those type of operations do require a command post covertly secreted away nearby. Sometimes that needs to be in a van or truck, with live feeds for electronic surveillance, but that is mostly because the command post needs the ability to go mobile. Static public demonstrations can be, and are usually, highly dynamic events. Height advantage and view of the field of operation is an extreme advantage in such situations

The Strike Force Neil report also raised questions about the risk of the command post being subjected to attack by demonstrators. This, in our view, lacked appreciation of the context and circumstances facing commanders at the scene. The Command Post was the local surf club, a beach icon of the community, and the notion that it might have come under attack was not realistic in our view. The crowd were there to fight for 'their' beach, 'their' surf club, its lifesavers and the whole local surf culture, not to attack it. The report failed to emphasise that all day, people were milling around the beach and in front of the Command Post, whilst singing "Waltzing Matilda" and "Advance Australia Fair", often added in for good measure, *"Cops are Tops"* and *"Three Cheers for the Cops"*. This was a gathering to 'reclaim the beach' from uncivil visitors, and not a morsel of intelligence, or a shred of evidence suggested it was going to be a protest directed at police. The comparison of the North Cronulla Surf Club Command Post of 2005, with the Police Command Post of Bathurst 1985, is not sustainable in our view. The mood and intent of each set of protestors was completely different.

Later in the Strike Force Neil report, to justify a finding that more education and training was needed for public order commanders, the issue was canvassed again: *"There was no appreciation in when, where and how to set up a command post and how it should be resourced".*[54]

"No appreciation"! Not an inadequate or even a limited one, but simply none!

Predictably, the media reacted negatively, aggressively and often to this finding that police commanders effectively didn't have a clue when it came to a Command Post. This was devastating to Goodwin both professionally and personally, and given the issue was never raised with him by the inquiry, procedurally unfair in our view.

Goodwin had a wealth of knowledge in setting up command posts over several decades and physically being present as he commanded literally hundreds of both complex covert undercover stings, major crime arrests, hostage situations and overt uniformed police operations during major public events, protests and demonstrations.

The Sydney Police Operations Centre

In fact, part of Goodwin's everyday role as Assistant Commissioner and as the Sydney Regional Area Commander was to manage and, as required,

---

[54]   Strike Force Neil Report, Volume One, p. 95.

operate the Sydney 'Police Operations Centre' (POC).

Located in a concrete bunker in Sydney's CBD, it is the largest police command post in the country. Goodwin would make use of this Command Post throughout his tenure on an almost weekly basis to plan and respond to major policing operations, such as the 'revenge attacks' in 2005, or New Year's Eve, Australia Day and numerous Sydney protests, demonstrations, major events and VIP visits. As previously outlined, a number of these were actually commanded by Goodwin utilising the POC whilst Strike Force Neil was 'investigating' police decision making on this very aspect.

Additionally, during the exact same time the Strike Force was coming to a contemplative view that the Cronulla commanders had *"no appreciation in when, where and how to set up a command post and how it should be resourced"*, Goodwin had overseen a $1M upgrade of the Sydney Police Operations Centre, which involved him chairing an implementation steering committee that actually included members of Hazzard's own CT command. Goodwin was well aware of when, where and how to locate a Command Post, and when and how to use the Police Operations Centre. However, his views on this were never sought.

The Command truck

In some limited circumstances, such as a remote non-urban location, a stand-alone hi-tech police semi-trailer type truck could be useful, but rarely would that then be of any assistance in the built up urban areas of Sydney, where virtually all police public order events occur. Despite its significant limitations it was never-the-less recommended:

> *"Police will get a hi-tech mobile command vehicle following a scathing report into the handling of the Cronulla Riots. The urgent need for a purpose-built vehicle was highlighted in the final volume of the report, released to Parliament on Friday night...Norm Hazzard, pointed out that 'What is missing from police operations, and has indeed never existed, is a purpose-built vehicle for use by command teams to manage a major operation,....The problem with an inappropriate command infrastructure at Cronulla would not have occurred if such a vehicle had been available'".* [55]

Not surprisingly, less than a year later on 30th April 2007, the *Daily Telegraph*

---

[55] M. O'Neill, *Sun Herald*, November 5, 2006.

ran an article regarding the NON-use of this truck.

> *"It's a riot doing nothing - $12,500 a month for idle police command post"*
>
> *"A GIANT command-post semi-trailer leased by police for $12,500 a month after the Cronulla riots is sitting idle in a police holding yard. The Daily Telegraph can reveal it was rejected for use as a command post during the security operation for the visit of US Vice-President Dick Cheney... it was deemed too large and unwieldy for the purpose. There have been no other public order incidents requiring its use, with some officers describing the semi-trailer as a 'waste of space'...the owner of the semi-trailer leased to police, admitted the 20m-long 23 tonne semi-trailer was not ideal for use by police in Sydney.*[56]*"*

Command structure

The report in a number of quite broad negative findings about command, effectively traduced the skill, experience and contributions of senior police engaged during the Cronulla Riots:

> *"The command structure and facilities to assist the commanders during that day were inadequate."*[57]
>
> *"Police on the street had to respond on many occasions without command direction to intervene and prevent assaults."*[58]
>
> *"Knowledge of the three levels of command appeared to be lacking."*[59]

We would of course, not imply or assert, that either command or its supporting command structures were flawlessly perfect on the day. Few organisational leaders would assert that even during the best of times.

Accordingly, it is appropriate for us to again emphasise that not all that is said in the Strike Force Neil report regarding command and structure/s is in dispute. The overall 'Cronulla Riots' operation was extremely varied, volatile, challenging and complex. It was not a single operation requiring the basic traditional command structure for a one-off day's event. It developed rapidly from a 'protest' in a single beachside suburb, to 'revenge attacks' across multiple geographic locations, right through to an 'extreme risk'

---

[56] K. Lawrence, *The Daily Telegraph*, April 30, 2007.
[57] Strike Force Neil Report, Volume One, p. 9.
[58] Strike Force Neil Report, Volume One, pp. 8 and 49.
[59] Strike Force Neil Report, Volume One, p. 95.

operation the following weekend utilising new Parliamentary powers and 2000 police in 7-zones from Wollongong to Sydney to Newcastle.

Things developed rapidly, requiring quick change and adaptability in command structures. Goodwin and other experienced police commanders made decisions that best suited the prevailing situation in a fast-paced and ever-changing environment never before experienced in Australia. A multitude of command structures were utilised to best suit the expanding situation, especially as issues rapidly escalated and the operation increased in size and complexity. It is not alleged by the authors that all command structures utilised were perfect and could not be improved, or that all commanders were of an equally trained and experienced standard, or that some police did not become confused. Sometimes command structures were rapidly put in place with little to no forewarning, utilising the best resources available at the time, to suit the ever-changing and expanding operational environment. In our view, it is important to conduct open and transparent debriefs, hear from all those involved and tease out improvements in command and control issues. And indeed, we agree the more command training, mentorship and exposure to complex situations the better.

However, the very public manner in which the Strike Force Neil report was released, together with some disparaging sweeping comments made within it regarding commanders and command structures, fed and caused a tsunami of media negativity. Unfortunately, in our view, this 'draft' report lacked a thorough documented analysis quoting and referencing actual individuals interviewed. It also lacked a contra-narrative, alternate opinions or balanced transparent counter-argument by those most affected by its provisional 'findings'.

Unsurprisingly, these types of sweeping assertions caused a great deal of sensational career destroying media Here are some examples:

- "The riot blunders verdict: no one in command" *(Note: A "verdict" regarding "blunders", as if opinion expressed in the report was equivalent to a Court Judgement of fact).*
- "Police leaders let public down"
- "Front Line Police Left in Mortal Danger"
- "No-one in Command"

And the following text in the report gave journalists plenty of encouragement to disparage the Cronulla Riots commanders:

> "Critical to an effective command system is the knowledge of roles... It would appear that there has been a presumption that commanders... come with knowledge and understanding of command and control. Also, that they possess an understanding of the principles and structures that make it work. The evidence is to the contrary".[60]

What "*the evidence*" was to support this "*to the contrary*" claim is simply unknown, as this detail is not revealed in the report, nor is any attempt made at a proper analysis of any material to support the claim. The report should have had excerpts of transcripts of interviews with senior police commanders, properly referenced, and an Appendix listing all the interviewees which were drawn upon to support the findings and recommendations. No such excerpts or Appendix was provided. Certainly Goodwin was not consulted at all on this issue. Even at this late stage, it would be interesting to know the list of interviewees and documents perused by the inquiry's team of investigators to support their arrival at such a damning conclusion.

A comparison with the Lindt Café siege commanders

A comparison of how the Lindt Café Siege Coronial Inquiry examined and reported on senior police commanders, with that of the Strike Force Neil Inquiry and the Cronulla Riots commanders, is an interesting yet sadly demoralising exercise.

In December 2014, two people were tragically killed during the Sydney Lindt Café Siege, one of whom died as a result of ricocheting gun fire from police. Police performance during the siege, especially that of commanders and their decision making, came under intense public scrutiny. This contrasted significantly with police performance and police commander decision making during the Cronulla Riots, which only came under any public scrutiny at all, when Commissioner Ken Moroney announced a 'Strike Force' investigation into it.

There were many police command issues that arose during the Lindt Café Siege examination, which could have resulted in career damaging findings. But it didn't. In perusing the sheer volume of tabloid newspaper headlines that the Strike Force Neil Report generated, a reader would be forgiven for thinking that the primary cause of the violence and fear which swept the streets and suburbs of Sydney in late 2005, was in fact poorly performing

---

[60] Report of Strike Force Neil, Vol 1, p. 95.

police commanders, rather than the real culprits, the rioters and revenge attackers themselves.

By way of stark comparison on this score, the coroner in the Lindt Café Siege Inquiry emphasised:

> "...the deaths and injuries...were not the fault of police...Man Monis deserves to be the sole focus of our denunciation and condemnation.
>
> This report...should not and will not be used to blame particular officers for outcomes beyond their control".[61]

And in getting the notion of the 'armchair general' spot on:

> "Officers who...faced terrible pressures can understandably feel indignant that they should be publicly called to account for every action and decision by people who were not there and can never fully appreciate what it was like for those who were".[62]

The Lindt Café Siege Commanders got a public hearing, due process, proper legal representation, and a detailed analysis of their oral and written evidence, quoting and referencing individual testimony from all involved parties. What a difference the outcomes could have been if the Strike Force Neil investigation had followed the same approach.

So how does Police Command work?

There are three levels of Command:

Strategic – This position/person deals with the higher-level issues of planning, logistics, resources, strategy, equipment, briefings, media etc. When an operation is rated as 'High Risk' this Command position would normally be occupied by an Assistant Commissioner. In the Cronulla Riots this was Goodwin. His logs clearly show that he occupied and carried out this high-level strategic command role.

Operational – This person is the hands-on operational commander, literally issuing orders from a command post directing teams on the ground, and seeing to it that the higher-level strategic commander's intent and strategy

---

[61] Coroners Court of NSW, 'Inquest into the deaths arising from the Lindt Café siege', May 2017, p. 5.
[62] Coroners Court of NSW, Inquest into Lindt Café Siege, p. 5.

are competently implemented. In a 'High Risk' operation such as at Cronulla on 11 December, 2005, this would normally be a Superintendent.

During the daytime events at Cronulla this was Superintendent Robert Redfern. Again, Redfern's operational logs were provided to the investigation team and they clearly show Redfern competently carrying out this Operational Commander role and nothing else. Supt. Redfern had recently completed the new Public Order Management Commander's Course.

In addition, to assist Redfern in his decision making, Goodwin had ensured an experienced Public Order Tactical Advisor was by Redfern's side throughout the entire operation – that person was the newly appointed head of the Public Order and Riot Squad, Superintendent Steve Cullen. Later that evening, Goodwin activated a well thought out Escalation Plan and called out several other Operational Commanders to take charge of Revenge Attacks developing in various geographic areas of Sydney. These operational commanders and their support staff were rotated on shifts, and reported to a Police Commander on duty 24/7 in a strategic command capacity at the Police Operations Centre throughout the remainder of the entire operation.

Tactical – These are the team leaders actually in the field, on the ground, carrying out supervision of their troops, whether that be generalist or specialist units. They are usually Inspectors or Sergeants (depending on the team size and nature of duty). They communicate with and obey the Operational Commander's orders. They also give their own directions, supervision, and sub-orders to their specific individual teams within their own areas of expertise. There were a large number of these present, fully briefed and on the ground on the day at Cronulla and later throughout the entire wider operation in other metropolitan areas. At Cronulla, all were clearly recorded in the staffing list attached to the Operational Orders, as were they recorded in multiple other orders and staffing lists later prepared for the ongoing operations over the ensuing days and weeks.

We accept that any confusion regarding command positions at the time of the Cronulla Riots may have been contributed to by a proliferation of terms being used in either frontline uniformed, or specialist units, of the NSW Police at that time to describe various command roles.

Some of the terms being used included:

- Operation Commander
- Police Commander
- Major Incident Response Team Commander
- Police Operations Centre Commander
- Forward Commander
- Tactical Commander
- Event Commander
- Incident Commander
- Site Commander
- Precinct Commander
- Region Commander
- Local Area Commander
- Duty Officer
- Specialist Commander, etc.

Varied terminology being used at that time throughout the NSW Police to describe command positions and roles in either frontline uniform operations or specialist police squads, ought not in our view justify a finding that the command structure used during the Cronulla Riots was inadequate. We submit the three levels of Strategic, Operational and Tactical command were clearly in place throughout the entire operation. Simply a finding and recommendation to standardise the use of terminology being used to describe command roles throughout various parts of the NSW Police at that time would have been appropriate and welcomed. Improvements in command education were recommended and would always be welcomed.

Regional vs Specialist command

Being designated the Strategic Commander for the Cronulla riots, and subsequent 'Operation Seta' that summer, were natural concomitants of Goodwin's everyday role as Regional Commander.

Goodwin was commander of Sydney's 'Central Metro Region' 24hrs a day, 7 days a week. It was an extremely busy and dynamic front-line uniformed role. In this Assistant Commissioner position, Goodwin was required to strategically oversee all operational police activity and to personally command 'high risk' events & public-order/demonstrations, as well as large/complicated emergency management situations. Significantly, in this front-line role, unlike a Specialist Commander, he was often up at all hours of the night/early-morning being briefed on significant issues that will hit the headline AM news; or being briefed on police seriously injured on-duty; or exercising delegated authorities regarding police arrested off-duty; or approving special weapons and tactics for sieges and hostage incidents unfolding in his region; or providing general advice, mentorship and/or occasionally directions to on-duty frontline commanders who had called him after hours in the 'heat of battle' and were facing difficult dilemmas.

Front-line uniformed policing command is a very dynamic constantly changing and challenging environment, most unlike the somewhat predictability of plain-clothed covert specialist units and their pre-planned operations. Being a uniformed Region Commander is not like a Specialist Commander, who on most occasions finishes their shift and is rarely disturbed after-hours unless there is a pre-planned operation at night by their Unit. And when such Specialist operations are conducted, they are meticulously planned, often for weeks or months. Conversely, the volatility and unpredictability of frontline police operations and situations under the control of a Region Commander are polar opposite. The role often requires immediate decisions, often in the middle of the night, that cannot be dwelled upon for extended periods, and such a commander needs the flexibility and autonomy to set up command wherever and whenever they want and need. That can literally be anywhere day or night as required. Goodwin well knew and appreciated the vast difference. He had been both a specialist and front-line regional commander.

Goodwin's decision to initially set up his 'Strategic Command' role at the Command Post at Cronulla during the daytime event was based upon this sound autonomous individual and experienced judgement of a Regional Commander. Firstly, at that stage the incident was confined to a singular suburb. Secondly, judging by the inordinate media interest in the preceding days, Goodwin well knew the absolute media & political frenzy and briefing demands that would (and did) occur at the actual incident site. He knew the Operational Commander, Rob Redfern, would be otherwise completely swamped, overwhelmed and distracted from his core role by these demands, which would be highly detrimental to the conduct of the actual operation. To this day Goodwin stands by that decision. What actually unfolded at the scene (in terms of such demands) is exactly as per what was anticipated.

Goodwin was Rob Redfern's 'strategic level' region commander on a 24/7 basis, 365 days a year and it is submitted there simply was no confusion between them at Cronulla as to their roles nor chain of command. Goodwin was never consulted on this issue, nor given the opportunity to explain his actions, respond or be heard. We submit his reasoning for so-acting should have been sought and included in the report.

Later in the evening, when issues quietened at Cronulla (including media, executive and political briefing demands), and the revenge issues began to emerge on multiple geographic fronts, Goodwin quickly and sensibly moved his Strategic Command role to the Police Operations Centre, which he'd already had activated anyway in a support role to himself. As evidenced by these Cronulla Riots operations, the autonomy of a frontline Region Commander about where best to command from, based upon the volatility and unpredictability of frontline policing with rapidly developing situations, needs to exist and should remain in our view.

The rapidly expanding nature of this police operation over the ensuing days (and weeks) necessitated intense planning and substantial police resources being suddenly required. Goodwin needed to oversee this planning and negotiate the resourcing of huge police operations, whilst also being available for briefing political, community and policing leaders, as well as managing the media firestorm that had erupted. These demands were extremely high. There was criticism in the report about command structures used, confusion about who was in command and Goodwin always remaining in strategic command whilst installing a separate Commander to run the Police Operations Centre on rotating shifts. We respect these opinions, but he was never asked the reasons why, never asked to explain, nor given the opportunity to respond to 'findings' regarding this issue before a 'draft' report was released to the media/public.

We emphasise this was not your average 'run-of-the-mill' police operation. It went on for days and weeks, with ever increasing complexity and unprecedented media, public and political scrutiny. It required an overall Strategic Commander with total continuity of issues to oversee the planning, resourcing & logistics of the largest public order operation ever conducted in Australia. It required that commander to conduct competent media & political briefings. It required that commander to negotiate with unions over suddenly placing the entire NSW Police force into 'Olympic Mode' and transferring hundreds of police from regional areas to the city. It required that commander's advocacy to Government for greater police powers to deal with extreme risk intelligence that was (by then) being received, etc. All these taxing, tough and onerous issues required attention by Goodwin, whilst the actual operation also ticked along in the background.

And for this reason, Goodwin chose to install an additional layer of strategic command and appointed a separate Police Operations Centre Commander on 24hr rotating shift basis – to solely focus upon the operation without being totally distracted and consumed by these other overwhelming high-level strategic issues and negotiations. To manoeuvre resources, equipment and logistics between various front-line geographic locations and operational commanders in the field as threats emerged, conditions changed and as required and requested.

This dire situation absolutely required a singular recognisable overall Strategic Commander to remain in charge, to be the face of it to the media, public and government, to have total continuity of issues, and to at all times be accountable to the Commissioner and Minister for Police. That was Goodwin. To suggest otherwise would be unrealistic in our view. There is no possible way that a band of rotating commanders taking charge of the Police Operations Centre on a shift-by-shift basis could have dealt with these massive strategic issues, as well as meet the actual operation demands required. On so many levels it would have been totally unsatisfactory and an absolute disaster. Given the passage of time, Goodwin does not back down from that decision one bit, nor would he ever abrogate that necessitous responsibility, given the extreme risk prevailing situation at that time and the enormity of the overall strategic decisions, planning and operations that were required. We submit Goodwin's above reasoning and perspective on Command and Control during the entire breadth of the Cronulla Riot police operations should have been sought and his response inserted into the Strike Force Neil report.

As stated, we do not allege these command structures were perfect, nor all commanders utilised were trained and/or experienced to a similar standard. Due to the number of command personnel required, some regional and other commanders were new to the Police Operations Centre environment and had to learn and adapt on the run. These are very good debrief points for improvement. And yes, this was a shift from traditional command structures as an additional command layer was inserted, but we strongly submit the prevailing conditions well and truly warranted it. The enormous complexities being faced required thinking 'outside the box' in the 'heat of battle'. This operation was far different from anything previously experienced by NSW Police, thus requiring extreme adaptability and resourcefulness. Most importantly, these command structures put in place by Goodwin actually worked. Could it have been done differently or better? That is subjective and there will always be varied opinions on the issue. The answer is 'yes' we can always improve and do better, which is why transparent debriefs are so valuable in capturing what worked well (even if that was a new strategy or method), what failed, what could be done better and what should we do next time.

The demanding nature of these high-level strategic issues were far in excess of anything a specialist unit might traditionally encounter in the midst of, and during, their rather predictable pre-planned operations with standard command structures. It is highly unlikely any specialist commander has, or ever would be, confronted right in the middle of their operation with the sheer level of overwhelming strategic planning, briefing demands, negotiations with unions over continued resourcing, advocacy to government regarding legislative reform, etc, that was encountered during the Cronulla Riots operations. Specialist Unit operations are simply not the same as these types of large-scale public order issues and are usually conducted behind the scenes. They do not attract the same level of intensity, immediate scrutiny and overwhelming distractions and demands of a commander at large scale public order incidents.

In this particular incident at Cronulla, the media over-exaggeration of issues for days leading up to the 'event' was unprecedented in Australia. Thus it was Goodwin's sensible choice (in our view) to initially physically locate himself at the incident site to take the heat, pressure and unwanted distraction away from the Operational Commander Robert Redfern. Likewise, the strategic command demands that unfolded over the ensuing days and weeks would have totally overwhelmed any individual commander operating out of the Police Operations Centre trying to also focus on the needs of operational commanders in the field and moving resources around to respond to emerging threats. This necessitated Goodwin installing a separate Police Operations Centre Commander on duty 24/7 on rotational shifts to handle this load.

It is our view you cannot simply uplift command policy & procedures from a relatively small specialist unit, with is somewhat standard predictable single-day pre-planned operations that require standard command and control structures, and force it to fit all frontline uniform operational policing scenarios, which, as these Cronulla Riots operations clearly showed, are vastly different and dynamic in nature. What works for them does not necessarily mean it can be, nor should be, jammed to fit all other frontline operational policing scenarios. Conversely, perhaps the NSW Police Force and other jurisdictions should take note and could learn a lot in hindsight from the Cronulla Riot commanders of what actually did work and what was actually achieved back in 2005 to quell riotous behaviour and bring the streets of Sydney (and beyond) back under control.

Charts depicting command roles given to Strike Force Neil

At one stage during its investigation, Strike Force Neil sent charts depicting what they thought the command arrangements were, to Goodwin's Staff Officer, Inspector Martin Hayston. These charts were so inaccurate that Hayston drew up nine organisation charts for the 'Investigation' team, depicting command on the day of 11th December 2005; command that night as the operation grew onto multiple fronts due to 'revenge attacks'; command the following days as the operation grew bigger; command the following weekend when new police powers were used after a special sitting of Parliament (during which Goodwin commanded 2000 police in 7 x zones from Wollongong to Newcastle utilising new powers from an urgent recall of State Parliament); and command of the following six weeks of Operation SETA throughout the rest of summer.

The three levels of command (strategic, operational, and tactical) were clearly depicted in all these charts supplied to the Strike Force.

Police left without command direction

> *"Police on the street had to respond on many occasions without command direction to intervene and prevent assaults".*[63]

Unsurprisingly, this extraordinary claim also led to significant career diminishing and personally devastating media: *"No-one in command'* and *"Frontline police left in mortal danger".*

The power and discretion of the Police Constable

The extraordinary notion that police officers were effectively wandering around in a rudderless, directionless state is disputed. The report made no

---

[63] Strike Force Neil Report, Volume One, p. 8.

mention nor any analysis of individual frontline uniform police officers exercising their 'Office of the Police Constable' discretion to prevent a 'breach of the peace', or arrest and charge an offender. The notion that individual police officers couldn't be expected to take action in the middle of a disturbance, whilst awaiting *"command direction"* is contested.

Video footage during the day of the Cronulla Riots clearly shows police in large numbers acting properly and appropriately, as did Sgt. Craig Campbell with his baton at Cronulla Railway station. Not one copper can be seen waiting idly by for command direction.

Bottle throwers, and the hooligans on Cronulla Railway station were met, as required, by the swift response of uniformed police exercising their sworn powers and discretion. There were no individual police wandering around the riot unsupervised. They were all in carefully pre-selected, substantially resourced and fully equipped teams. Each and every team was deployed under their respective field Tactical Commanders. We cannot recall a single image of a 'lone ranger' officer standing around the crowd wondering what to do, nor acting in isolation.

Police officers were acting in tandem with their colleagues, in accordance with the well understood Concept of Operations for the event. These police teams had been strategically placed throughout the crowd by police command. The briefing prior to the event was for those police officers and teams on the ground to take prompt action against any violent behaviour they observed within the crowd. Intervening to *"prevent assaults"* when observed by individual police officers and/or their team is not necessarily an immediate command issue but is at the core of that individual police constable's discretion to act or not. That discretion was exercised quite appropriately on the day by individuals within teams, but not by lone-ranger cops in the crowd left isolated, unsupported or without command direction. The narrative continues: *"Visual records of those incidents depict the individual initiative and courage of police officers"*.[64]

Exactly as it should be!

On every single occasion that violent behaviour occurred within the crowd, police took immediate action, arresting and extracting those offenders away from the melee, exactly as they had been briefed to do by police command. And as soon as any problematic behaviour within the crowd became known

---

[64] Strike Force Neil Report, Volume One, pp. 8 and 49.

to command, additional resources were immediately dispatched to that location under the Operation Commander's and/or Tactical Commander's direction. Crowd dynamics were being monitored and relayed by radio to the command post from police on the ground and via aerial top cover surveillance provided by the police helicopter.

This fact was very well documented by the mass of media coverage of the day.

The bravery of some police present was highly commendable. So much so, that Goodwin later lodged a written application that individual Commissioner's Commendations should be awarded to several police for their actions that day. None were awarded. Why?

The only difference between responding to a pub brawl, or a domestic violence situation and to this 'main event', is the planning, resourcing and personnel put into place ahead of time, and that each rostered police officer well knew that something may happen requiring more from them than just turning up with a group of their colleagues. Like a general duties shift, they knew what was expected of them as individual officers protecting the peace. On a 'normal' shift police have been trained, equipped, rostered, briefed at the start of their shift, deployed on a car-crew, directed to attend (say a Domestic) by Police Radio, and are under the supervision of the Shift Commander (Sergeant), the Duty Officer (Inspector) and to a lesser immediate level the Local Area Commander (Superintendent). They then attend these jobs all shift and take appropriate action in accordance with the law, their powers and their discretion.

At Cronulla, at all times, the police attending were trained, rostered, briefed, equipped and deployed in teams under explicit command direction. As in a 'normal' shift, after these important preliminaries were in place, a police officer would not expect a commander to direct them on every single occasion when to *"intervene and prevent assaults"* before they'd even act. That's their job at the scene, it is their discretion as a 'Constable of Police' doing critically important front end law enforcement, whether that be at a 'domestic', at a pub brawl, or during a disturbance.

There was a robust command structure in place at Cronulla, as outlined earlier in this chapter. Claiming that individual *"police on the street had to respond on many occasions without command direction to intervene and prevent assaults"*, is demonstrably unsustainable in our view, but never-the-less led to headlines such as: *"no-one in command"* and *"front-line police left in mortal danger'.*

Static lines at Redfern and Macquarie Fields

Footage of either the Redfern or Macquarie Fields Riots of February 2004 and January 2005, depict images of static police lines being pelted with rocks, Molotov cocktails, bricks and other objects, and in the latter case for days on end. There is no such footage of any of this happening at Cronulla. Goodwin's *"command direction"* during briefings on the day to front-line police were very clear – Any criminals who started any fights in the crowd were to be immediately and forcefully extracted. And this is exactly what occurred.

Major Incident Response Team (MIRT)

"After the events of 11th December, the MIRT policy was enacted."[65]

This claim is contested. A MIRT was enacted by Goodwin on the 9th of December 2005, before the riots began on the 11th of December not *"after the events"*. This had been put in place as soon as the risk rating was raised to High. This was good police practice, sound planning ahead of an event rated at 'High Risk", and was in accordance with recommendations from the review of police performance following the Macquarie Fields riot in January, 2005.

A MIRT is as it sounds, the deployment of a team to plan and respond to major incidents.

The following headings (in bold text) are the components of a Major Incident Response Team. Listed next to them is what was actually utilised by Goodwin at Cronulla, on and from the 7th of December:

- **Command** – Assistant Commissioner Goodwin (Strategic Commander), Superintendent Redfern (Operational Commander), Superintendent Cullen (Tactical Advisor), plus numerous Tactical Commanders (uniform and specialist) deployed in the field on the day at Cronulla.
- **Planning** – Superintendent Hutchings (Region Operations

---

[65] Strike Force Neil Report, Volume One, p. 75.

Manager) plus the entire Metropolitan Planning Unit (who were the most experienced Major Police Operations Planners in Australia and planned the police response to over 300 major events annually).

- **Logistics** – Inspector Wayne Laycock (Metropolitan Planning Unit Commander) plus his entire Unit of specialised operational planning and logistics personnel.
- **Intelligence** – Inspector Lenzo (Region Intelligence Commander)
- **Investigation** – A decision was made not to specifically deploy Cronulla Detectives to aimlessly wander around the crowd in plain clothes during the daytime events at Cronulla. This was due to their existing workload dealing with significant issues and arrests in the preceding days. Detectives were however rostered on duty at Cronulla and throughout the wider Sutherland Shire as part of their normal duties and ready to respond if necessary to any criminal investigation issues. There are alternate points of view on this, but those views and criticism are always welcome and encouraged in any transparent debrief to improve police operations and performance. A Strike Force was set up that evening of 11th December to investigate criminal offences committed on the day at Cronulla and was later substantially increased in size due to the subsequent 'Revenge Attacks'.
- **Riot Police Commander-** Superintendent Cullen (Commander of newly formed Public Order and Riot Squad) was appointed Tactical Advisor to Superintendent Redfern.
- **Media / Public Information** – A very senior Police Media liaison officer was briefed and engaged immediately after the 2nd Life Saver assault and was widely consulted by Goodwin & Redfern in the lead up to, and during, the day at Cronulla. Throughout the actual day, a whole media liaison team were deployed and were physically at the Command Post on-site at Cronulla.

Missed opportunities

Significant opportunities to improve Public Order Management in police operations were missed in our view because of the narrowed 'Terms of Reference' for Strike Force Neil to examine just 11th to 13th December 2005, whereas the actual operation lasted for weeks, at least from the 4th of December 2005 through until at least the end of January 2006.

It is unknown who wrote or influenced those Terms of Reference to limit the inquiry to just those dates, or why? But what it meant was, that important and noteworthy new public order strategies and massive police operations used to quell the 'Cronulla Riots' were excluded from the investigation, its report and any subsequent media publicity or ongoing academic analysis, research or literature. These very 'positive' policing issues therefore remain relatively, or sometimes completely, unknown to the public or even law enforcement personnel themselves. Instead, most public knowledge and ongoing commentary of the 'Cronulla Riots' police operations is drawn solely from the almost seismic level of negative media criticism unleashed when the 'draft' report was released.

The actual sheer magnitude of threats that police commanders faced and how they competently dealt with them, together with the expanse of police operations that were actually conducted, have never before been reported upon and are therefore simply not known. Until now.

We submit this was a substantial missed opportunity by NSW Police to debrief and highlight the most significant strategies that actually quelled riotous behaviour for the future good of police operations and generations

These missed opportunities include:

(a)   Rapid Response Riot Police:

The singular most effective and significant police strategy that quelled the riotous revenge attacks was the design and use, for the very first time in Australia, of Rapid Response Riot Police. Yet this strategy apparently deserved zero analysis, commentary or feedback (good or bad) in a review undertaken by NSW Police.

During the revenge attacks Sydney faced unprecedented violence from highly mobile rampaging gangs. The speed, agility, randomness and savagery of these revenge attacks in multiple locations throughout Sydney had never before been experienced in Australia. Goodwin came up with the idea of attacking these marauding gangs head-on with similar highly mobile law enforcement teams. He brought together several teams of highly experienced and trained highway patrol pursuit drivers and their V8 vehicles in convoy, with riot police and all their gear onboard each vehicle. That meant these gangs would then be stopped in their tracks by 40 x police in 10 cars at once. Several of these teams were strategically placed in multiple locations in the southern, eastern and western suburbs of Sydney, ready to rapidly respond. And respond they did – with great success. Physically fit riot police dealt with angry, intimidating and 'mouthing off' individuals, whilst highway patrol police dealt with drivers, traffic infringements, defects and seizure of vehicles. All frontline police and the radio network were told to inform the Police Operations Centre immediately they saw or detected a convoy of these suspect vehicles anywhere, so these highly effective mobile police teams could be deployed.

This strategy literally crushed these predatory convoys and stopped them in their tracks. It was a highly successful strategy, different and never before used. It received wide attention and notoriety in overseas policing jurisdictions. Yet, it remained un-debriefed and not part of a report by its own jurisdiction, the NSW Police. Why?

It is believed a significant opportunity was missed to examine and highlight the success of this strategy for the good of future police operations and generations. The opportunity to study how it worked, how it could be improved, methodology deployed, policy regarding its deployment etc, was all but buried and lost.

(b)   New Police Riot Powers:

An urgent recall of the NSW Parliament saw the introduction of unprecedented new public order and riot control legislation for police to deal with the riotous revenge attacks. These powers were extensively utilised by police in massive police 'public order' operations. Yet those operations were excluded from the Terms of Reference, investigation and report. Why? Opportunity was therefore lost to critically examine and document how these new powers worked for the good of future police. Were they judiciously utilised? What effect did they have? Could they be improved? How could they be used better in the future? All lost.

(c)   Resourcing Large Scale Public Order Operations:

A strategy was implemented to free up considerable police resources for redeployment into public order police operations. It was achieved by placing the entire state's police force into what we've called 'Olympic Mode', where its 80 x Local Area Commands were joined into bigger areas plus leave & other commitments deferred. It was a massive logistical operation in itself, even just housing the hundreds of country police that were brought into the city for these operations. The NSW Police Association were highly consulted and involved in the planning. But yet again, no mention is made in a review report commissioned by the NSW Police Force itself of this extraordinarily large and complex public order strategy. Why not? How did it work, what was done well, how could it be improved, etc – all lost.

(d)   Thwarting of hand-grenade and machine gun attack at Northies Hotel:

This significant operation, with its extremely positive outcome, was not reviewed and thus not mentioned in the report due to the narrowed Terms of Reference. Why?

(e)   Thwarting of massive damage and assaults at Westfields:

Again, the police response to this significant threat was yet another example of an extremely positive outcome in the overall Cronulla Riots operations. Yet again, not reviewed nor mentioned due to the narrowed Terms of Reference and therefore completely unknown to the public until now. Why?

(f)   Largest Ever Public Order Operation Sat 17th – Sun 18th December 2005:

This operation saw 2000 police deployed in 7 zones from Wollongong in the south to Newcastle in the north. It was the largest deployment of police ever by the NSW Police Force in respect of public order management. It was also the most intrusive police operation ever to date, with extensive geographic areas placed into complete 'lock-down' utilising the new special powers conferred upon police after the urgent recall of NSW Parliament. Entire suburbs were locked down, beaches and roads closed, phones, cars, knives, guns, bats, clubs and a vast array of home-made weapons were seized and taken off the streets.

Why were these operations excluded from the Terms of Reference? Why weren't they examined as part of a debrief review? One would think that an organisation the size of the NSW Police (one of the biggest in the world) would want to examine what worked and what could have been done better in the largest 'public order' police operation ever conducted in Australia? Yet again, we submit this was a significant missed opportunity to inform future generations of police and their operations.

Lost Learnings and the interview with Supt. Ron Mason

As mentioned in the Preface and in Chapter One, we decided to test the creditworthiness of our perspectives and opinions on a whole range of matters by conducting a number of interviews with people who at the time were MPs, police officers and community leaders.

And in particular, to test our position that the Strike Force Review process had led to lost learning opportunities, we interviewed NSW Police foremost expert on the planning and response to major public order events, Supt. Ron Mason. Why he was not interviewed by Strike Force Neil investigators, despite twice offering to do so, is not known. Whilst the opportunity for police to learn early on from his contemporaneous reflections on police performance during the riots is long past, we never the less, found his perspectives on the review process as both revelatory and confirming. This is set out in more detail in Part 4 'Reflections from the Field'.

Conclusion

The sensational media fanfare generated after the 'draft' Strike Force Neil report was released, left an indelible mark and skewed impression on the public's psyche about what happened regarding the Cronulla Riots and police performance. It continues to this day to be the only source of information. It therefore continues to feed journalists, academics and literature alike, especially every time a 'racist' issue occurs in Australia. However, we submit a gaping hole was left in that 'publicity', and thereby public knowledge, of the sheer extent and actual complexity of the wider police operations. The absence of material or information publicly released by NSW Police on the above matters makes it almost seem as if these extremely important and notably positive parts of the overall police 'public order' operation didn't even exist nor happen. It's almost like they were erased from history. For some reason, unbeknownst to us, they were outside the narrowly framed 'Terms of Reference', so they were not debriefed, not mentioned in the Strike Force Neil report and thereby completely brushed over by the media in their tsunami of negativity.

It is hoped this new material helps to better inform readers and will give a far greater balance and appreciation of what police commanders and their frontline troops actually faced and did, and what actually happened in Sydney back in December of 2005 when it seemed the whole city was under attack.

12

Operation Pendennis: CTC a Role Model

Norm Hazzard was a highly experienced and very well regarded Strategic Commander in Counter-Terrorism. Unsurprisingly, when writing his report into policing of the Cronulla Riots, he drew heavily on his experience in this specialist command as the 'go-to' position for how things ought to be done in all other front-line operational NSW Police commands, including during a major public disorder event. Assuming or requiring that Counter-Terrorism operations can or should be the role model for General Duties policing is, in our view, an unsustainable proposition.

Just 33 days before the Cronulla riots began, a police counter-terrorism operation unfolded in Sydney during which an unsuspecting general duties police officer from Green Valley Police Command was shot.

Operation Pendennis

Operation Pendennis conducted on the 8th of November 2005, was a broad and bold initiative focussed on a cell of very violent people. It involved ASIO, the Australian Federal Police, Victoria Police and NSW Police, and was a targeted, intelligence based, cross jurisdictional specialist counter-terrorism operation involving hundreds of specialist police, directed at taking out a major terror cell operating in both Melbourne and Sydney. It was an almost universally successful operation. Almost!

There were simultaneous raids across Melbourne and Sydney arresting a total of 16 men across several different locations. As at Cronulla and beyond in December 2005, police in November 2005 during Operation Pendennis, responded to intelligence, planned operations, used all available resources, found the culprits, and brought them before the courts. Many are still rotting in gaol. This was exemplary police work and deserved the commendation it received.

In 2011, six years after this operation, *The Sydney Morning Herald* Newspaper managed to finally obtain a copy of the NSW Police internal report into what had happened at Green Valley in South West Sydney during Operation Pendennis:

> "In NSW, seven men were arrested across Sydney under instructions of the Counter-Terrorism Co-ordination boss, ...who was at the time at the Police Operations Centre at Surry Hills. But an eighth suspect, Omar Baladjam, was still at large.[66]

> ... they (ASIO) tailed him (Omar Baladjam) to a mosque in Wilson Road, Green Valley, and then watched as he loitered nearby. These covert operations were relayed to [the CT Operational Commander – name redacted]. From this moment forward, his decisions would prove critical. With Baladjam positioned only several hundred metres from Green Valley Police Station, he dialled through to local command and spoke to Chief Inspector Robert O'Connor. He advised there was a person of interest nearby, adding he wanted a car crew to respond. Armed with no information other than a brief description of a man wearing sunglasses and carrying a backpack, an unassuming crew of two male sergeants and two female senior constables climbed into a marked police sedan tagged Green Valley 14.

> The team comprised Sergeant Wolsey, a supervisor at the station, an education and development officer, a local traffic cop and a crime prevention officer who usually spoke at community meetings".

Despite the extraordinary cross jurisdictional planning for Operation Pendennis, carried out by highly trained and well briefed police, it would seem that no risk assessment was carried out on the possibility of needing to draw on uniformed General Duties Police:

> "As Green Valley 14 pulled out of the station, the vehicle's mobile phone sounded. It was [the CT Operational Commander] who informed them the person of interest was now walking south along Wilson

---

[66] E. Duff, 'The police sent in blind to catch a terrorist', *The Sydney Morning Herald*, December 11, 2011.

> Road. With seconds to spare before they reached their target, [the CT Operational Commander] added there was no 'information' to suggest the man was armed... the advice was incorrect. In a Person of Interest 'Risk Assessment' compiled just six days earlier by [the CT Operational Commander's] own counter-terrorism intelligence unit, Baladjam was rated as a 'medium' risk to approach. Under the heading 'warning', he was identified as a person with a 'history of carrying weapons' who attempted to acquire a 9mm pistol recently. It later advised: 'Fully brief police on background... entering police use caution and utilise defensive tactics'."

Given the available intelligence that Baladjam had a "history of carrying weapons", had "attempted to acquire a 9mm pistol recently" and was part of a terrorist cell intent on mass violence, it seems simply extraordinary that this individual was left at a rating of "medium risk". If this had been elevated to 'high risk', then presumably, the counter-terrorism command would have planned better 'treatment options' for implementing this 'on-the-run' policing which occurred at Green Valley. Uniformed front-line police officers may well then not have been put in harm's way.

The irony of the following text in the Strike Force Neil Report on Cronulla, when compared to this Medium risk rated individual, was not lost on us:

> "The suggested treatment options were then in line with a risk assessment of 'Medium' when it could be argued that based on this risk assessment for... violence... the risk assessment rating should have been 'High'. The treatment options for 'High' would have reflected that planning should have been relative to dealing with a significant event".[67]

Despite what occurred at Green Valley as a direct result of CT Command decisions, the CT Command was still presented by Strike Force Neil in their report as the go to command for effective risk assessment during a major public order disturbance:

> "...a formal threat and risk assessment process was designed, tested and implemented by the Counter-Terrorism Command... There is no reason why this process cannot be applied to general policing and Local Area Commanders and Regions".[68]

---

[67] Strike Force Neil, Volume One, p. 64.
[68] Strike Force Neil, Volume One, p.85.

> "The Joint Intelligence Group (JIG) is a formal group devised by police nationally under the National Counter-Terrorism Arrangements. The head of the Intelligence Unit, Counter Terrorist Co-ordination Command (CTCC) is the JIG Co-ordinator for NSW".[69]

> "It is recommended that a review be conducted of the Joint Intelligence Group arrangements to broaden it from counter-terrorism to public order management and any other major police operations".[70]

The account of Operation Pendennis by the Sydney Morning Herald continues:

> "About 8.55am, Green Valley 14 pulled up behind Baladjam as he walked along Wilson Road. Oblivious to the danger, none of the officers wore body armour, although there was a bullet-proof vest in their car.
>
> One of the officers failed to get out of the car because a child safety lock trapped her in the back seat. The other three got out and one called, 'Police...mate, hang on a minute. Can we have a word'? In a flash, Baladjam's right shoulder dropped, he spun round and pulled out a Browning high-power, self-loading pistol from his pants, then fired three shots.
>
> 'He hit me'! Sergeant Wolsey cried. He was shot in the hand.
>
> His male colleague returned fire with two shots, one of which struck Baladjam in the neck, sending him straight to the ground. Unaware of the suspect's links to explosives, one of the officers then naively grabbed Baladjam's backpack and moved it away from him."

It was a sheer fluke that Sergeant Wolsey was not killed that day. On these two major police events, just 33 days apart, perhaps the counter-terrorism command could have learned much from Operation Seta (Cronulla) as to how to properly manage risk, use intelligence and keep uniform police in the field out of harm's way.

The Pendennis Report

The internally conducted NSW Police report into this aspect of Operation Pendennis would normally have gathered dust and in time forgotten, except

---

[69] Strike Force Neil, Volume One, p. 80.
[70] Strike Force Neil, Volume One, p. 84.

that the four officers affected by the behaviour of the CT Commanders that day, refused to go quietly. However, unsurprisingly for NSW Police, it did take years before any of this saw the light of day.

Some 6 years, 4 Premiers, 2 Police Commissioners and 5 Police Ministers later, a copy of the Green Valley report was obtained by the *Sun Herald* newspaper in December 2011:[71]

> "In a section headed 'The role of [the CT Operational Commander]', the counter-terrorism boss stated during interviews that the situation developed over a 'very short period of time'. He said the option of using the nearby ASIO surveillance team to arrest Baladjam was dismissed because they were unarmed. He added that in his mind, there was an 'urgent need' to apprehend Baladjam as he was the only target not to have been arrested that morning, and the location of the stockpiled chemicals and weapons was unknown.
>
> He said that, in the end, he decided to use police from the Green Valley command because they were 'only 500 metres away'.
>
> The report stated: 'The fact that Baladjam was carrying a backpack which might contain weapons – or even an explosive device – was never considered by [the CT Operational Commander] as an issue he should pass on to police he was sending out'.

The *Sun-Herald* journalist then quoted from a complaint lodged by one of the female police officers with damning effect:

> "Four officers could have been killed due to the complacent attitude of the Counter-Terrorism Co-ordination Command and its commander. This command placed our lives in this situation and the subject officer is still working normally with no care in the world, no loss of income or any sort of acceptable punishment".

Ironically, to our knowledge, these four officers, like Goodwin and the Cronulla Local Commander Redfern, never received formal apologies for how they were treated.

Had Sergeant Adam Wolseley been killed on 8 November 2005 during Operation Pendennis, as he quite easily could have been, then almost

---

[71] E. Duff, 'Police sent in blind to catch a terrorist', *The Sydney Morning Herald*, December 11, 2011.

certainly this 'event' would have led to public scrutiny, senior police excoriation, and an extensive Coronial Inquiry. However, the far more laudable performance at Cronulla just three weeks later, was the one which was excoriated.

The all but buried report into Green Valley found that the CTC Operations Commander reporting directly to Hazzard had *"failed in the duty of care"* by not *"adequately warning"* the affected police officers, thereby putting their lives at risk.

Commissioner's commendations for Pendennis but not Cronulla!

Police Commissioner Ken Moroney gave out many Commissioner's Commendations for Operation Pendennis. These were warranted, despite the incredible and little known 'dip' in performance during the Green Valley 'event', for outstanding and tenacious work done over an extended period of time by a number of police officers in the CT Command. Many very dangerous individuals were taken off the streets and the work put in to ensure this happened deserved recognition.

However, not a single Commissioner's Commendation was given out for the Cronulla Riots, nor any for the huge Operation SETA that Summer, which with over 2,000 police officers restored peace and order to Sydney following unprecedented public disorder and violence. It took courage, organisation and effective leadership to ensure this, in the face of quite frightening possibilities based on what occurred, and what the intelligence indicated could have been a lot worse.

PART 4:
REFLECTIONS FROM THE FIELD

13

Interviews: MPs, Police and Community Leaders

Background and the questions

As mentioned earlier, prior to completing this book we decided to test the credibility of our claims and opinions against twelve key players who had important roles during the 'Cronulla Riots'. Far from challenging and confronting our views as expected, we found they confirmed them. This was a very surprising aspect of our research.

We determined that local members of parliament (MPs), senior police and Middle Eastern community leaders would provide a good cross section of the views of important key stakeholders at the time. They provided a range of perspectives and deepened our own thinking and understanding.

We selected some and others were recommended to us, as part of our sample. Each interview was conducted in a semi-structured way with a series of questions to guide discussion, but also in part, as circumstances warranted it, a more freely flowing discussion.

Whilst only twelve is a small sample and does not allow us to make any statistical generalisations, the process was both rewarding and enlightening.

In total, 12 interviews were conducted, 11 in person and one online as follows:

Name	Role in 2005/2006	Role in 2024
MPs		
Malcolm Kerr	MP for Cronulla	Retired living locally
Barry Collier	MP for Miranda	Retired living locally

Name	Role in 2005/2006	Role in 2024
Michael Daley	MP for Maroubra	MP for Maroubra
Jihad Dib	Dep. Principal Punchbowl Boys HS	MP for Lakemba
Police		
Craig Campbell	Sergeant Cronulla Transit Police	Retired
John Richardson	Commander Campsie Police LAC	Retired
Ron Mason	Supt Sydney	Retired
Lee Howell	Police Operation Support/ Diversity Manager Surf Lifesaving NSW	Trainer
Community leaders		
Dr Jamal Rifi	Director Belmore Medical Centre	Director Belmore Medical Centre
Stephen Stanton	Barrister	Barrister
Fatima Karouche	Project Coordinator Dept Sport	Consultant Settlement Services
Mecca Laallaa	Uni Student/ 'Share the Wave' participant	Community liaison Dept of Education

We were trying to find out from the interviewees, the answer to the question: **What caused the Cronulla riots?** Additionally, we wanted to hear their perspectives, on some of the wider issues surrounding that significant event.

Members of Parliament

The four retired or current MPs we interviewed, were all at the time of the riots, working and involved in communities around which these troubling events occurred.

Police

Highlighting the performance of police in the summer of 2005/2006 in restoring order to the streets of Sydney, and allowing people to feel safe again, has been a core part of this book. We have reflected at length about this performance as it went under the 'torchlight' of the Strike Force Neil inquiry.[72]

Whilst our view of that performance is at considerable variance from what the Strike Force Neil Report found, we firmly believed that the issue of police performance and the credibility of the findings, as well as our own views, ought to be also tested during the interview process.

---
[72] Strike Force Neil Report.

Possibly one of the most memorable policing contributions during the Cronulla Riots, was the Cronulla Railway station baton wielding Sergeant, Craig Campbell. To hear his first-hand account on that day, of what he needed to do to protect the lives of two individuals from a marauding mob, was both fascinating and inspiring. This alone, made the interview process a rewarding one.

We also interviewed Supt. John Richardson, who as Campsie Local Area Commander at the time, was critical for the essential community liaison and effective policing around that part of Sydney, including the response to the threat to the Lakemba Mosque.

We also decided to interview former Supt. Ron Mason, as he was inexplicably omitted from the Strike Force Neil Inquiry interview list (if there was a list) despite being one of NSW Police most experienced public order police officers.

Finally, Lee Howell, who by December 2005 had had years of policing experience in emergency management and dignitary protection and was then working closely with the Miranda Local Area Command. In that role he provided support in assessing crime trends and determining the best police response in dealing with them.

Mr Howell has lived in the Cronulla area all his life, has been a member of North Cronulla Surf lifesaving club for over fifty years, and by the time of our interview provided both an eyewitness account to some of the early events of the 11th of December 2005, but more importantly, his perspective on the significance of the 'Share the Wave' programme with which he became heavily involved in his post policing career. This programme brought Muslim surf lifesavers, men and women, to the beach at Cronulla in a critical cultural reaching 'across the aisle' in Cronulla itself.

Community leaders

Dr Jamal Rifi, Director of the Belmore Medical Centre, and justifiably recognised as a significant Muslim community leader of Southwest Sydney, provided invaluable insights and perspectives on what happened and why, around the Cronulla Riots and why the 'troubles' have not returned.

Likewise, Christian Lebanese barrister, Stephen Stanton, gave us an account of his perspectives on why Middle Eastern men were motivated to react as they did, and his thoughts on the policing response.

On the suggestion of Dr Rifi, we interviewed two Muslim women, Fatima Kourouche and Mecca Laalaa, both of whom played critical roles, with Surf Lifesaving NSW, in the training and introduction of Muslim lifeguards on the beach. Given the 'attack' on the lifeguards was for many, the 'lighting of the fuse', this programme was worthy of our attention.

Methodology and broader findings

Interviews were conducted in person with one exception online, and on average lasted approximately one hour. With the consent of each participant, the interviews were audio recorded and transcribed via a professional transcription service. Where required, we checked the audio file against the transcript, and each participant was sent a copy of their own interview transcript to review.

An exhaustive process was then undertaken to analyse the extensive information contained within each interview transcript for repeated patterns of ideas, which then informed the assigning of codes to these ideas. Similar codes were then drawn together into separate collective themes. All of this initial analysis was then migrated to a detailed landscape scaffold setting out both the clustered codes and themes, from which further detailed analysis was undertaken to inform the final narrative. Where we directly quote the words of a participant, the words are italicised. Where appropriate within a quote, we have added our own non-italicised words.

It is hoped we have done justice and given a real voice to these views and perspectives.

In the interviews, we explored with many participants the extent to which the Cronulla Riots were a racist event, and if not, then what?

A wide-ranging discussion also occurred in varying degrees, depending on the participant, on the role of police, community leaders, the media, how to properly define the 'event', cultural 'reaching across the aisle', scapegoats and finally, what it all meant for the status and validity of the Strike Force Neil report itself.

These themes which emerged from the interviews are summarised as follows:

Number	Theme
1	It wasn't racism
2	If not racist, then what?
3	East meets West
4	The media amplified it
5	That's not a riot
6	Containing the rage of revenge
7	Law enforcement
8	Scapegoats of the riots

All of the themes, except for part of theme 8, emerged from an analysis of patterns of repetition of participant views drawn from the interview transcripts. Our naming of the themes, as listed above, reflect what became apparent from that detailed examination of those collective views, rather than any pre-conceived notion of what we thought they might represent.

In theme 8 we explore the personal and career consequences of the Cronulla Riots for Sergeant Craig Campbell and Superintendent John Richardson.

We also explore in theme 8 how the lack of a NSW policing expert driven no-blame approached enquiry, led to a loss of any real and long-lasting learnings for police planning and operations for future riots. Our interview with Supt. Ron Mason has given voice for the first time, to the views and perspectives on the Cronulla Riots from the vantage point of a riot policing expert.

As the first two themes formed a significant part of what transpired in the interviews, and a very important part of understanding of what underpinned the breaking out of conflict all those years ago, we have separated these two themes into a chapter on their own. We have also included in this chapter the 'reaching across the aisle' Muslim Lifeguard programme launched just a few weeks after the riot and revenge of the 2005/2006 Sydney summer.

Apart from 'Scapegoats of the riots', which we believed warranted a chapter on its own, we have included the balance of the themes, 4 through to 7, in their own chapter.

14

What Caused the Conflict?

A critical part of a fuller understanding of what led to, contributed, or underpinned the Cronulla Riots, requires a deep dive on whether or not it was actually a 'race riot' as labelled by many, or maybe something else.

We have bundled the three themes on this area of discussion and analysis in sequential order in this chapter as follows:

Number	Theme
1	It wasn't racism
2	If not racist, then what?
3	East meets West

These three themes which have been drawn from participant interviews, centre upon racism, cause, containment and rapprochement, and in our view, are appropriately clustered in this chapter.

Theme 1: It wasn't racism

Everybody was a local

One fascinating and very unexpected finding from the interviews, was the extent to which the interviewees could be regarded as Cronulla locals, and saw themselves, at least in part as locals. Muslim long-term residents of Southwest Sydney Dr Jamal Rifi, Fatima Kourouche and Meccaa Laalaa, all talked at length about how for years they visited Cronulla Beach, almost every weekend, as children and then as parents.

> **Laalaa:** "I grew up on the beach. Every weekend, my family and I would spend time at the beach...since I was a kid...that's how I learned to swim...That was my childhood...I'm like any other girl. I was born in Sydney, Australia, I grew up on the beach".

> **Kourouche:** *"Cronulla Beach is where we grew up as children. Every Sunday we'd go there for picnics".*
>
> **Rifi:** *"You're talking to someone who used to go to Cronulla every week... it was our favourite destination".*
>
> **Dib:** *"The idea of reclaim Cronulla Beach... is crazy... it's the beach [where many in the Lebanese community] ...grew up at".*

Jihad Dib actually spent his early years living and being schooled in the Sutherland Shire itself, residing at Heathcote and attending Heathcote High School. Barry Collier, living in Revesby as a young man, travelled like many 'westies' then and now, on the train to surf at Cronulla Beach.

In fact, apart from Maroubra MP Michael Daley, all interviewees have long and fond memories of growing up on Cronulla Beach. This alone was an unexpected finding. However, what was more unexpected, is that during their long years of visiting Cronulla Beach on innumerable occasions, none ever experienced firsthand racism. None!

A racist Cronulla?

When asked if interviewees believed that the Cronulla riots were underpinned and driven by racism, this is what they had to say:

> **Rifi:** *"It wasn't driven by racism, without any doubt".*
>
> **Laalaa:** *"I wouldn't say racism is at the forefront of somebody's lives. There's always an underlying issue".*

Mecca Laalaa was asked what racism she or her family experienced through all the years of regularly visiting Cronulla Beach. Her answer sums up not only our surprise, but ought to question the easy and convenient stigmatising of Cronulla and the Sutherland Shire, as a deeply racist Caucasian bastion:

> **Laalaa:** *"Nothing. You hear about racism... I can only go by what I've experienced... in particular Cronulla... going there every weekend and having never experienced that. You just kind of try and work through it... I was like, how much of it is true".*

When Dr Rifi was asked if anyone had ever been rude to him during his countless visits to Cronulla Beach, his reply was suitably succinct:

> **Rifi:** *"No. Never".*

What Caused the Conflict?

Local Lee Howell had at least a dozen local friends and acquaintances who attended and 'participated' at North Cronulla Beach on 11 December, 2005, and soon afterwards expressed regret to him, with the typical response being:

> **Howell:** *"Wow, I don't know what happened to me. It just totally got out of control".*

Both local MPs at the time, Malcolm Kerr, and Barry Collier, along with then local police officer Lee Howell, rejected the notion that their community was a racist one, or that the events of the 11th of December 2005 were underpinned by racism. They were joined in these views by Muslim interviewees Dr Jamal Rifi, Fatima Kourouche, and Jihad Dib.

> **Rifi:** *"I never believed it before. I never believed it after. Because I met the people* [of Cronulla] *before, and I met the people after".*

> **Kourouche:** *"The people of Cronulla themselves are good people, that's what I know. My sister had a restaurant there, a Lebanese restaurant at the time. Whenever we went there, we never had any problems. So, if there was a really racial issue regarding Muslims ongoing then, really, we wouldn't have been going there in the first place. I think from a long time".*

> **Dib:** *"I don't believe we are a racist country".*

Malcolm Kerr provided an excellent summary of this widely shared perception, by drawing on the fact that the 'Cronulla Troubles' came and went, never to return, as proof enough that the original event and the violent responses were not driven by racism:

> **Kerr:** *"If there had been ingrained racist attitudes then* [the conflict] *wouldn't have gone away.... look at what's happening in other parts of the world when there are racial divides and there are racist attitudes. You get repeat offenders all the time. It doesn't go away. It's not eradicated. If racism was an underlying cause, then you would have had this situation repeated. Maybe not on such a scale, but it would have been repeated".*

Racially hijacked?

Lebanese Christian barrister Stephen Stanton, had an interesting perspective on the racialised image of the Cronulla riots and the revenge attacks. He argued that:

> **Stanton:** *"It may not have been racially inspired but it was racially hijacked...racially fuelled, racially inflamed, and racially driven, only in order to get focus, you had to put a badge on it".*

If Mr Stanton is right, and each tribe in this conflict was not racist per se, then they only drew on racial badges and motifs, for their chants, placards, tattoos, and thousands of text messages, as an effective means to fuel and motivate their side of the battle.

In other words, the racialised emblems and slogans were not the badges of battle but simply, the means by which the forces for that battle were corralled and encouraged. If he is right, then this goes a long way to explaining why so many 'scholars' and social commentators, have naively assumed that these racialised calls to arms, were in fact just racist behaviour, rather than something warranting a little deeper examination.

As Jihad Dib said rather more eloquently, we need to look beyond the obvious!

> **Dib:** [The two tribes in the conflict] *"...weren't at the opposite ends of the spectrum but if you consider like a horseshoe, they actually had the same issues...directly opposite each other.... sometimes we don't see what's behind the picture...that could easily be considered a racism view".*

The broader context

A number of interviewees expressed the view that the larger local, geo-political and criminal environment, directly played into the fears of some Caucasian Sutherland Shire residents about the threats of Muslims tolerating or committing major crimes here and overseas.

The early 2000s was certainly a time when Western developed countries had serious violent crimes undertaken by Muslim extremists brought to their doorsteps.

The 11 September 2001 attack in the USA killed 2,977 people and left the developed world a fearful place to be in.

At the Sydney level, in 2002, the Skaf brothers were sentenced to very long terms of imprisonment for violent and despicable gangs rapes committed upon young Caucasian women in Southwestern Sydney. This made a huge and very unfair dent in the image of Muslims across Sydney:

> **Dib**: *"The way it was reported was like it is an acceptable thing by the Lebanese community and it certainly isn't".*

In October 2002, 88 Australians died following a terrorist attack on a nightclub in Bali at a well-known tourist night club. In all, 202 died in the attack. In a second terrorist attack in Bali in 2005, 19 were killed including 4 Australians.

In July 2005, a number of co-ordinated Islamist suicide attacks occurred in London, directed at commuters during the morning peak time, killing 52 people and injuring more than 700.

So, by December 2005, when the Cronulla riots occurred, it is challenging to believe that all this which occurred on our own doorstep, to Australians overseas, or to communities with which we have a close affinity, would not have played on the minds of some as they expressed an intolerance to the Muslim 'Other'. This was certainly a view expressed by Dr Jamal Rifi, Jihad Dib and Sergeant Craig Campbell.

But in their minds and ours the conflict was underpinned by tribalism not racism.

Theme 2: If not racist, then what?

Several interviewees proffered views on what they believed caused the initial disturbance at North Cronulla Beach in late 2005, which also unexpectedly, largely aligned with our own.

We have captured these perspectives in the following sub-themes below:

Number	Description
1	Tribalism
2	Territoriality
3	Incivility and disrespect
4	The Aussie identity
5	Contempt for the law

We will now discuss each in turn.

1. Tribalism

Jihad Dib, Malcolm Kerr, and Jamal Rifi were all of the view that tribalism played an important part at Cronulla.

> **Dib:** *"I felt...that for years preceding...there'd been more of a rise of what felt was a bit of and us and them mentality, the creeping, more and more language of you're either an Australian or not, you're either one of us or you're not".*

Malcolm Kerr referred to the years of inter-tribal conflict between 'visitors' from the Western suburbs of Sydney coming to Cronulla by train, and local surfers and beach goers. This of course, started years before any Lebanese migration to Australia, and for a long time was an ongoing conflict between Caucasian 'Westies' and Caucasian 'Locals'. Once it became a Caucasian vs Arabic contest, the tribal histories of the past were forgotten, and the racialising stigma was brought forth to superficially explain it all.

> **Kerr:** *"You'd have the surfies and the westies going back to the sixties and seventies, the bodgies and so forth. So, you had that insider and outsider culture there. Now, at the time, that culture was Caucasian, whether you're in one tribe or another...They came from Bankstown. The bankies...were white".*

> **Howell:** *"There's always been a degree of tension down there...degrees of tribalism about people and there were blues on the beach".*

2. Territoriality

A clash for spatial domain at Cronulla was certainly a long-term expression of inter-tribal conflict between locals and visitors, as seen by some participants.

> **Kerr:** *"local residents* [felt] *they sort of had a proprietary right to the beaches".*

> **Campbell:** [The] *"...surfing community, they're very territorial".*

Jamal Rifi thought it was adolescent territoriality at North Cronulla rather than anything more serious, whereas nearby things were quite peaceable:

> **Rifi:** *"We used to go to Gunnamatta Park...you would have 500 Muslim families, 500 Lebanese families. We occupied the whole park. So, the locals, they only just came to buy ice cream and left. Now we*

had that park to ourselves one day every week".

However, a truly extraordinary and until now virtually unknown territorial claim, was put forward by one lone Muslim leader to his Middle Eastern peers, just as they were about to go into a meeting designed to contain inter-tribal tensions. This meeting was just a few days after the initial riot and revenge attacks.

Lebanese Christian Barrister Stephen Stanton has brought this fascinating vignette into the light of day. Mr Stanton had been asked by his Arabic colleagues to be their lead spokesperson for the meeting, when one amongst them dropped this territorial clanger:

> **Unknown bidder:** *"Steve, if you could just ask them to give us 400 metres of Cronulla Beach for the Islamic community, that'll be a big thing".*
>
> **Stanton:** *"I said: 'I think we should ask the Aboriginals if they'd like to reconsider the beach as well, because it was theirs in the first place. Just 400 metres... that's the whole effing beach'".*

Unsurprisingly, Jamal Rifi exclaimed:

> **Rifi:** *"Whatever you do, don't mention it, for God's sake".*

3. Incivility and disrespect

During the participant interviews, incivility and disrespect played a significant part in fomenting discontent at Cronulla which eventually percolated to breaking point. These centred on two important but separate aspects as to how to behave in public. First, misogynistic language directed at young bikini clad Caucasian women from young Lebanese men congregating in groups, in the local car park near the women's change rooms. Second, the acculturated differences as to how to use the beach. What we have termed the towel versus the soccer ball.

We will deal with each in turn.

Misogyny

> **Howell:** *"They would sit in their cars. They'd have their very loud exhaust, duff cars... any girl who happened to walk past... would cop a bevy of all kinds of comments about inappropriateness... to do with having extremely large breasts or different things... or what* [they'd] *like to do to* [them].

> *I definitely remember talking to a couple of dads...even after the event, who felt incensed that the ridicule, or the abuse, or the sexual suggestion, that had been made to their daughters, or wives, or girlfriends".*

> **Campbell:** *"...there was a small percentage of Middle Eastern young men that were coming over...harassing...the girls...wearing their bikinis and things like that. They just had no respect for the girls. And that sort of thing just kept simmering and simmering and simmering* [and] *ended up becoming...the Cronulla Riots".*

Barrister Stephen Stanton provided an explanation:

> **Stanton:** *"What caused it, in my view, was the fact there was, regrettably, an arrogance in the members of the Lebanese community in terms of how they perceived they could behave.*

> *...the perception as to how women were to be treated was culturally out of kilter with what was the accepted norm within the Australian community".*

Mr Stanton argued that to not like the dress standards, or the immodest attire of women was one thing, but using a forum such as a popular beach location to express it directly, certainly generated strong negative reactions.

The towel versus the soccer ball

> **Supt. Richardson:** *"...guys from Middle Eastern backgrounds were going to Cronulla beach and chatting up girls and kicking footballs around and people getting annoyed...young guys going to the beach... causing trouble".*

> **Howell:** [There were] *"...some arguments where groups would turn up to play soccer or football right in the middle of where people were sun baking...that...definitely had been going on for years".*

Malcolm Kerr as both the local MP and a local resident, was also of the view that this clash of how to use the beach had caused a simmering tension:

> **Kerr:** *"It was a build-up...there was...anti-social behaviour on the beach. For instance, a family might be playing a ball game and...a group might throw sand at them. Or there would be some antisocial incident which you could hardly report to police. But there were a number of these things".*

It is one thing for two tribes having different acculturated views on how the beach ought to be used and quite another to disrespect the use by one over the other. The constant 'misunderstanding' that one could ride roughshod over the other, certainly led to simmering resentment.

Incivility drives simmering tensions

A number of interviewees referred to the simmering tension which had been in place for years at Cronulla between locals and visitors.

The tension was almost entirely around local angst directed at Middle Eastern visitors who they regarded as disrespecting the space of others on the sand, disparaging and offending women, disregarding others, and a conflict, we have summarised, as the towel versus the soccer ball, combined with deeply sexist commentary.

It should of course, not be assumed that the incivility was a one-way trip. Quite the contrary. Some of the things said to Lebanese visitors by local surfers and lifeguards from time to time, could hardly be classified as respectful or civil.

It may sound harmless relative to more violent tribal interactions both here and overseas, but civility and respect matter. It was the lack of these critical ingredients for polite and enjoyable sharing of the beach, combined with a tribal territorialness, which long fuelled simmering tension and discontent which eventually boiled over in late 2005. Racist slogans and the claim for what constituted the Australian identity, followed, but these were not the driving forces underpinning that tension or the conflict.

Interestingly, Lee Howell whilst volunteering as a lifeguard at Cronulla Beach, observed several of these 'interactions' between rival interpretations of how the beach could or should be used. In most cases, when folks were asked to move away from families and young children they did so. However, sometimes the police had to be called with the tension a constant recurring theme: *"It was always simmering in some regard"*.

Stephen Stanton also agreed that it was just a few who caused most of the problems: *"But it's that minority, that menacing minority that want to make it so hard"*.

Stephen Stanton blamed the incommensurateness of the action and reaction of riot and revenge squarely on our multicultural model failing to adequately vent the simmering discontent of the two tribes at the beach:

> **Stanton:** "...*the disproportionateness...on both sides, came about, because there was a pent-up frustration that had never been effectively accommodated. We've talked about multiculturism, but nobody had effectively brokered real multiculturalism*".

4. The Aussie Identity

The conflict and tension surrounding what it meant to be an Australian, was certainly a new addition to the decades long battles for the sand at Cronulla between 'Westies' and locals. The bodily wrapping of the Australian flag, tattoos suggesting that only Caucasians were truly local born Australians, and the xenophobic chants from more than a few, certainly added to the 'us' and 'them' tension of the inter-tribal battle which unfolded in late 2005.

Whose flag is it anyway?

The local MP for Miranda at the time, Barry Collier, was none too impressed and nor was the now MP for Lakemba, Jihad Dib that our national flag was sequestered by some rowdy Cronulla locals as a vehicle to express not national unity, but tribal separateness.

> **Collier:** "*I was appalled at the drunks who wrapped themselves in the Australian flag and pretended to be down there...protecting our way of life in the Shire, or our way of life as Australians*".

Jihad Dib was unimpressed with the many in the Cronulla crowd, effectively saying, "*this is my flag and you're not part of this flag*". Likewise, with the purloining of the stars of the Southern Cross to somehow indicate anyone not born under them can't be a real Aussie. The "postcode tats" of the Cronulla postcode of 2230 just added to this corralling of who was and was not an Australian.

> **Dib:** "*I'd always had this fear of this rising...we're the Aussies and you're not, and it didn't help that some kids from the Arabic community were saying 'we're not Aussies, we're Lebanese or whatever', well mate, you're Australian.*
>
> *So, there was...this issue of identity* [which flowed from the attack on the Lifeguards] *...it was like, oh...what do you mean lifeguard, you were attacking Australian icons and Australian symbols and you're... un-Australian*".

What Caused the Conflict?

Jihad Dib also raised an interesting point about Arabic Australians, without an Anzac story or connection, being no less Aussie than the Caucasian Australians who do have that connection:

> **Dib**: *"I can't tell an Anzac story because I have no lineage to Anzac but don't say I'm un-Australian because I don't have an Anzac story...we need to make sure we define what being an Australian is, not just by the bronzed Aussie image...but the image that we're all part of the Australian story. And we've made big progress since that time, but at that time, no.*
>
> *...about our understanding of one another...maybe that was the wakeup call that we needed".*

A fascinating story of despair and then hope was the burning, by a young Lebanese man, of the Australian flag he had pulled down from the flagpole of the Ramsgate RSL (Returned Serviceman's League) Club.

> **Dib**: *"Everyone was going... 'we've got to lynch this kid'. Well, that kid did that because he goes' 'this is not my flag' and no one in Australia should ever feel that that's not their flag. And then what the RSL Club did was terrific...they sent this kid to* [the] *Kokoda* [track in New Guinea] *and the kid came back with a new history".*

Mr Dib emphasised the point, that if a story is important to belonging, such as the Anzac story, and you're not part of that story, then how can you feel you belong.

The BBQ Aussie

Lee Howell had quite a different perspective on the almost gauche expression of Aussieness at Cronulla Beach. He felt it was far more about expressions of patriotism like an Australia Day event until alcohol, the sun and egging on from White Supremacist agent provocateurs sent the day awry.

Jihad Dib was a little more dismissive:

> **Dib**: *"...people had come all over to Cronulla,* [with the mantra] *'come down, we're going to have a barbie, let's try and be the most Australian we can' because they think Muslims don't have barbecues".*

The SUV and national pride

> **Howell**: *"...there were definitely some of the Utes. They reminded me very much, because they were so high, like straight out of the*

American SUV, American type vehicles. Vehicles that were very uncharacteristic...for the Cronulla area...probably 4 or 5 I saw...They were right wing extremists...barbies on the back. Flags all over the place. And... chants".

5. Contempt for the law

We have discussed earlier what might have happened in late December 2005, had the NSW Police Task Force Gain not already locked up 15-20 hard core very violent Lebanese criminals, and they had been available, and on the street, contributing to the 'leadership' of the revenge attacks.

However, it still took a lot of effort on the part of Arabic community leaders and police to ensure, that the would be 'replacement' leaders, did not step up from within their own community to fill this violent void.

Barrister Stephen Stanton has given a scathing perspective at the contempt which young Lebanese Muslim men had for police and law and order, which he believed fuelled a greater reaction in revenge than would have otherwise been the case:

> **Stanton**: *"Certain sections of the Lebanese community...effectively flout, and more importantly, disrespect law and order. Not only with police, but within all society sectors. And there was a terrible intolerance of the police force...Greenacre Bankstown...the crucible of discontent in that area was inflamed by the riots".*

Ethnic exceptionalism

Mr Stanton also put the case for an arrogant self-appointed ethnic exceptionalism, as the reason for young Lebanese Muslim male propensity for violent overreaction.

> **Stanton:** [In relation to Lebanese law breakers] *"It's not just a question, of race or culture or otherwise, it's regrettably a failure on the part of the family units concerned, and ultimately the monitoring of those people who were encouraged to be ethnically exclusive. And encouraging their ethnic exclusivity, they fuelled their right, unbridled, in terms of arrogance, to act whichever way they liked".*

The academic scholars and social commentators, who have in large number since late 2005, stigmatised Cronulla as simply a bastion of Caucasian privileged racism, would be a little perturbed by Mr Stanton's confronting analysis. However, in the face of any better one, it goes a long way to explaining why the revenge attacks were so swift, so violent, so geographically comprehensive, so disproportionate, and so terrorising of Sydney.

That there would be some kind of tribal response to the provocations unleashed at Cronulla could be regarded as unsurprising, but the violent disproportionateness of that response does require some explanation. Mr Stanton, we believe, has provided such an explanation.

Who turned up?

Before concluding our discussion on this theme, it is important to consider just who were in the crowd mix at Cronulla Beach on Sunday 11th of December 2005. The excesses of the day were primarily blamed upon an allegedly racist Sutherland Shire.

However, there were many White Supremacist visitors who took the opportunity to foment xenophobic discontent. Just as Stephen Stanton has suggested that young Muslim men, angry with police and the world, took the Cronulla provocation as an excuse to act as they violently did, it was argued by some of the interviewees, that White Supremacists also took the opportunity to stir up a reaction out of keeping with what might have been the case, had locals been left to their own version of protest, chants, and tattoos.

> **Howell:** *"There appeared to be people [who had] arrived with megaphones that were in the crowd and started to yell and scream. And sort of whipping some intensity about Australianism. They were very pro: I'd say that's when I realised...this has gone a little on the cusp of being right wing extremism...Almost the White Australia policy type of thing".*

In other words, the initial 'riot' and then 'revenge' were fuelled by factors far broader than what superficially looked like a reaction to a provocative event. Life and events, as always, are usually more complicated than they at first appear, even if academics and social commentators say otherwise.

According to Messrs Howell, Kerr, Dib and Collier, the people who fronted Cronulla Beach on that day were a mix of White Supremacists, disgruntled locals, visitors attracted to the clarion call sent out in text messages, and finally, local 'rubberneckers' who turned up to look.

> **Collier:** *"A significant number of people were down there doing the*

> damage didn't come from the Shire and had no association with it...I think that's pretty significant".
>
> **Dib**: "It was when the others who were not from the area who don't regularly go to Cronulla Beach who just wanted to use the opportunity... for...wog bashing...They were the ones that in my opinion caused [what] went from being a get together barbecue into where it got more violent and inciting. Their intention was to get into a fight. No other intention.
>
> ...they called themselves locals, but they weren't locals. Many of them were coming from all over Sydney".

Jihad Dib believed that most who turned up were overwhelmingly 'rubberneckers' looking at everyone looking. In respect of the non-local visiting troublemakers on the day, in fifty years of living at Cronulla and as a local Police Officer, Lee Howell had never seen these people before.

Lee Howell's perspectives on the visiting troublemakers and local rubberneckers makes for an interesting contrast. One local just a few days after the initial 'event' had this to say to him:

> "I have no idea what happened to my mind. I just got whipped up in the whole thing and I would never have acted like that, behaved like that, listened, or carried on like that. But I just got taken along with the mood of that day. And the intensity of the spruikers".

If Howell and Stanton are right, on the reasons for the level of disproportionateness of both sides to the conflict, being either initially spruiked up on the day at Cronulla, or those already in an angry state using the provocation of Cronulla, as an excuse and not a cause, for revenge, then we may well have a good explanation for why this allegedly racist event occurred and never returned.

If it were otherwise, then surely we would have had many repeat 'performances'. It came and went, never to return.

Theme 3: East meets west

An important message which pervaded a number of interviews was the positive engagement between the Muslim and Caucasian communities rapidly after the breaches of the peace in late 2005.

There was a strong commitment from government and the police to quickly quell the discontent and lawlessness, but also a strong commitment from the Lebanese Muslim community to reach out to the Caucasian community in Cronulla to achieve an enduring peace.

There were a number of different aspects which emerged from the interviews, as to how and where the 'elders' of the Caucasian and Middle Eastern tribes reached 'across the aisle'. They are discussed as follows:

Police liaison

Given the great work done by Campsie police commander, John Richardson and Muslim community leaders like Jamal Rifi and others, the police and Southwest Sydney's Muslim community were already well known to each other in a positive and productive way, well before the 'riots'.

In some ways, this is effective community policing and expected, but it did make a big difference in drawing on the best aspects of police and community leadership to bring passions under control, and the lawlessness to an end.

Whilst an assumed and important role of a local police commander, this valuable and valued community outreaching, was the first 'East meets West' in the wider Lakemba area.

The Comancheros and the Bra Boys

Just a few days after the events at Cronulla an extraordinary meeting took place on Maroubra Beach between leaders of the Comancheros Bikie Gang, and the Bra Boys Surf Gang. Anyone passing by may have mistaken the "meeting" as a film setting for a comedy episode of the ABC Chasers programme, rather than anything remotely approaching an 'East meets West' rapprochement. We have a little more to say on this in Theme 6 "Containing the rage of revenge'.

Interfaith on the beach

Barry Collier spoke of religious interfaith meetings on Cronulla Beach, just a few days after the 'events' of late 2005. He believed the 'prayer for peace' meeting *"where participants used stones to write 'peace' on the sand"* had a positive impact on community healing.

Barry Collier also referred to the exchange programme between school pupils at Grays Point Public School and Auburn Public School which involved visits and writing letters, as well as a 'Harmony on the Beach Day' in April 2006.

These all contributed in their own way to reconciliation.

The Lifeguard programme

A number of interviewees acknowledged the wonderful inter-community positive impact that the training of Muslim surf life savers had on societal healing. The idea was generated by Jamal Rifi and NSW Surf Life Saving, and involved the training of young Lebanese men and woman as lifeguards on Cronulla beach. *(See photo on the back cover of this book).*

Coming so soon after the 'Cronulla troubles' it had a lasting impact. The programme was called, *'On the Same Wave* A Living in Harmony Initiative', which Jamal Rifi believes had enormous symbolic impact and greatly contributed to a lasting peace between the two tribal communities:

> **Rifi:** [The programme] *"...sent a few messages. First of all, the communities are not at war: the communities are on a friendship path. Symbolic definitely. Second, it sent a message to everyone who are non-Anglo Saxon-blonde with blue eyes-that those Cronulla clubs are not a bastion of the blonde, blue eyed Australian. Third, they also sent a message we are open door clubs. We are not going to exclude anyone.*
>
> *Finally, it sent a message to our community: these are not our enemy. These are fellow citizens. Whatever prejudices you have against them, go, meet them. Same thing for their community. It said, 'we are fellow citizens; we share this country; what you heard of us is totally different than when you meet us'".*

Jamal Rifi also fondly recalls the Kokoda trip attended and promoted by him, and co-sponsored and attended in 2007, by then new back bench MPs Jason Clare and Scott Morrison. However, the Lifeguard Programme had the greatest impact.

In the end, seventeen young Lebanese men and women completed the gruelling training programme and became certified lifeguards. However, Lee Howell remembers well some of the funnier aspects to this journey:

> **Howell:** *"To say they could swim was a great exaggeration.* [Some had water polo experience which didn't exactly translate to ocean

swimming]. *So, we took a lot of time. We had to engage with some swim coaches... introduce rescue. How to paddle a board... they had no concept of how to paddle a board... they were going in every direction... it was hysterical... they were actually getting rescued by the patrolling lifesavers.*

[Instead of the usual 10 weeks] *it took... about... 14 to 16 weeks.* [But] *the passion never drained... They were committed. They were focussed".*

Stephen Stanton best summed the sociological impact of the programme as follows:

Stanton: *"The lifesaving movement... accepted Lebs into their ranks, and willingly and very enthusiastically embraced them as members. The Lebs in turn realised what a great movement the lifesaving movement was, and what it meant to act on the beach in the right way".*

Malcolm Kerr was also very positive about its impact.

Kerr: *"The way in which the* [local] *surf lifesaving clubs welcomed new recruits and provided training and assistance to them... was seen as integrating that ethnic community into the surfing culture".*

There were three Muslim women on the programme, but many will remember that one of them introduced the new Burkini swimming costume to the world, which has enabled scores of Muslim women, the world over, to enjoy the wonders of swimming comfortably and modestly by the sea.

However, the expectations and symbolic load upon the young shoulders of then 19-year-old Mecaa Laalaa were enormous:

Laalaa: *"I was doing interviews with the New York Times, and I was just going international as well as local, and I had no idea and couldn't grasp the idea that it was that big".*

Kourouche: *"Just to see the Burkini, the red and yellow Burkini* [the surf Lifesaving colours]. *This Muslim wearing an Australian icon. That's great for us, for Muslim women and women. And it was on a billboard".*

Compared to the memes, tattoos, and text messaging war cries of the tribes following the 'attack' on the red and yellow outfitted lifeguard on the 4th of December 2005, and the alleged sexualising of women at the beach by Muslim men leading up to it, the extraordinary appearance of a young Muslim Lebanese woman in lifeguard colours wearing a Muslim costume, cannot be underestimated for its impact on healing and renewal.

Role models

Stephen Stanton referred to the very well-known and much-loved Lebanese Australians, Nick Shehadie and former NSW Governor, Marie Bashir, as "*templates of tolerance...*[and] *role models, on the headland of what you could do and be in this country if you preferred to co-operate and live with each other with respect, and more importantly civility*".

However, it was Jihad Dib who pointed out that in 2005, unlike now, there were very few Arabic leaders in the professions immersed across mainstream Australian Society, who could shine a light on the way to succeed, to behave and to peaceably live amongst fellow citizens.

The change from then to now, in the educational and professional landscape of Arabic Australians, is both profound and positive. One would presumably be able to draw a conclusion, that with so many fine examples of educated, successful and articulate Arabic Australian contributors, that there ought to be less need to feel abandoned or disenfranchised by the 'system', than may have been otherwise the case several years ago.

The 'Social Contract'

Stephen Stanton believed that Jean-Jacques Rousseau got it right in his 1762 book 'On the Social Contract', where Rousseau argued that for civil life to work effectively, and for each of us to achieve our self-centred goals, we need to look out for one another co-operatively and meaningfully.

To put the case convincingly to warring tribes that they are both fundamentally better off by working together rather than warring and fighting, has been the challenge of mankind through the centuries. The Cronulla Riots and the inter-tribal conflict of Caucasian surfers and Arabic soccer players is no different.

Jihad Dib was certainly of the view that a realisation of this has been a strong positive outcome of the Cronulla Riots:

> **Dib:** "*I think we've had a positive from it, there's been changes and I think we've actually been better as a society in terms of understanding*

What Caused the Conflict?

one another...I think people will always have their heritages and things like that and [the] *Cronulla riot itself is a terrible blight on our country.*

...but it's really, really positive...I see positive things I never used to see. I see so much interfaith.

I see more young people engaging with others in good things...as more kids interact because more are going to uni or TAFE...there's more interaction going on".

The Anzac spirit

We have already discussed the confronting burning of the Australian flag, after it was stolen by a young and angry Lebanese youth from the flagpole of the Ramsgate RSL, and how that club sent him to the Kokoda track so he could better understand the Anzac spirit.

We also canvassed Jihad Dib, who could have been speaking for all Australian migrant families, when he opined that like many, he did not have an Anzac story.

However, he put a fascinating case for us all to own the Anzac sprit even if some of us, like him, cannot have or relate to an Anzac story. This quote best captures this notion:

> **Dib:** *"I can own...the Anzac spirit of mateship, the camaraderie, you see that at Kokoda, the endurance, sacrifice, isn't that good values for everyone. This is what shapes us as an Australian.*
>
> *I don't care if you pray to a God in a church, in a Mosque, in a Synagogue, in a temple, or whether you don't pray to God. What I care about is what you do to make this a better place and what you do to make everyone feel that they belong".*

What and how we relate to the Anzac story, and what and how we believe, go to important aspects of what contributed to the Cronulla Riots and why, with a better understanding of each, we all might be able to prevent this kind of conflict ever happening again.

15
Broader Perspectives

For convenience of discussion, we have split the interview perspectives between what the interviewees believed caused, or did not cause the riots, with that of their much broader and wider perspectives.

As we shall see, these further perspectives dealt with a whole gamut of things covering media impact, whether or not it was really a 'riot', how Muslim community leaders helped contain the revenge attacks, and policing and law enforcement.

The consequences flowing from the Cronulla Riots for the careers of a number of police officers and law enforcement generally have been addressed in a separate chapter, 'Scapegoats of the Riots'.

The themes to be discussed here in order are as follows:

Number	Theme
4	The media amplified it
5	That's not a riot
6	Containing the rage of revenge
7	Law enforcement

Theme 4: The media amplified it

In the final Part 5 of this book 'Explaining the Riot', one of the issues we critically examine is, 'Did the media cause the riots?', We conclude that serial text messaging, angled and 'edited' TV 'news' coverage on the evening of 11 December 2005, and the Daily Telegraph's publication of the Bra Boys dare regarding Maroubra Beach, all contributed to some degree, towards the initial riot and follow up revenge attacks.

The notion that the media played a role at Cronulla well beyond just reporting the news, was a recurring theme amongst a number of interviewees. Based upon those perspectives, we have set out three broad aspects to the media amplification of events leading up to and after Cronulla.

They are as follows:

- The broader negative presentation of Muslims being a risk.
- The 'overreaction' to the attack on the Lifeguards.
- The edited and deceptively angled TV News coverage of the initial 'riot'.

We will deal with each in turn.

The broader negative presentation of Muslims

Dr Rifi expressed strong concern that in the broader context, the few years leading up to December 2005, of global Muslim terrorist attacks, the appalling local Skaf brother's rapes and of course, serious drug and violence offences committed by Lebanese men in Southwest Sydney, that the media did not miss any opportunity to paint the local Muslim community as dangerous to society.

> **Rifi:** *"...there was a simmering event, one after the other, and the media had a field day in always projecting the light into every negative in our community. They did not publicise anything positive. So, there was a tension and the media played it. Radio talkback and shock jocks inflamed it.*
>
> *...the young people in Cronulla, they were being fed ideas, wrong ideas against us. And that didn't happen overnight. It took years".*
>
> **Dib:** *"...after 2001...it seemed everybody was blaming the Muslim community for what happened in the States...the media wasn't...highlighting the good...the only thing you ever saw was very negative, very narrow perspective and I think that sort of helped to heighten tension".*

The 'overreaction' to the Lifeguard attack

Former police officers Craig Campbell and Lee Howell have given a clear picture of this issue.

> **Campbell:** *"The media played a very big role in hyping it up...*

it was just a common assault. It should have been dealt with as a common assault under the Crimes Act and that should have been it.

But once it got out and the media got hold of it...they blow it up out of all proportion...it absolutely had a very large bearing, the media did.

...had [the media not] carried on like pork chops about...the original assault, it wouldn't have happened. It would have been sorted out and that would have been it."

Howell: *"I just thought 'you are kidding'...when someone... said along the lines of:*

> *'This is an attack against an Australian iconic institution... attacking our lifesavers...who are an institution...they've attacked the very standing of what is Australian down on the beaches'.*
>
> *And so many different comments...from [radio] shock jocks...or [news] papers...I thought, this is outlandish that it had got to that, outrageous that it got to such hype and build up over something that was just so small".*

It was after all, just a minor scuffle at a beach carpark but it provided enormous overkilling copy for newspapers and 'Shock Jock' radio hosts. Elevating what should and would have been a long forgotten and inconsequential tribal skirmish at the beach, to a question about being Australian or not, seems all these years later, to be simply absurd. But that is what happened.

Jihad Dib also believed that the social media of the day, text messaging, combined with Shock Jocks repeating their content, certainly incited reactions, and discontent, beyond what the messages may have done on their own.

> **Dib:** *"So then, when there's this issue about two stupid boys having a go at a lifeguard, it was...what do you mean a lifeguard, you were attacking Australian icons...and you're un-Australian".*

Broader Perspectives

Angled and spliced TV news coverage

Former senior police riot commander, Ron Mason, was astonished at the degree to which the TV news media exaggerated the events of 11 December 2005. Supt. Mason planned and commanded the police response to the significant public protest to the Sydney inauguration, as a Catholic Cardinal, of George Pell at St Marys Cathedral in 2003. However, this 'event' hardly received much news coverage in significant contrast to that of the Cronulla riot.

> **Mason:** *"The...one thing I learnt* [is] *if there's no media it didn't happen. The so-called Cronulla Riot...there was more action and violence at the George Pell inauguration at St Mary's* [Cathedral] *than there was at Cronulla".*

Former Supt. John Richardson was of a similar view with regards to the TV coverage of events on the beach: *"It was overkill...the media made it worse than it really was".*

> **Kerr:** *"...the media coverage, the optics were out of proportion to what had actually happened...from memory there was only a cracked window in terms of property damage as a result of it. And I'm not sure anybody was hospitalised on the day at all.*
>
> *My reaction* [to the TV media coverage] *was this wasn't representative of what happened on the day...*[but] *the 'news' was made for television in broad daylight. That had a bigger psychological impact than the revenge attacks which were, in fact, more serious in terms of the lawlessness".*

The day after the Cronulla 'riot', Jihad Dib started in his new role as deputy principal at Punchbowl Boys High School. He was astonished to witness a number of teenage boys in the playground reading the news section of the Daily Telegraph newspaper, and thinking to himself: *"How good's this?",* until realty set in:

> **Dib:** *"I didn't think kids would buy the paper, but then you could just see it, there was anger. Like, look at what happened here...look at what's being said about us... palpable anger...you could just feel more and more of the tension rising".*

Theme 5: 'That's not a riot'

This theme is of course, a take from the well-known New York City street scene in the movie Crocodile Dundee 2, when the famous Australian actor, Paul Hogan, is confronted by a would-be robber holding a puny pathetic looking penknife. Hogan snorts contemptuously at the young man: *"That's not a knife"*, while he at the same moment pulls out a huge knife of his own with a rather self-confident: *"This is a knife"*!

As Ron Mason said to us rather dismissively of the 'riot' label attributed to Cronulla:

> **Mason:** *"The so-called Cronulla riot, there's probably four or five incidents that were viewed heavily by the media and pumped up as this is exactly what happened all day, and it scared people. And it drove the Lebanese community to retaliate through emotion. **That's not a riot, I'll show you a riot**"!*

John Richardson the former Campsie Local Area Commander was equally dismissive on the point:

> **Richardson:** *"That was no riot in Cronulla. It was a disturbance that got a bit out of hand, but it was in no way, in my view, a riot".*

When asked to compare the so-called Cronulla Riots of December 2005, when no-one was killed, limited property damage occurred, just a few hospitalised and only 200 arrests, with what occurred in July 2021 in South Africa, with the loss of over 300 lives including an alleged 170 murders, 3,400 people arrested, 132 cases of alleged arson, massive looting, destruction, and wholesale property damage to shopping malls, warehouses and factories with police simply overwhelmed and 25,000 troops deployed,[73] this is what John Richardson had this to say:

> **Richardson:** *"Cronulla wasn't a riot. That's a riot".*[74]

Lee Howell as both a local resident and local police officer at the time

---

[73] *'Unrest death toll rises to 337'*, South African Government News Agency, Thursday, July 22, 2021; SAnews.gov.au; S. Mkhwanazi, *'Mapisa-Nqakula: We have deployed 25,000 troops'*, July 15, 2021. www.iol.co.za; L. Prinsloo and R. Henderson, *'As Rioters Overwhelm Police, South African Civilians Step in'*, Bloomberg. July 14, 2021.
[74] Communication between John Richardson and Carl Scully, email, July 25, 2021.

put a similar view. He believed that the case simply couldn't be made for accurately calling what happened at Cronulla as a riot:

> **Howell:** *"We actually refer to 'the Cronulla disturbances'... like a riot is a riot. And we didn't have a riot. There was a disturbance. And that's the way we looked at it".*

In Part 5 of the book we also examine the misnomer of calling the events of late 2005/early 2006, as the 'Cronulla Riots', given the geographical coverage of the mobile attacks in revenge. This, combined with the relatively limited level of personal injury or property damage, and the media exaggeration of both, has left several interviewees wondering whether or not the term 'riot' can be used at all when describing those events at Cronulla and beyond all those years ago.

> **Mason:** *"I'll give you an example* [of a real riot]. ***The Bathurst riot in 1985****. I was one of a six-person team* [and] *out of that six...five* [coppers] *had broken bones that included three legs and an arm... One* [got] *helivaced out of Bathurst to the hospital because he was hit with a house brick to the chest* [which] *knocked him out...and stopped his heart. Everybody in my team got set on fire at least once with Molotov cocktails.*
>
> [On another occasion] *I remember standing toe to toe in fights with the Builders Labourers* [in the Sydney CBD] *and it was a punch up. There was no movie there, no-one saw it, but I know it happened, and all the people I know that I was working with* [know] *it happened, and it could've been very serious if we didn't get on top".*

Malcom Kerr was similarly of the view, that compared to the mayhem at the same time in Paris, where many people were being injured and vehicles being set alight, our own riot was hardly worthy of that name: *"...there was very little property damage, very little physical harm compared to what was happening in...Paris".*

Lee Howell also made the comparison between the Parisian violence and mayhem of 2005 with that of Cronulla the same year and made the strong point that at Paris *"over 200 cars were burnt on the first night compared to maybe a single bonnet at Cronulla".*

> **Howell:** ...[aren't] *riots when they turn cars upside down? I've*

been to Bathurst riots...seen other riots...and this [at Cronulla] *wasn't a riot. It was nothing like that".*

Lee Howell also made an interesting point distinguishing Cronulla from other more violent and damaging public disturbances, in that at Cronulla, there were a number of White Supremacist 'agent provocateurs', stirring up local passions beyond what might have been otherwise the case. He believed that these very sober *"agitators"* were *"preying"* on alcohol affected young males and *"whipping them into a frenzy"*.

In summary, perhaps the stigmatising descriptor given to this suburb of Sydney, ought to be removed from our historical lexicon, and replaced with a far more accurate one: 'The Sydney Breaches of the Peace'. Alternatively, if we can so easily have the multiple suburban conflagrations of Paris in 2005, conflated by its media into 'The Paris Riots' then likewise, why not have our local media, conflate our multiple suburban troubles also of 2005, into a more accurate 'The Sydney Disturbances'.

However, the truth is unlikely to ever get in the way of such a succinct and colourfully damning descriptor as: 'The Cronulla Riots'.

Theme 6: Containing the rage of revenge

What it took to limit, contain, and then end, the sheer volcanic rage in revenge of young Muslim men, in response to what they perceived as attacks on their community, their honour and even their valour, is too little known and too little acknowledged.

The violence, the random attacks on Caucasian strangers, the damage to property, and the fear and terrorising of the suburbs of Sydney which this all instilled within just twenty-four hours of the initial Cronulla 'breach of the peace', and what it took community leaders to bring it to heel, is worthy of a theme on its own.

In Part 5 we analyse and discuss in more detail the one sided and extensive focus by academics, social commentators, and the general media on the allegedly racist 'riot' at North Cronulla on Sunday 11th of December 2005. The paucity, if not almost completely absent focus on the far more violent, property damaging and racially badged attacks in revenge, over the following several days, is simply extraordinary.

Given that the revenge attacks were conducted by a mobile marauding convoy of angry young Muslim men, unsurprisingly, it was almost entirely elder Muslim community leaders who put in an heroic effort to contain the rage, lower the temperature and working closely with other Arabic leaders and the police, helped remove this awful threat to the peace of the streets and suburbs of multicultural Sydney.

Fear

The immediate reaction of Dr Jamal Rifi when he saw the evening news on 11 December 2005 was the violent backlash that it may generate from within his own community for revenge and that the reaction *"was going to be deadly"*.

Jihad Dib was worried that the *"pent up emotion"* which had been generated within his local community would result in non-Arabic locals being bashed. He recognised the sad irony of this fear, as it is exactly what had happened the day before at Cronulla in reverse. However, young angry Muslim men did in fact carry out awful violent attacks on non-local non-Arabic looking people simply because they didn't look like them.

Stephen Stanton had a different perspective. He believed that his Muslim Lebanese community leader counterparts in Southwest Sydney were compelled to contain the scope and spread of revenge for fear of being *"societally crushed"*.

> **Stanton:** *"...the Islamic community realised that if they allowed this to occur, they were too small, too insignificant, and they'd be rubbed out".*
>
> **Rifi:** *"We didn't want the bad elements in our community to take a leadership role. We needed the calm, coolheaded community members to take the leadership role in how to respond to the riot".*

The phones ran hot on the evening of 11 December 2005 amongst Muslim community leaders, and between them and police and senior government members, about what was to be done to put a lid on an angry response.

But they were all too late. Whilst talking, convoys of indignant young Muslim vigilantes carrying their version of how to protect and exert masculine honour and respect, had already left Punchbowl for Maroubra,

Cronulla, and Brighton-le-Sands, to begin a spree of aggrieved violence and property damage which would terrorise Sydney.

> **Rifi:** *"Unfortunately, the gathering point, we didn't know about it until later on. A lot of hot-headed people went to Punchbowl Park, and they actually formed a convoy, and they went down".*

Jamal Rifi was *"ashamed"* and appalled by the unwarranted and unjustified randomness of both the revenge attacks and the initial Cronulla attacks. But from the outset, he and his colleagues were clear that they would be supporting the police and the government in bringing the lawlessness to heal.

> **Rifi:** *"The fear was manifested later on by the retaliations that took place. The shameful retaliation. The cowardly retaliation. We tried to do our best to put a lid on it, not to happen".*

The sad and frightening irony of what then unfolded is that it left both beach side and Lakemba residents in a state of fear.

Maroubra

The revenge attacks were launched across many suburbs but the standout for its organised and fearsome detail occurred at Maroubra.

Michael Daley MP for Maroubra was an eyewitness to part of the attack on his suburb:

> **Daley:** *"I saw the gang coming back up the hill from Maroubra Beach...a number of cars, ten or so, driving very slowly with young men walking next to them screaming at people with baseball bats... and smashing everything on the way out...they hopped in their cars and then just left".*

As for what we have called 'the Maroubra Dare', being the boast by Koby Abberton reported in the Daily Telegraph, that the Lebanese troublemakers would be effectively too scared to face off with the much tougher Bra Boys Surf Gang:

> **Daley:** *"It might have been meant as a boast. I'm sure it was. But it appears that it was perceived as a challenge and the challenge was accepted...One of the locals apparently a surfer, ran out* [from the Maroubra Bay Hotel] *to meet them.* [He] *didn't come off very well*

and...went to hospital with some broken bones [after being hit in the chest with a baseball bat]".

However, Daley was somewhat bemused as to how a rumour was disseminated and given such Muslim community currency, that the next night the Bra Boys would travel by convoy to smash up the Lakemba Mosque:

> **Daley:** *"I don't think there was ever any contemplation. People criticise people from Maroubra for never leaving the area. Well, we weren't going to leave that night".*

And according to Daley, if the Bra Boys had decided to launch their own violent and property damaging convoy to Lakemba, they would have struggled to even find the Mosque.

The Lakemba Mosque

It is almost breathtaking, that having launched an attack on a suburb, and then across a number of Caucasian vantage points for violence and property damage by over 100 convoying Muslim youths, that these same attackers and literally thousands of their fellow community members, were outraged that in response, the allegedly equally violent youth of Maroubra were preparing to defile a place of Muslim religious worship in Lakemba.

Had an attempt been made on the mosque, it would have failed, but the inter-tribal tensions would have escalated to an almost uncontrollable level. Thankfully, the attack was just a rumour. The Maroubra Bra Boys had been busy weaponizing their suburb, but to defend not to attack.

However, the calming down of the angry preparations for the defence of their religious citadel, did require a lot of careful work from several Muslim community leaders.

Jamal Rifi and Jihad Dib, along with about ten other Muslim community leaders, just a day after the initial 'event' at Cronulla, shouted, cajoled, and encouraged their fellow Muslims on the steps and surrounds of the Lakemba Mosque, to calm down, to go home or to just pray. With their effort and that of police, and the positive response of their community, a very grave risk to escalated violence in Sydney was avoided.

Little is known of the great work they all played in achieving this.

Jamal Rifi described three waves of mosque 'supporters' who travelled to the mosque that evening to share in its 'defence':

> **Rifi:** *"First, people were starting to just walk in, standing in Wangee Road and saying, 'we're going to protect the mosque; we're not going to let anyone come in'. Then we saw another wave of cars come in and without any doubt, there were some guns in these cars, in the boot and inside. Then the third wave, we saw non-Lebanese, non-Muslim; they came in because they wanted to show solidarity with their friends in the second or first wave".*

Jamal Rifi described how he witnessed one young man lift a blanket off the load in his car boot, to show off a collection of machine guns. Jihad Dib witnessed thousands of people gathered at the mosque where *"the tension was just unbelievable"* and then seeing one young man pulling a large block of wood out of his car, clearly meant as a weapon.

For Jamal Rifi, *"it was touch and go* [with] *many people* [losing] *their voices by shouting at troublemakers to calm down"*. As there were so many, so few community leaders and tensions so high, he and his colleagues were simply unsure how it would all end.

Jihad Dib still recalls the exquisite timing of the Muslim 'Call to Prayer' which just happened to occur in the middle of all this, folks went into the mosque, many prayed, some began to go home, and the crisis slowly passed. It could have been a lot worse for the people of Sydney.

NSW Police Task Force Gain

We earlier considered the extent and ferocity of Middle Eastern crime in the 1990s and onwards, and the degree to which violence, commercial drug dealing, rapes, and murders, had led to a significant police focus on tracking, arresting, and locking up the perpetrators. This focus led to the setting up of a well-resourced stand-alone police task force known as Task Force Gain. Prior to December 2005, this very successful effort in policing had locked up around twenty very violent and serious criminals, most of whom had come from the Muslim Lebanese community of Southwest Sydney. The views of police and Muslim community leaders was that had Task Force Gain not already done its work, then these violent criminals would have been free to do their 'work' across Sydney, protecting their concept of personal and community valour and reputation. Thankfully, we were all spared that outcome.

Jamal Rifi in particular, emphasised that these dangerous individuals were off the streets but the worry he and his colleagues had was that some of the revenge attackers may have sought to fill the leadership void. However, this was successfully avoided:

> **Rifi:** *"...if Task force Gain didn't do what they did, our job would be 100 times harder...many people were innocently attacked. But it could have been a whole lot worse".*

Former Supt John Richardson believes that without question, had these violent criminals been on the streets, the revenge attacks would not have just been with knives and baseball bats, but with firearms as well, with deadly results. *"I have no doubt about it"*.

Working with police

Stephen Stanton argues that the Lebanese Muslim community had no choice and were compelled for reasons of self-interested survival, to quell the anger from their midst. He believes that the dominant Christian Caucasian community would have acted with political, communal, and legislative repression, had they not done so.

Whatever the reason, the Muslim community leaders certainly did their bit.

> **Rifi:** *"...those who went down there from our community and came back, they weren't treated as heroes. They were treated as criminals... by the community.*
>
> *...we managed to get into everyone's mind; 'Now we did not escape the Lebanese War to create another war and we're not going to let the thugs in our community dictate the future of our community'".*

Much of the great work done locally by Muslim community leaders in calming tensions was the manner in which they worked closely with local senior police commanders.

John Richardson talked at length about the extent of constant and close communication throughout the crisis between himself and community leaders like Jamal Rifi:

> **Richardson:** *"I started to get...intelligence...[and] phone calls... from the local elders, expressing some concern relating to the younger members of the community and their anger.*

...it was settled down".

Richardson was in regular contact with Jamal Rifi and the Lebanese Muslim Association immediately after the events at North Cronulla Beach and reached agreement on an early and effective response:

> **Richardson:** *"We'd organised a tactic...where we were able to spread these senior members of the community out throughout the crowd, get a good view of what was happening from within, and we responded accordingly".*

John Richardson went so far as to claim that the relationship between police and the local community *"pretty much saved the day"*:

> **Richardson:** *"...people didn't know...that here I was at 6 o'clock in the morning, in my pyjamas in my home, speaking to community leaders about calming the young people down at a very vital time...it didn't just happen overnight...it...went on for that full week.*
>
> *...nobody knew the sorts of things that were being done in the background that really stopped something major from happening".*

A strange rapprochement

Perhaps one of the strangest 'community leaders' gatherings at the time, would have to be the self-styled rapprochement meeting at Maroubra beach, a few days into the revenge attacks, led by Lebanese Mick Hawi on behalf of the Comancheros bikie gang, and Caucasian Sunny Abberton on behalf of the Bra Boys surf gang.

The gathering was indeed useful for police intelligence.

Michael Daley happened to be nearby, meeting up with then Federal MP Peter Garrett and was an eyewitness to this rather bizarre event:

> **Daley:** *"The messaging was good:*
>
> *'Peace brother. The beach is open for anyone of all races and creeds to come and surf. We just love surfers so come on down. But we don't want any trouble with the Lebanese community'."*

Mick Hawi then added to the message: *"Well, we don't want any trouble with the Bra Boys and it's over and lets all love each other and be very peaceful".*

Daley felt that *"it was bizarre, but...had an effect of cooling things down in a funny way"*. He also felt that Sunny Abberton would have had a very influential role in calming down the Bra Boys. Mick Hawi, of course, apart from the Comancheros, would have had no impact on what several hundred young angry Muslim Lebanese men might have still been planning for Sydney.

Theme 7: Law enforcement

We have discussed at length elsewhere, the extraordinary policing and law enforcement response to the 'Cronulla Riots', including pervasive new police powers and the resourcing of over 2,000 NSW Police personnel. A number of participants had interesting insights into the role police played.

Police performance

The interviewees all put forward very positive accounts of policing performance. Jamal Rifi and Jihad Dib best summed it up:

> **Rifi:** *"Police...were extremely effective, careful and they communicated very well".*
>
> **Dib:** *"Credit to the police...they...got onto* [the threat to the mosque] *straight away...they had to because this had the potential to be really bad".*

These views line up squarely with former Police Commander John Richardson, who believes that effective community engagement by police, a strong police presence and arresting law breakers, all contributed to quelling lawlessness and reassuring the public into the future.

> **Richardson:** *"I think the manner in which the police in particular handled the whole situation was exemplary...we'd...pre-empted that it could get pretty nasty, so we'd arranged for Operations Support Group* [to assist] *...PolAir as well...to give us an overall view of what was happening, both on the ground and from the sky".*

John Richardson regards the police response as *"swift and appropriate"* and that *"it would have gotten a lot worse had we not responded that way we did"*.

Stephen Stanton eloquently captured the record:

Stanton: "...*it is the just and unstinted praise of all our police officers who silently and valiantly and stoically and steadfastly observed and performed within their command of all of the tasks that they undertook to preserve peace, law, and order.*

And it is to their credit, that our society never devolved into what would've been a far more grotesque landscape and state of anarchy.

And to Mark Goodwin and his officers, we owe that debt and recognition, which we so much take for granted".

"The only thing we have to fear...is fear itself".[75]

We discussed in the last theme, participant commentary around the fear which pervaded Sydney after the violent launch of random mobile revenge attacks. It only takes a few acts of arbitrary violence and property damage to terrorise a whole city. And fear of harm was pervasive for a period of time in late 2005/early 2006.

Police had to focus on preventing serious breaches of the peace but equally, restoring confidence in the people of Sydney that our streets were safe again. Ron Mason believed that the public's fear of harm was greater than any other riot he had policed throughout his long police career.

Malcolm Kerr also put the view that people seeing on TV, the violence and baton wielding police officer on Cronulla Railway Station, *"had a psychological impact. People were genuinely concerned about their safety going out"*. He believes it was the strong and effective police response that soon enough made people feel safe again.

However, before police and the use of new legislative powers made that possible, the focus was on dealing with weapons that each tribe had cached ahead of their terrorising use.

Maroubra weaponised

We mentioned earlier Jamal Rifi observing a car boot load of machine guns, and Jihad Dib, seeing one young mosque protector brandishing a wooden weapon.

Maroubra MP Michael Daley also witnessed the weaponizing of his suburb,

---

[75] President Franklin Delano Roosevelt, First Inaugural Address, Washington DC, March 4, 1933.

as the Bra Boys prepared for the defence of their territory:

> **Daley:** *"...the next morning,* [after the Maroubra attack] *I went down to the beach...and saw they were arming themselves. They were secreting weapons on awnings and in laneways...I was told that they were preparing for a return visit from our friends from the west...they were rostering people on to be there at certain times of the day and night...outside the pub, in the square, on the beach".*

However:

> *"The police heard about it...searched the joint and took half the weapons away* [which included crates of Molotov cocktails and baseball bats]*".*

In response, police closed off all the streets and *"Maroubra was locked down"*. As Goodwin put it: *"We didn't* [then] *actually have the power to do it-we just did it"*. But it worked!

Meanwhile a more violent turn was taking place in Lakemba.

Lakemba weaponised

Stephen Stanton made a fascinating claim that the Lebanese Drug dealers began using drug receipts, not to buy more drugs to trade, but to purchase weapons.

> **Stanton:** *"The presence of prohibited weapons... of the greatest lethal power...using receipts from drug proceeds to build up the cache of weapons...hand grenades and machine guns.*
>
> *The machine guns were Uzis, they were the weapon of choice...places like* [name redacted] *Avenue, Greenacre...every garage had weapons... firearms...it is no wonder that the Middle Eastern Crime Squad* [was] *generated as a result of all this nonsense".*

Legislative reprisal

Much has been spoken and written about the rapidity with which the NSW Government responded to the violence and fear of the 'Cronulla Riots', with what at other times, may have been regarded as punitive new police powers.

We earlier referred to Barrister Stephen Stanton describing the statutory improvements to police powers enacted in mid-December 2005, as a necessary "*legislative reprisal*".

> **Stanton:** "*The Islamic community was effectively polarised, and there were those that wanted to use to flame, ...and fan, what was an attempt by groups within society to rebel against law and order.*
>
> *The response that was undertaken in terms of a legislative reprisal... was both necessitous...and timely. Because if you didn't have those powers for cordon, search, and seizure, detain and other matters... If that power wasn't in place, you couldn't have detained those cars*".

He believes that whilst "*appeasement*" and "*rapprochement*" played their parts, it was this law-and-order initiative which made it possible to achieve a lasting peace.

> **Stanton:** "*If that legislation wasn't passed* [as quickly as it was] *...the whole place would've been a blood bath. Men like Goodwin would've had war, not riots on their hands*".

Jamal Rifi was equally emphatic of the value of this legislation, particularly its lockdown powers: "*Now we're talking about the pandemic. Everyone is talking about lockdown. But 15 years ago, nobody had heard about a lockdown*".

For John Richardson, the expansion of police powers made a significant difference:

> **Richardson:** [Prior to the passing of that legislation] "*I couldn't stop people from leaving Punchbowl Park and going somewhere else. This legislation would have allowed me to have the power to do a lot of things that I couldn't do that night...like lockdown areas...* [search vehicles, take mobile phones]".

Sgt. Craig Campbell

Perhaps some of the most famous footage of the initial Cronulla 'riot', was a baton wielding Sergeant Craig Campbell, protecting the lives of two visitors in a train carriage from a marauding mob. However, before giving voice to his perspective, we thought an amusing explanation from him would be appropriate as to why he called his police issue baton, "*Milo*".

> **Campbell:** "*When I was a young bloke, there was ad on TV for the Milo drink and their catch cry was, 'marvellous what a difference Milo*

makes.'

So, I thought...well it's a good name for the baton as its marvellous what a difference that will make in a situation like that. So, it's called Milo because it's marvellous what a difference Milo makes".

Marvellous! We obtained a fascinating first-hand account from Sgt. Campbell of what is perhaps the most memorable recorded event of the Cronulla Riots. Rather than paraphrase his narrative we have decided to leave much of this in his own words.

The recounting of his day all those years ago is as follows:

The radio call for help

Campbell: *"I had about six of my crew on...for the shift...I was just patrolling around and...taking water supplies to the troops...when an alert came over and it was two Middle Eastern males being beaten up on a train in the Cronulla Train Station.*

So, I expedited there, I was driving, and when I pulled up there [were] *people just pouring over* [a] *little* [fence]*...and...into the front of the station and I thought, well what's going on here?*

I pulled up...onto the footpath...and got out. I took my baton out and I gave the other one to Sergeant Smith. I thought if we've got to get out of this, we might have to use these, you never know. I had no capsicum spray left, I'd used that at several other skirmishes prior to it and we had no more brought down so I was out of that, and I wasn't about to pull my gun out of the holster".

What happened next ought to be the stuff of police legend and what brings such Muslim leaders as Jamal Rifi to say: *"...there are heroes like Craig Campbell in the police force".*

Entering the train

Campbell: *"So, I went in and as soon as I cleared the turnstiles, I could see two young men being attacked by a heap of young yahoos and I knew I had to get up there because it was not looking good.*

...I've gone in [to the train] *and I'm yelling at him, get out, get out, get out. No one could hear me; they were too busy yelling and screaming and throwing bottles and kicking these guys. So, I just* [thought]*, 'what*

do you do'? I know it's a defensive weapon OK, and I used it in an offensive way, however, I was using it like that in the defence of those two young men that were getting, basically beaten to death. So, I have no regrets about using it and I will do it again today".

Using the police baton

Campbell: "So, I give them [the rioters] a reason to leave. I mean 130kg, six foot and 26 inches of spun aircraft aluminium in my hand, those shire kids should have had more brains. So, I give them a good tune up with Milo. OK? And I got everyone in that carriage, so we could look after the two young Middle Eastern boys and then they wouldn't get off the railway platform, they were carrying on, throwing bottles through the windows, we had to shut all the windows. So, I thought, well, you are going to learn the hard way so I just started cracking people, give them a reason to leave".

The riot squad

Campbell: "And as soon as the Public Order [and] Riots [Squad]... saw the big sergeant wielding a baton, they all went, 'well it's obviously OK', so they got their silly little collapsible batons out and started whacking them with those... we got the job done because I needed to get those boys off and get some medical treatment. So, the only way to do that was to get everyone off there and not wanting to come back and then I put them into the Stationmaster's office in their meal room and I had the ambos go in there and treat them where no one could get to them".

When asked how many attackers he had to deal with in the train and on the Railway station that day, his reply was suitably succinct: *"Didn't have time to count them, just whack them"*.

And so, as the famous TV footage played thousands of times over shows, it certainly was marvellous what a difference Milo made.

We will discuss later, the sad end to Sergeant Campbell's policing career, and despite being the hero of the Cronulla Riots, having a completely absent recognition of this from NSW Police.

The Police response

Ron Mason, by the time he retired was perhaps the leading public order police commander in the country and played an important role in operation

Seta throughput late 2005/ early 2006. When advised that Scully had to challenge Moroney with bringing the army in, if he and NSW Police were not up to the job, as earlier mentioned, his response was somewhat succinct: *"I think it worked...I had 1,000* [police] *at Cronulla* [in the days following the initial disturbance]".

On the criticism by Strike Force Neil of locating the initial Command Post at the local Surf Club above and overlooking the crowd on North Cronulla beach: *"It was a great location"*.

The Campsie Supt. at the time, John Richardson, believed that placing Riot Squad personnel in Highway Patrol vehicles was a very effective means of dealing with what he called: *"A moving breach of the peace...a great idea... we had police who were experienced...in riot control...a smart move, it was appropriate"*.

John Richardson also strenuously rejected any notion by 'Shock Jock' radio hosts, that Police had not been monitoring in and around Punchbowl Park, on the evening of 11 December 2005:

> **Richardson**: *"I had police in plain clothes in unmarked cars around Punchbowl Park. They were giving me up to date feedback on what was happening at the time. We were on a special radio channel...I was always asking, how many people, how many cars? Cars were coming and going in ones and twos, going in different directions...* [Until the special powers] *...the only thing I could ask police to do is, if you see any traffic offences...If you see any offence, stop the car, arrest, or take action"*.

This account of on the ground real and effective policing, is such a contrast to how the ABC and Ray Hadley 'reported' on his management of Punchbowl Park as to defy belief. We will consider this further, in more depth, as part of the discussion in the next chapter, 'Scapegoats of the riots'.

16

Scapegoats of the Riots

"I did my job...we took an Oath of office... I upheld that"[76]

Name	Theme
8.	Scapegoats of the riots

Theme 8: Scapegoats of the riots

As we have already discussed, a number of interview participants lauded the performance of NSW Police in restoring peace and order to the streets of Sydney following the 'Sydney Disturbances'. Despite that performance, a number of senior police careers came to unexpected ends as a result of a range of factors, but mostly, we believe, from unfair and unwarranted public exposure and disparagement.

The leadership positions held by these senior contributors to responding and resolving the 'Cronulla Troubles' included a police sergeant, superintendent, assistant commissioner and finally, a police minister.

As much of this book has dealt with what happened to Assistant Commissioner Mark Goodwin and Police Minister Carl Scully, we do not intend to repeat ourselves and will concentrate instead on Messrs Campbell and Richardson, as well as 'lost learnings'.

Craig Campbell

The Commissioner commends and then doesn't

In the last chapter we gave voice to Sgt Craig Campbell, on what he saw and did in the railway carriage at Cronulla train station on Sunday 11th of December 2005. In this chapter, we deal with what happened to his policing career at the hands of NSW Police.

---

[76] Sgt. Campbell, Transcript of Interview, 22 November 2020.

Just a short while after Sgt. Campbell was forced to use his baton to protect two individuals under physical attack on a train, Commissioner Moroney happened to be visiting the police command post at North Cronulla and introduced himself to Sergeant Campbell:

> **Campbell**: *"Moroney came over to me...called me by my first name and said: '...you've got no problems with me; it was a good effort'. He actually had a bit of a laugh that he should put me in charge of his Weapons Training Unit".*

Campbell, not surprisingly, was recommended at all stages of the police chain of command, for a *'Commissioner's Commendation for Courage'*, by his local Superintendent, Robert Redfern, by his Regional Assistant Commissioner Mark Godwin and finally, by the internal NSW Police Reward Evaluation Committee. Sadly, and unexpectedly, it was not signed off by the commissioner himself, and the award was never made:

> **Campbell**: *"...somewhere along the way, someone decided I didn't deserve it. And when I heard that they wanted to charge me with the excessive use of force that just crushed me...to think that...the hierarchy, would do that to you when you've put your life on the line. I ended up having a breakdown and that was it, I was gone...it ended my career, it ended my marriage and, basically it ended my life as I knew it.*
>
> *...I was starting to go to Vinnies and places like that trying to get food".*

Craig Campbell has a copy of his own employment file which clearly has as a last entry: *"Awarded Commissioner's Commendation [for] Courage...in relation to civil unrest at Cronulla on the 11th of December 2005"*. But the award was never actually bestowed.

The pertinent details directly from Craig Campbell's *'NSW Police Individual Profile'* is set out in the table below and makes for interesting reading:

Date	Title	Description
31.12.9999	Commendation - Courage	*Awarded Commissioner's Commendation – courage and devotion to duty in relation to his actions in response to civil disorder incident at Cronulla on 11 December 2005 – nswp/d/2006/21360.*

Apparently, the administrative recording practice of the NSW Police Force, is that when an award has been recommended and approved for bestowing on an individual police officer, the details are recorded on file prior to it being personally presented, but the date is later inserted on the personnel file, on the day it was actually bestowed. Hence the use of the year 9999 to simply complete that cell on the records pending the actual date of presentation being inserted after the ceremony. However, *'betwixt cup and lip'* of Craig Campbell being 'given' the award, it was 'ungiven', by persons and processes not yet known.

When Craig Campbell put in a Freedom of Information request, under the Government Information (Public Access) Act 2009 (GIPA), for this same material, it was refused, only for him to subsequently learn via police sources, that the last entry on his personnel file regarding the awarding of the *'Commissioner's Commendation* [for] *Courage'* had then been deleted from his file. These same sources advised Goodwin, that the entry was removed.

We also lodged our own GIPA application, in an attempt to obtain documents setting out details of anyone recommended for commissioner citation or commendation, for both operations Pendennis (counter terrorism) and Seta (Cronulla). We wanted to learn what had been recommended on one and not the other, and why Sgt. Campbell's commendation for courage had disappeared. Our request was rejected for a myriad of 'secret government business' reasons, the most amusing being that disclosure would involve the release of *"personal information"*.

Hazzard's Operation Pendennis vs Goodwin's Operation Seta

As we have discussed in chapter 13, Operation Pendennis, conducted a month before the Cronulla Disturbances, by the NSW Police Counter-Terrorism Command (CTC), led to one general duties officer being shot in the hand, and it was just a sheer fluke that he wasn't killed on that day.

No explanation has been forthcoming from NSW Police as to why that operation led to individual commendations from the commissioner, yet none for an operation, just a month later, when police stepped up and delivered the restoration of peace to the streets of Sydney.

Recognition from the Muslim community

In an act of both irony and generosity, the Lebanese Muslim community were appalled at how poorly Craig Campbell had been treated by NSW Police, that he had fallen on tough times, and put on a couple of fundraising events for him.

> **Campbell:** *"The Arabic community couldn't believe the way I'd been treated after saving two of their own...*
>
> *They gave me some clothes...money and food...to...assist me, I was struggling at the time. Without their assistance, I wouldn't be where I am today".*

His Oath of Office

> **Campbell:** *"I did my job and that's what I was paid to do, and we took an Oath of Office, so I upheld that as well. And the Arabic community has recognised that, but my own peers have gone the opposite way".*

John Richardson

Supt. John Richardson, Commander of Campsie Local Area Command and the leader of the police response to the Southwest Sydney revenge attacks, also had his exemplary performance humiliated and denigrated, not by police, as was the case with Sgt. Craig Campbell, but externally by unfair, unwarranted, and probably defamatory media attacks.

The attack on John Richardson essentially boiled down to this:

> As Commander of the Campsie Local Area Command, he should have known in advance that angry young Lebanese Muslim men would use Punchbowl Park as a vehicle convoy staging point.
>
> He should have met them in advance in force.
>
> He should have then ordered police to detain them and to confiscate their vehicles, even though police then had no legislative power to do so.
>
> Finally, by failing to do so, he allowed an angry mob to violently terrorise Sydney, which was effectively his fault due to his inexcusable inaction.

A 'Shock Jock' never needs to be logical, sound or fair, but this extraordinary and tortuous path of reasoning was at the more extreme end of argumentative gymnastics.

It will surprise many that the police media unit played in March 2006, at best, an inadvertent role in the demise of John Richardson's enviable reputation as a hero of the Cronulla revenge attacks. For those who have had firsthand experience of this unit, it will not come as a surprise. For others, it is worth outlining how they 'function'.

The inside story on the NSW Police Media Unit

The Police Media Unit, now known as the Public Affairs Branch, is primarily staffed by civilian journalists with a police officer presence, and usually nominally headed by a senior police officer. A naïve audience may often not pause to wonder each evening during the TV news hour, how yet another police door busting take down just happened to have a media camera crew at the ready to provide full graphic details. That's where Police Media steps in to ensure cops get a good wrap generally in return for a constant flow of crime fighting copy. It is a long 'time-honoured' contract which has served very well, the mystique of cops doing their duty, and TV news editors who have an hour of action to fill for an easily distracted audience.

However, on occasion, the media unit uses this 'relationship' with journalists and media organisation, to meddle in police politics.

Before assessing the role of the Police Media Unit in the demise of John Richardson we thought it worthwhile to shine an even brighter light upon their operations.

A Police Minister's perspective

Carl Scully recalls his less than joyful experiences with the Police Media Unit:

> *"I was astonished to find, quite early in my tenure as police minister, that the media unit pretty much did as it pleased. However, and also astonishingly to me for a public sector CEO, was that the Commissioner for Police, Ken Moroney, also had his own stand-alone media advisor who was located in the commissioner's wing, just a few metres from the commissioner's desk.*
>
> *This created competing dual Police Media Units. One consisting of one individual serving the commissioner only, and the other, a whole unit with a plethora of media savvy individuals feeding journalists wanting good crime and police stories. This certainly resulted in the not infrequent strained functions when either I, or the Unit, wanted the commissioner to be involved in something about which his adviser disagreed.*
>
> *However, mostly I worked well and productively with the Commissioner's*

media advisor, but on a few occasions, it was hard work, as I tried to make a case for the commissioner to do an appearance. And only I could turn her around, when her preference was for a non-appearance of the commissioner, as my staff would be simply ignored. On these things, Moroney deferred to her, so on media matters, I only dealt directly with her. In my first 10 years as a minister, in many different portfolios, I had never come across such an unusual arrangement in securing a CEO's public appearances.

Whereas I could at least directly appeal to the commissioner's 'one woman media unit,' usually with some degree of success, the Police Media Unit was a whole different kind of minefield. On more than a few occasions, when either I, or my senior staff, asked for something to be done, and this was not something the unit agreed with, the request was simply ignored, or a 'Yes Minister' obfuscation invoked. On occasions, unwelcome leaks would appear in the press, and we usually suspected but of course, could never prove, that the source was the Police Media Unit. They were a law unto themselves.

I am sadly unsurprised, that John Richardson feels he was not protected by his own organisational media unit. Why should he have been when that, rather incredibly, was never its role".

The media searching for a victim

Journalists never need much encouragement in their search for negative angles to run, or to find suitable victims to target and blame, as they produce daily copy. Unfortunately, positive stories lauding the performance of leaders and individuals don't sell as many newspapers, or attract TV audiences, as much as a good dose of negativity. Radio 'Shock Jocks' are no different in kind, but are usually far more expansive in degree, during their exhortations of who in their view, is the guilty party of whatever it is they are exhorting about.

Supt. John Richardson, a valued and valuable servant of the community, was caught in the crossfire of this approach to keeping ratings and selling 'stories', his reputation besmirched, his performance in quelling and containing the revenge attacks unrecognised, and sadly, driven from the police force.

The journey to a media driven demise

After the initial demonstration, then the revenge attacks, and the uncertainty of that summer all being brought to a peaceful norm for the people of Sydney, the media generally as usual were simply not exhausted as everybody else was from weeks and weeks of reporting every various angle of every morsel of story on this, and now felt free to explore new angles. One 'new' angle initially given low level coverage, almost not worth responding to in terms of its relevance and impact, was that the Campsie Police Command should have, allegedly, known that the young angry men of Lakemba would launch their attacks from Punchbowl Park on the evening of Sunday 11th of December. Much of this was 'midnight to dawn' radio commentary and unworthy of response.

However, in mid-March 2006, some three months after these events, the ABC TV Four Corners programme decided to explore the issue. The Police Media Unit contacted Supt. John Richardson and requested that he be interviewed. He was initially reluctant and certainly concerned about the risks of putting himself in such a position. However, it simply didn't occur to him that the Police Media Unit would have neither properly assessed the risks to him personally, nor been concerned about his interests. His appearance on Four Corners on the advice of that media unit would lead to a 'Shock Jock' forum and the end of his policing career. It is a sad tale.

We have captured John Richardson's perspective on this in the following table:

Subject	Quote
Police Media Unit	[The Police Media Unit]... *called me about the proposed interview and said: 'I think it will be a good thing to do and you'll get to do your side of the story'. I was reluctant to do the interview but foolish enough at the time to believe that the Police Media Unit was going to give me the right advice".*
ABC TV Interview	*"The interview* [on the Four Corners programme] *went for about an hour and only near the end, did I get asked about what I think was their original purpose...to* [allege] *that it was really the Local Police Commander who had allowed the revenge attacks to occur, rather than the attackers themselves who had committed the crimes and terrorised a swathe of Sydney".*
Police Media Unit	*"And there I was sitting in the target line on the advice of Police Media. It was an outrageous piece of journalism and one I am inclined to believe was, or ought to have been, reasonably foreseeable* [by the Police Media Unit]*".*

Subject	Quote
Punchbowl Park	"*I was grilled* [on the Four Corners programme] *about Punchbowl Park and whether I knew or ought to have known that young Lebanese troublemakers were or might be congregating there.* *My response of 'It is a public park, people are allowed to meet there, and until the special powers were enacted on 15 December 2005, I had no statutory power to prevent people moving about Sydney in motor vehicles', became for me, an inadvertent piece of malicious ABC copy, as they presented me as either a liar or a fool. I was neither, either then or now".*

Ray Hadley and 'Shock Jock' journalism

The day after the Four Corners programme, 14 March 2006, a caller rang 2GB radio host Ray Hadley, to advise of what had happened on Four Corners. The 2GB radio transcript is set out in the table below:

Name	Quote
Caller	"*Punchbowl Park is the normal meeting ground for Middle Eastern youth. He was blatantly lying saying, 'no...we're not aware of it'".*
Hadley	"*We didn't see Four Corners last night. But...if the officer has said that there's no conclusion that anyone can draw that he lied".*
Caller	"*How can he be the Local Area Commander and then say on national television that the police are not aware that that park is a meeting ground for these youths".*
Hadley	"*...Strike me pink, he has to resign now, John Richardson. If he's so bereft of any knowledge of what happens in his own LAC, well he ought to resign. There isn't a person in Sydney that doesn't know that Punchbowl Park is a known meeting area for people of Middle Eastern appearance...and you've got the LAC saying no, it's not...blissful ignorance I think they call it".*
Caller	"*...he's either one of two things, a totally incompetent fool, or a liar".*

This is an extraordinary attack without so much as giving a moment's thought to giving Supt. Richardson an opportunity to defend himself.

And the attack, given its irrational premise, would have nonetheless been hard to overcome. Talk back radio hosts have a habit of upping the fulmination dial whenever a victim tries to defend themselves. As mentioned, Sydney had never before had a violent mobile breach of the peace which had unleashed random violent attacks and property damage across our city, and all emanating from a small area of south-western Sydney. Yes, the police had expected and planned for a reaction to the North Cronulla provocation, but nobody knew where groups of Middle Eastern men would congregate. In actual fact, there were countless places these hordes met before travelling in convoy to wreak havoc across Sydney. Their actual reaction was off the charts, it was mobile, it was random and it was in multiple locations. It could hardly be rationally blamed upon a single police officer for causing it all. But that was no barrier to the police superintendent then being trolled on air by callers.

The subsequent damage to the target was inversely proportional to the logical validity of what was being asserted.

The aftermath

John Richardson never fully recovered from this attack. He was shattered, soon after going on medical leave and never returned to duty as a serving police officer.

Supt. Richardson expressed appreciation for the support he received at the time from the Commissioner and the Deputy Commissioner who had been *"both singing my praises about what I did* [in managing the revenge attacks]". However, and also disappointedly, the NSW Opposition Leader joined the Hadley chorus in attacking the Campsie Police Commander, who also appreciated the defence provided by the Minister for Police in parliament:

> **Scully:** *"I'll not have the Leader of the Opposition criticise the commander at Campsie, John Richardson. What a great field commander. He's out there doing a terrific job".*

The Police Chaplain at the time, Reverend David Warner, was also concerned about the impact of these attacks upon the health and wellbeing of Supt. Richardson and informed the Commissioner of that concern by email on the same day of those attacks.

Barrister's advice on defamation

One thing that was of partial assistance to the Superintendent, was that Police Legal was requested to obtain the advice of a barrister on whether or not these broadcast attacks were defamatory.

That advice concluded that the claims made on 2GB that Supt. Richardson, had told *"a knowing and blatant lie"*, that he had *"performed as a grossly incompetent fool"*, and that he needed to *"resign"*, provided *"reasonably strong prospects"* of establishing that the *"meanings"* conveyed were defamatory.

However, as is too often the case with good public servants under attack, there was a sting in the tail in this advice in the form of the recommendation given by Solicitor Mark Hicks, which was accepted on 1 May 2005, by the NSW Police Director of Legal Services, Asst. Commissioner Lee Shearer:

> **Hicks:** *"This matter has been investigated by Legal Services on behalf of Superintendent Richardson. Legal Services will no longer play an active part in this matter and any further steps Superintendent Richardson may wish to take will be a matter for him and require his personal funding".*

What this meant, and not demurred by anyone from the Commissioner down, was that despite the appalling attacks upon John Richardson, and despite Counsel's advice that there were strong prospects of proving they were defamatory, he was not going to be supported any further. Not surprisingly, John Richardson was devastated. Defamation proceedings are long drawn-out affairs, involving exorbitant legal costs and with a serious risk of bankruptcy if a case is lost. He simply couldn't put his family home on the line, so he copped it on the chin, left the Police Force and tried as best he could to move on.

What really happened?

Perhaps a very well respected and renowned leader in the Middle Eastern Community – Dr Jamal Rifi – best summed it up when outlining what happened from his perspective during the evening after the 'event' at Cronulla on Sunday 11 December 2005:

> **Rifi:** *"The shameful retaliation. The cowardly retaliation. We tried to put a lid on it, not to happen. Unfortunately, the gathering point-**we didn't know about it until later on**. A lot of hot-headed people went to Punchbowl Park, and they actually formed a convoy, and they went down".*

No-one ever suggested that Punchbowl Park is not a place where local residents of Middle Eastern background choose to meet and mingle. It's a local park and people visit and use its facilities. Superintendent Richardson was well aware it was a park and that local folks used it. His thoughts are outlined below:

Event	Quote
Punchbowl Park	"I had police in plain clothes in unmarked cars around Punchbowl Park. They were giving me up-to-date feedback on what was happening...I was always asking how many people, how many cars? Cars were coming and going in ones and twos, going in different directions".
Incorrect information	"Some police officer put a COPs entry on the police computer relating to a commander telling police to leave the Punchbowl Park area. What I actually said was: 'we need the police to be a little further back so that they're not too obtrusive to be able to actually see what was going on'.

It is clear from this account that Supt. Richardson was commanding and acting as he should have, in properly leading the police response to a very volatile and unpredictable situation. That a police clerk put in a wrong entry about police fleeing from trouble would have only added accelerant to journalists and 'Shock Jocks' but that doesn't make the 'story' any less the 'Fake News' it was then and remains to this day.

It simply stretches credulity to breaking point by claiming that everybody knew, or ought to have known, that Sydney's first and only mobile riotous convoy would emanate from Punchbowl Park and then terrorise Sydney. This is probably best summed up by the below 2GB quote versus another quote from just up the road from Punchbowl Park, at Belmore Medical Centre, run for over 35 years by Dr Jamal Rifi and repeated here for valuable emphasis:

Name	Quote
Hadley	"There isn't a person in Sydney that doesn't know that Punchbowl Park is a known meeting area for people of Middle Eastern appearance".
Rifi	"Unfortunately, the gathering point. We didn't know about until later on. A lot of hot-headed people went to Punchbowl Park...and formed a convoy".

It is generic knowledge that Punchbowl was a highly populated area of people of Middle Eastern appearance who occasionally use the park. So what! Local people use local parks! There are literally dozens of other outdoor and indoor meeting places for Middle Eastern people in the Lakemba/Punchbowl/Bankstown area too. It is then a giant leap to mix those two elements of demography and topography to make an absurd and unsustainable claim on the name and reputation of Supt. John Richardson, that somehow he ought to have known this is where some revenge attacks would be launched from. For Supt Richardson, his policing career was over. And like Sergeant Campbell, there would be no commissioner's commendations for him either.

Lost learnings

We discussed in earlier chapters how Goodwin had quickly put into place, in early 2006, the well tried and valuable no-blame 'debrief' process which NSW Police had long done after a major event. The views of police in the field were being sought, meetings held, consideration being given on where to improve and where things went well and why. Then unexpectedly, Commissioner Moroney announced a 'Strike Force' to investigate senior police performance during the Cronulla Riots.

The following claim appears in the subsequent Strike Force Neil report:

> *"From the command-and-control structure and the overall command of the operation as outlined in this report, it could be perceived that the report is being critical of the performance of individual commanders. This is far from the case".*[77]

This probable yet hardly effective nod to journalists was on page 76 of the report and can be juxtaposed with the assertion made on page 4 of his report that the Police Executive had: *"...made it clear that the review was not an investigation into the actions of individual police officers".*

However, the manner in which a 'draft' report was released, ignited a media frenzy of career destroying blame, which reigned down upon individual police commanders thereby limiting the policing value for improving the police response and performance around future public order events. This was a significant opportunity lost for police to learn what went well and what went wrong, and to learn and improve through an interactive, inclusive and transparent, no-blame process. For this reason, we have designated this lost opportunity for police to learn, alongside Messrs Campbell, Richardson, Goodwin and Scully, as a 'scapegoats' of the riots.

The expert ignored by 'investigators'

In coming to our opinion that the Strike Force Neil investigation was a somewhat lost opportunity for police to learn and improve, we drew heavily upon our interview with Supt. Ron Mason, who not only had a

---

[77] Strike Force Neil Report. Volume On. p. 76.

leading role in Operation Seta in late 2005/early 2006 in the stymieing of the revenge attacks, but was at the time the most experienced riot control police commander in the NSW Police Force. Despite the senior leadership role he had in protecting Cronulla from revenge attacks, and his wealth of experience in the planning, commanding, and responding to major public order disturbances, the Strike Force Neil team, omitted to interview him.

Ron Mason

We interviewed and obtained fascinating details of his lengthy police career, in literally facing the front line of countless violent public confrontations. But for his evidence, we would have left our narrative on the Strike Force Neil report to the body of this book rather than in this part. However, the perspectives of Ron Mason were simply too relevant to leave out.

Ron Mason's policing career is littered with major public disturbances, riots, and violent breaches of the peace. He dealt with these as a front-line police officer and a commander over a sustained period of years. In his later years, if anyone in NSW Police wanted advice on public order planning and management, he was the *'go to guy'*.

Below is a sample of the countless number of serious breaches of the peace dealt with by Ron Mason throughout a long police career:

Event	Detail
The stolen army tank	In 1985, at the approaches to Sydney Harbour Bridge, Mason climbed onto a military tank stolen from Holsworthy Army Base, lifted the lid and saw that, *"he had a gun in his hand"*, was shot at, and then shot back and killed the assailant.
The first Gay Mardi Gras	In 1978 this was a violent start to achieving gay rights, police were assaulted, and 50 demonstrators arrested.
Bathurst Riots	Mason attended all the Bathurst riots of the 1980s, including the especially violent one in 1985, when 5 of his team of 6 officers had to be hospitalised with broken bones. One had to be Helivaced *"because he was hit with a house brick to the chest and that stopped his heart"*.
Builders labourers protest	He and his police colleagues went *"toe to toe"* with angry building workers in Sydney's CBD, *"and it was a punch up"*.

Event	Detail
George Pell protest at becoming a cardinal	In 2003, at St Mary's Cathedral: "...*it was a bit of a fight... There was more action and violence...than there was at Cronulla*".

He then put these rather confronting public disturbances into perspective:

> **Mason**: *"There are 400 roughly a year events that are major events, demonstrations, protests, and they can relate to a car crew attending, just oversighting right up to you need a couple of thousand police on the ground".*

In 2005 he was the Superintendent Police Commander in charge in Sydney's CBD and was called on by Goodwin, his Region Commander, on every occasion to plan, oversee and command the police response to public order incidents in Sydney's CBD.

Ron Mason's experience in riot control and response has been long recognised by both senior NSW Police and interstate Police forces. "*I seem to be approached every time there's... a major event*".

When asked why he believed he was not consulted on any aspect of the Cronulla Riots investigation, including its findings and recommendations before they were publicly released: "*I might have been critical of the report*".

After the initial day of 'disturbance' at Cronulla and beyond, Supt. Mason was put in charge of over 1,000 police officers stationed at Cronulla, to restore order and protect the community. Quite apart from his extraordinary career in the policing of very challenging public disturbances, this very senior policing leadership role during the revenge attacks and located at 'Cronulla Central', ought to have been enough on its own, to warrant an extensive interview with him by the Strike Force Neil team.

> **Mason**: *"I approached* [the Strike Force investigators] *twice... I saw them at the Sydney police Centre...people I had never seen before* [or seen anywhere near a riot], *but I was told they were doing the investigation for Hazzard.* [So, I approached one of them and] *told him who I was...what my role was in the city and what I've done, and also told him that I also did a report for the Macquarie Fields riot, and they said they'll get back to me.*

> *No-one spoke to me for weeks, so I tried to ring up and get somebody and said, 'listen I'm still here' and they said, 'yeah, yeah, we've got your request' and no-one got back to me. Next thing I know the report is out".*

Advising on the Macquarie Fields Report

In sharp contrast to the Cronulla Riots investigation, when the then Deputy Commissioner and ex-Tactical Response Group member, Dave Madden, was quietly tasked by Commissioner Moroney to conduct a review of the policing of the January 2005 Macquarie Fields riots, not surprisingly, the Deputy Commissioner turned to Ron Mason to undertake a review of the tactics and planning used by police during that 'disturbance'. This work formed an important part of police learning from their performance during that riot and improving for any future events. Ron Mason's contribution informed a substantial part of the final Macquarie Fields report released publicly in August 2005. Had a normal learning process been followed here, then Ron Mason would have (and should have in our view) again informed and underpinned a large part of a review into police performance at Cronulla.

No-blame learning at Macquarie Fields – vs – Blame no-learning at Cronulla

> **Mason:** [The Macquarie Fields report] *"... was* [about] *how can we improve...how can we gain something out of this report...One of the first things you do is have a debriefing and you're involving critical people in relation to that debriefing... You identify areas that went wrong, you identify areas that went well. This was something I did in the Tactical Response Group (TRG) every operation.*
>
> *...It's a no blame...it was such a great thing we did, we identified areas where we could improve, and we included it in our training and development".*

When asked how useful and what is learnt from a 'Strike Force Investigation' such as the one used in the Cronulla Riots review approach, he replied:

> **Mason:** *"You learn nothing. You learn not to trust...I am really disappointed about the whole process in relation to the review* [of the Cronulla Riots]*".*

Mason finally gets interviewed

Sadly, any opportunity for real 'Learning' for NSW Police in a no-blame environment, was lost long ago with the substantial passage of time, and the methodological approach of the 2006 inquiry.

We concluded that the best approach would be to interview Supt Mason about his perceptions and reflections on some of the main findings and recommendations of the Strike Force Neil report.

These are set out below:

Strike Force Neil Assertion	Our Assessment	Ron Mason Perspective
The risk rating ahead of the riots was kept at MEDIUM	It was elevated to High and not kept at Medium	*"It was elevated. It was initially elevated to MEDIUM with the one assault but then with the second assault I got a phone call* [from Goodwin] *to say that the rating had been increased to HIGH"*.
Proper planning for a higher risk event did not occur	Planning was for a higher risk event	[The NSW Police planners involved prior to the 2005 riots are] *"the best...I've ever seen... no-one comes near it...after the* [Sydney] *Olympics...I was flown to* [Queensland] *to review what* [they] *had in place for a major public order demonstration and what they did was good, but it was nowhere near as good as what we do"*.
During the daytime events at Cronulla, Goodwin should have been located 30km away at the CBD Police Centre or in a Command Truck	Disagree	*"At Cronulla...it was a great location... to command,* [as with this kind of] *single event you need to be there on the ground... If you've got the one area* [as was the case at Cronulla] *rather than multiple ones,* [as was the case with the revenge attacks] *it's by far the better approach...far better than being stuck in a command vehicle watching CCTV"*.

Strike Force Neil Assertion	Our Assessment	Ron Mason Perspective
Use of hostage negotiators not considered	Raised by Hazzard in discussion but contested	[At the initial demonstration and the revenge attacks which followed] *"there was no apparent leader or leaders to negotiate with...First off to negotiate, you need someone to negotiate with. Who are you going to negotiate with? Who's in charge? Who do you talk to? Do you talk to Alan Jones and negotiate with him? Who do you talk to?*
Police need a command vehicle	Of limited benefit.	...*they got a vehicle...I don't think it was ever used"*.
NSW Police needed a Public Oder Commander's Course	One already existed	*"How would he know"*?

Discussion

On the Strike Force Neil assertion of poor planning ahead of the 'event', we asked for Supt. Mason's comment on whether or not the key police planning and operational personnel leading up to and during the Cronulla riots were interviewed by anyone on the investigation team. We have tabulated his response below:

Name	Position	Role	Interviewed
Mark Hutchings	Superintendent Operations Manager Sydney	Oversaw Planning of police response to all Public Order and major events in Central Metro Region, including Cronulla Riots	No
Wayne Laycock	Inspector, Sydney	Senior Planner Public Order Management	No
Ben Millington	Snr Sergeant, Emergency Management Coordinator, Sydney	Member Planning Team	No
Ron Mason	Superintendent, Sydney CBD Commander	Commander Operation Seta at Cronulla from 12 Dec 05 onwards	No

The lead NSW Police role for planning & logistics (at that time) of major & public order events, including Cronulla / Revenge Attacks, was allocated to Insp. Wayne Laycock. Supt. Mason regarded him as possibly the most capable public order planner the NSW Police had to offer. He was not surprised that no interview took place.

Supt. Mason advised that not a single police public order planner with whom he was well familiar in NSW Police was seconded to the Strike Force Neil 'investigation' and lamented that, *"even they couldn't deny that".*

Supt. Mason still believes now, that despite the criticism from Strike Force Neil, the planning and operation of policing at Cronulla and beyond in late 2005/early 2006, dealt very effectively with the fear of harm, the breaches of the peace and the restoration of order to the streets of Sydney. In his view it was and remains an excellent plan, despite what may have been said on the matter to the contrary:

> **Mason:** *"I've been involved in thousands of operations from New Year's Eve to even the Olympics, involved with planning. I was in charge of all the demonstrations in the Olympics. I've never seen a more effective plan* [than the one prepared ahead of the Cronulla Riots]*".*

When advised that the second in command of the Strike Force had openly acknowledged he had never planned or commanded the police response to a major public order disturbance and that the investigation would be a great experience for him:

> **Mason:** [Would] *"you get* [police officers to] *do a motor vehicle investigation that have never seen a motor vehicle before... You've got all these people that have never* [commanded a public order event],*all of a sudden they're testing and judging performance of people who have. It's ridiculous. Why would you do that?"*

PART 5:
EXPLAINING THE RIOT

17

Was it Really a Riot?

"That's not a riot. I'll show you a riot".[78]

The events at Cronulla and beyond in late 2005/early 2006 have been almost universally labelled by media, scholars, social commentators and the general community by the nomenclature of a 'riot' or, given the revenge attacks, as 'riots'. But what does it mean for an event such as this to be labelled in this way? Is it an accurate one, or a misnomer?

To be able to properly consider and answer these questions we need to first consider what is meant by the term, where it fits in the continuum of human protest, how that lines up with our recent history of riots, and finally, is it an accurate descriptor for what happened at Cronulla.

In assessing these questions, the following pessimistic account of 'scholarship' on past collective protest is pertinent:

> *"Much of what has passed for the analysis of violent crowds, riots and similar collective action has been characterised by a failure to define precisely what it seeks to explain,* [and] *a lack of empirical evidence to* [either] *support its claims...* [or understand] *the meaning of* [the]... *actions* [of those involved]*".*[79]

Hopefully, our own 'analysis' will pass muster.

---

[78] R. Mason, Transcript of Interview, 9 March 2021.
[79] P. Bagguley, and Y. Hussain, *Ethnic Conflict in Multicultural Britain*, Routledge, 2008, p. 36.

What is a riot?

Throughout modern urban and political history there have been countless examples of angry citizens taking protest to a level which confronts law enforcement personnel, government and the wider community. The causes and consequences of each are many and varied. A spectrum of collective human anger expressed in protest ranges from the very mild to the most communally convulsive.

A suggested range of that expression of collective anger is set out in the table below in ascending order:

No:	Name	Description
1	Meeting	A few people drawn together to discuss a contentious issue which can descend into conspiracy.
2	Gathering	A much broader audience, sometimes in the thousands, to support or promote an issue or cause with widespread appeal and support.
3	Protest / Demonstration	A large crowd, stationary or on the move, to bring a complaint loudly and publicly, to the attention of government.
4	Breach of Peace	Mild level lawlessness, some property damage with low level violence, usually quickly contained.
5	Riot	More serious levels of violence, injuries and even deaths, usually significant property damage, major confrontations with law enforcement, not easily contained.
6	Rebellion	Armed attack and massive protest in huge numbers, usually in many places, against government and law enforcement.
7	Coup	A quick and sometimes bloodless removal of government often by the military.
8	Revolution	A violent upheaval involving the societal destruction of the established political, religious and commercial norms and order.

On any reckoning of what occurred during the more serious acts of violence and property damage at Cronulla and beyond, it was more than just a placard wielding demonstration, and a lot less than a full armed rebellion against the state. Accordingly, we will focus on the kind of conflict which lies between the two, a breach of the peace and a riot. To get a better understanding of how best to describe what happened at Cronulla, it is of value to consider what these two terms mean, before considering our own more recent history of confrontational collective anger.

Breach of the peace

An ancient notion of English law, and inherited into Australian jurisdictions, has been that you are not entitled to behave in a way that disturbs the peace of the community, or individuals, by the violent or threatened violent behaviour to another, or damage or threatened damage of property of another. This notion was developed to ensure that citizens could peaceably go about their business, without harm, or the fear of harm to themselves, or their homes and possessions, without lawful excuse.

Where a threat, or actual interpersonal violence or property damage occurred, then Justices of the Peace, and later police, were empowered to take appropriate action to prevent the behaviour or to arrest offenders.

> *"The preservation of the peace has long been at the heart of public law and ultimately concerned with the prevention, control and limitation of spontaneous violence and its social and political consequences."*[80]

The NSW Court of Criminal Appeal in 2017 took this even further and found that "a breach of the peace includes 'a wide range of actions and threatened actions that interfere with the ordinary operation of civil society'".[81]

Riot

Given we never hear the term 'The Cronulla Breaches of the Peace', but an almost ubiquitous, 'The Cronulla Riots', we will concentrate our discussion on the latter rather than the former.

As at Cronulla, and just about everywhere else, when a group of protesters take their placard waving, chanting and demonstrating to something more confrontational, the word 'riot' is quickly thrown into the mix to describe what has happened. It is not always an accurate descriptor. Throwing a punch, hurling a bottle, swearing or shirtfronting police, and breaking a window or two, does not lift the event from common assault, vandalism and breach of the peace, to one of riotous behaviour warranting a substantial law enforcement response.

---

[80] B. Murphy, 'Retaining and Expanding Breach of Peace', *Criminal Law Journal*, (2017) 41 Crim LJ 1 pp.1-20, p. 1.
[81] New South Wales v Bouffler [2017] NSWCA 185, [164].

Reading the Riot Act

The first legislative steps to control riotous behaviour occurred in the UK with the passage in 1714 of the Riot Act, which was introduced following a series of public disturbances. The desire of *"political, social and economic"* elites for calm, order and *"public tranquillity"*, as opposed to the chaos, disorder and commotion of riot, is what underpinned this and later legislative measures to either discourage, or have the power to quell such outbursts of civil unpleasantness.[82]

The short form description of the original 1714 Act would have been clearly ominous for any gathering which might become unruly, disorderly, loud and breaching of the peace: *"An Act for preventing tumultuous and riotous assemblies, and for the more speedy and effectual punishing of rioters"*.

For us now, in a relatively more modern and tolerant era of general disdain for the death penalty, this Statute rather astonishingly, provided that the refusal to disperse by twelve or more persons, upon being ordered to do so by proclamation read to the crowd, was a capital crime punishable by death.

The words of the proclamation make for interesting reading:

> *"Our sovereign Lord the King chargeth and commandeth all persons, being assembled, immediately disperse themselves, and peaceable depart to their habitations, or to their lawful business, upon pains contained in the act made in the first year of King George, for preventing tumults and riotous assemblies. God save the King."*[83]

Not surprisingly, arguments ensued in the courts, as to whether or not the Riot Act was actually read in full, or only in part, or not at all, before police officers opened fire and began making arrests. In one infamous case, the UK 1839 Newport Rising, it was claimed that as the mayor stood from the window of the Westgate Hotel, he was prevented from completing the reading as he was shot and injured, mid-sentence.[84]

The Act was an effective means of addressing serious breaches of the peace by an unruly crowd acting in a noisy, threatening and disorderly manner. A 'Reading of the Riot Act' last occurred in England on the 3rd of August 1919 during a police strike, when troops had to be called in to restore order. The

---

[82] S. Body-Gendrot, 'Urban violence in France and London: comparing Paris (2005) and London (2011)', *Policing and Society*, (2013) 23:1, pp. 6-25, p. 7.
[83] UK Parliament, 'The 1714 Riot Act'.
[84] https://www.phrases.org.uk/meaning/read-the-riot-act.html

1714 Act was finally repealed in 1973, however, many jurisdictions around the world copied its provisions for dealing with troublesome law-breaking crowds.

The NSW Statutory definition of riot

The NSW Crimes ACT 1900 still contains the following provisions:

> **Section 93B:** *"Where 12 or more persons who are present together use or threaten unlawful violence for a common purpose and the conduct of them (taken together) is such as would cause a person of reasonable firmness present at the scene to fear for his or her safety"*

This is a useful starting point in NSW on what constitutes a riot: A common purpose of at least 12 people threatening unlawful violence such as to cause others to fear for their safety. The challenge, as is often the case, is in the interpretation of the meaning of the words, and the extent to which grouping, acting and threatening, all in concert might satisfy a judicial notion of riot.

Something more is needed, in our view, than a few people turning up, yelling offensive slogans, shaking a car or two, breaking a window and entertaining a fist fight. In our view, those actions constitute a 'breach of the peace', not a riot. We contend that any reasonable notion of a riot is usually a large gathering which is significantly violent and tumultuously confrontational. Let's look at some examples.

Ethnic violence in Northern Nigeria 2000/2001[85]

The riots in Nigeria in the cities of Kaduna in 2000 and Jos in 2001, are particularly apt for our assessment of the Cronulla Riots, as they involved, like Cronulla, an unexpected and quickly escalated conflict between local Christian and Muslim communities. However, in Nigeria, at both Kaduna and Jos, they were far more violent, deadly and destructive than at Cronulla.

Kaduna 2000: In February 2000, over a four-day period, Kaduna exploded into appalling levels of Christian-Muslim violence. It started as a peaceful protest by unarmed Christians opposed to the application to them of Sharia Law. However, much like at Cronulla with its fair share of bigoted anti-Muslim placards and body tattoos, there were a number of provocative signs making pejorative and disrespectful aspersions. One example: *"Shari'a is not Y2K Compliant"*.

---

[85] A. Scacco, 'Anatomy of a Riot Participation in Ethnic Violence in Nigeria', *WZB Berlin Social Science Center,* April 2021.

At some point stones began to be thrown by one group at the other, and almost unbelievably, within the hour, a full battle was underway in the local central market between Muslim traders and Christian protestors, with stones and wooden planks used as weapons. Churches and mosques were set alight and nearly 1,300 people were killed. The conflict could not be contained by local police and the military had to be called in to restore order. This was a full-scale riot.

Jos 2001: In a city of large Christian and Muslim residents, a long understood local practice of Christians not walking past mosques during Friday prayers, was breached on the 7th of September 2001, by a Christian woman, an argument ensued with a Muslim security guard who allegedly slapped her. Within minutes a rumour of the attack spread and before the hour was up, fighting began outside the Mosque between men of each religion, which within a few hours led to the Mosque being consumed by flames.

What followed over the next few days was both unexpected and frightening, as dozens of churches and mosques were burned, pitched battles between residents spread over a wide area, and over a thousand people were killed. This was a full-scale riot.

Political violence in South Africa 2021[86]

In July 2021, the Constitutional Court of South Africa issued a warrant for the arrest of former President Jacob Zuma, for failing to appear before, and give evidence to an inquiry into corruption during his nine years in office.

A combination of party and tribal loyalty to the ANC Zulu leader, political opportunism for settling scores, poverty, and a wider view of disenfranchisement, led to nine days of almost industrial scale looting, assassinating, murdering, and property damage. The ensuing conflagration led to the destruction of 160 shopping malls, 11 warehouses and 8 factories, as well as damage to numerous banks, pharmacies, and post offices. There was evidence of Indian and Black community members in Durban, racially profiling the other for entry restriction and vigilante action.

342 people died including 170 suspected murders, 3,400 arrested, 132 acts

---

[86] South African Government News Agency, '*Unrest death toll rises to 337*', Thursday, July 22, 2021; SA news.gov.au; S. Mkhwanazi, 'Mapisa-Nqakula: We have deployed 25,000 troops', July 15, 2021; www.iol.co.za; L. Prinsloo, and R. Henderson, 'As Rioters Overwhelm Police, South African Civilians Step in', *Bloomberg*. July 14, 2021.

of arson, thousands of jobs and small businesses adversely affected, 25,000 troops deployed, and a large part of the Republic of South Africa simply terrorised. It was the worst violence the country had seen since the end of Apartheid. This was a full-scale riot.

Compared to Cronulla

These almost insurrection levels of violence, killing and property damage, so put what happened at Cronulla into the pale, as to leave anyone considering a comparison wondering how the events in Sydney in late 2005/early 2006 were ever described as riots. Before further considering this point, it is useful to consider some scholarly definitions of riot.

Ethnic riot: Given that Cronulla involved what might be called an ethnic conflict, or racial profiling between tribal belligerents, a definition of an 'ethnic riot' may assist our consideration of how best to describe those events.

Following Hindu-Muslim riots in India two studies provided the following definitions:[87]

> "An event involving large numbers of massed persons from opposing ethnic groups engaged in assaults on persons, lives and property".
>
> "An intense, sudden, though not wholly unplanned, lethal attack by civilian members of one ethnic group on civilian members of another ethnic group, the victims chosen because of their group membership".

How do these definitions line up with what happened at Cronulla? The initial demonstration on 11 December 2005 at North Cronulla Beach was certainly a large mass of Caucasians expressing anger about Arabic visitors, and apart from the attack on the train upon two unsuspecting 'visitors', there was little by way of assault or property damage. The revenge attacks did involve the use of baseball bats and knives, some occasional serious injuries, about 30 cars smashed up but no-one was killed.

The point made by Alexandra Scacco is a sound one:[88] *"The term 'intense' evokes a similar image as... 'massed', suggesting that riots need to assume at least reasonably large scale in order to be classified as such".*

---

[87] A. See Scacco, 'Anatomy of a Riot', p. 9.
[88] A. Scacco, 'Anatomy of a Riot', p. 9.

The convoys of vehicularised revenge attacks marauding across the streets of Sydney looking for Caucasian persons and property to assault and injure, might struggle to fit into this definition. If not, then the 'Cronulla Riots' would become the 'Cronulla Riot', but only if the initial event at the beach was something more violent and sinister than the evidence suggests.

Generic riot: It would seem that the critical component here, is that for an event to be properly designated as a riot, there needs to be a significant collection of angry people exacting a serious level of personal violence and property damage both in kind and degree. In other words, a few acts of unpleasant violent criminal behaviour are just that, breaches of the criminal code, but not a riot.

It will be always a moot point, as to just what point the violence and property damage needs to reach, to then consider it a riot. Based on the case studies above, it would seem it is high bar never before reached in the Australian context. Additionally, we have no real examples of mass looting of shops and stores which is also often, but not always, a part of riotous behaviour.[89]

> "...all riots share common foundations and factors and must include violence and damage to public or private property to warrant the term and any confrontation between riots and police is a consequence of the incident".[90]

Given the challenge in accurately delineating the line beyond which collective protest moves from a breach of the peace to a riot, is a very subjective one, then not surprisingly, some scholars have even suggested, that such a descriptor is issued to an event as a political judgment rather than one reflecting an analytical determination. This could describe the almost universal application of the term to Cronulla.[91]

Before looking at our history of riots and what they mean for Cronulla, a couple of recent European 'riots' provide interesting comparison with our version closer to home.

---

[89] J. Havercroft, 'Why is there no just riot theory?', February 15, 2020, preprints. aspanet.org; G. den Heyer, 'What constitutes a Riot?', *Police Response to Riots*, Chapter 2, pp.15-47, see pp.16-18.
[90] T. Bateman, 'With the benefit of hindsight: The disturbances of August 2011 in historical context' (2012), referred to in G. den Heyer, G. 'What constitutes a Riot?', p.18.
[91] G. Den Heyer, pp. 17-18.

Paris 2005: The Paris riot of 2005, occurred just a few weeks before the events at Cronulla, involved thousands of angry Muslim young men protesting against unemployment, poverty, disenfranchisement and police harassment.

On the 27th of October 2005, police responded to a call that there had been a break-in at a construction site and a number of youths dispersed upon the arrival of police. Two youths who hid in an electrical substation died from electrocution. This set alight what had been long simmering tensions amongst many French economically poor Muslim youth, which quickly engulfed Paris and many other regional urban centres across France.

The conflict lasted three weeks leaving 3 dead, 2,990 arrested, 8,873 vehicles burned, 126 police and firefighters injured and 18,000 police needing to be deployed. This was a riot.

London 2011: As is often the case, a seemingly isolated but socially serious incident takes place which unexpectedly lights the kindle of conflagration. In this case, it was the death of one Mark Duggan on 4 August 2011, after being shot by police. Two days later, the Duggan family and 120 supporters peacefully marched to the local police station for answers from senior police who refused to meet with them. The crowd was very dissatisfied with this snub by police and reacted angrily. *"Bottles were thrown...two police cars were set on fire* [and] *looting took place in two large local stores which police were unable to stop"*.[92] The conflict then quickly escalated to towns and cities across the UK.

When it all ended just a week later, 15,000 had been actively involved in the disorder, 5 were dead, over 3,000 arrests had been made, 1,300 of whom received custodial sentences on average of 17 months each; 100 major fires; cars, homes and shops attacked and burned, a warehouse destroyed, 186 police injured, homes and shops looted, and a massive deployment of police.[93] This was a riot.

Our own history of riots

Throughout the 1970's in Australia, a culture emerged of rights movements,

---

[92] S. Bendy-Gendrot, 'Urban violence in France and England', p. 13.
[93] T. Newburn, 'The 2011 England riots in European context: A framework for understanding the 'life-cycle' of riots", *European Journal of Criminology* 2016, Vol.13)5) pp. 540-555, see p. 544.

protests, political activism, pop-culture and drugs. Demonstrations took place protesting Australia's involvement in the Vietnam War, Aboriginal Rights, Land Rights, Women's Rights, Gay & Lesbian Rights, Working Conditions, Multiculturalism, Immigration, Environmental issues, the South African Springboks tour and an array of other single-issue agendas. Free speech and anti-authoritarianism grew. Often police at the frontline were the target, as they were visible agents of government and the keepers of law and order. Better technology meant better media coverage, which in-turn sparked a greater and wider community interest in social justice issues, challenges to tradition, defiance of authority and calls for change. It was a somewhat snowballing effect, with media coverage of protests and demonstrations leading to more public awareness and participation, thus increasing the number, size and complexity of protests and demonstrations, and with that came confrontations with police.

We have set out below some well-known examples of our major collective protest in NSW since the late 1970s which have generally been given the moniker of 'riot':

Date	Place	Cause	Description
1978	Sydney CBD	Gay rights	The first major protest seeking decriminalising of homosexuality and an end to police harassment. Violent confrontations with police and 53 protestors arrested. It had a transformative impact on legal and social change.
1979	Newcastle	Star Hotel closure	An unexpected announcement by brewery company Tooth and Co. that the rundown working class pub known as The Star Hotel was to be closed, met with some considerable local angst. The scheduled last night of operations with music, alcohol and revelry with over 2,000 people in attendance did not react well to a police request to stop the music and close up at 10pm. It quickly descended into throwing of bottles and beer cans, police cars set alight, injuries and arrests of over 40 people.

Date	Place	Cause	Description
1980s	Bathurst	Alcohol	The Australian Motorcycle Grand Prix events at Bathurst every Easter long weekend attracted amongst its thousands of spectators, large numbers of heavily drinking campers who would confront police, their vehicles and compound, with rocks, bricks, bottles and even sticks of gelignite. It was an annual violent event with hundreds of arrests, but mostly curbed by alcohol being banned from the event.
2004	Redfern	Police engagement	A 17-year-old Aboriginal youth riding his bike in this poor rundown estate known as 'The Block' was killed when impaled on fence stake whilst eluding a routine police patrol. Locals reacted angrily; bricks, fireworks and Molotov cocktails thrown at police. Fire brigade hoses used to disperse the crowd, 40 police injured, a vehicle set alight and some damage to the local railway station.
2005	Macquarie Fields	Police engagement	A 20-year-old Aboriginal man being pursued by police within a Macquarie Fields public housing estate crashed his car into a tree killing his 17- and 19-year-old passengers. Locals quickly came out in anger, began abusing and throwing projectiles at police. This soon escalated to 300 people clashing with police over 4 nights, hurling rocks, bottles, bricks, petrol bombs and setting cars alight. It lasted 4 nights before order was restored.
2005	Cronulla	Inter-tribal conflict	Two Caucasian lifeguards assaulted at Cronulla Beach by visiting Lebanese men. 5000 locals protested; revenge attacks followed. Order restored after 2,000 police engaged, 200 arrests, some injuries and property damage.

If the five case studies above from Africa and Europe, set the standard of violence and property damage justifying a collective public protest warranting the description of 'riot', then it would seem that none of our own local 'riots' would meet it. However, given that apart from the annual Bathurst riots in the 1980s, we have had so few significant breaks in our civil 'tranquillity', it is little wonder that these unexpected challenging and confrontational acts of violence, unruly behaviour and property damage might be given such a description.

But just because we are not used to noticeable breaches of the peace, doesn't make them a riot per se. In many respects, it is the outcome when the dust is settled, as to how a public disturbance might be best described. How many killed and injured, how many vehicles, shops and buildings burned, and the level of police or military deployed to contain the rage.

The confronting TV footage of the 1985 Bathurst Racetrack attacks on the police compound, and the TV footage of the railway carriage attack at Cronulla, both encouraged a 'riot' descriptor. However, even these in our view, like the other 'riots' listed above would struggle, when compared to our international examples, to meet the level of violating and violent significance to life, limb, property and law enforcement, as to warrant use of the term.

The comparison of our 'riots' with those of the United States challenges our use of the term 'riot' no less than the overseas examples set out above.

The Los Angeles Riots 1992

Just a few days after the January 2005 troubles at Macquarie Fields, the Los Angeles Police Chief, Bill Bratton was visiting Sydney at the invitation of the NSW Police leadership. As the former Chief of Police of NYPD and then current Chief of LAPD, he was well used to major racial, ethnic and political explosions which would destroy whole city blocks, injure countless people, involve massive arrests and huge police deployment. He was savvy at media and did not disappoint when asked about the Macquarie Fields 'riot':

> "[It] *doesn't equate with some of my experiences...there was minimal damage, minimal injuries to police and civilians...I had to chuckle. I'm looking and I'm asking 'What's the problem?' I just don't see it...What you are dealing with here doesn't approach in any way shape or form the state of what we deal with in America."*

Was it Really a Riot?

Of the countless and far more conflagrating protests in the USA, the one which stands out amongst many, would be the almost insurrection levels of violence and property damage in Los Angeles which followed the acquittal on 29 April 1992 of four police officers charged with using excessive force during the arrest of Rodney King. The "flashpoint" here was the acquittal not the assault, unlike the igniting of the 'Black Lives Matter' movement in the USA, which quickly followed the police killing of George Floyd in Minneapolis on 25 May 2020.

In LA all those years ago, the video footage over many nights graphically recorded an event unimaginably confronting for us here in Australia: 63 people killed, 2,383 injured, 12,000 arrested, 3,600 fires lit, 1,100 buildings destroyed, widespread looting and a massive police response including the calling out of the National Guard.[94] This was a full-scale riot.

Thankfully, apart from Macquarie Fields and Cronulla, both in 2005, we have not had in NSW any major level of public disorder, and certainly nothing like what has happened overseas. We will now consider whether or not our 'riots' should be labelled as such.

The Macquarie Fields Riot 2005

The Macquarie Fields 'Riot' was the first real test of NSW Police responding to a significant community disturbance for an exceptionally long time and the response revealed several areas for improvement. It was also the first of two 'riots' new Police Minister Carl Scully had to deal with in his first 10 months in the portfolio.

Like Cronulla, the TV footage during the evening news was confronting but for different reasons; police too few in number, too tame, just holding their line, no arrests and no real effort to quell what looked like an unacceptable breach of the peace. The overall image and then of course, Shock Jock and tabloid newspaper presentation was one of a scared police force unable or unwilling to press the point. The new police minister met the next day with all the police senior leadership at the Macquarie Fields Police Station and made it clear that the police needed to do better, in greater number and with greater intention. It was hard to get the message through:

---

[94] A. Sastry, and K. N. Bates, 'When LA Erupted in Anger: A Look Back at the Rodney King Riots', *NPR*, April 26, 2017, www.npr.org.

Scully: *"I voiced these concerns to all the senior police brains in the room which included the Commissioner and both Deputy Commissioners, but I immediately felt underwhelmed with their responses. I said: 'Gentleman, I have only been in this job for just 7 weeks, and I must defer to your considerable experience in policing on how best to handle this but are you sure you have got it covered. You say 150 police will be enough tonight if the disturbance continues but I question that. Is that really enough?'*

Once I was back in the car I immediately rang the Commissioner: 'Ken, you blokes have got to be kidding. 150 cops tonight is simply not good enough. You need hundreds more to give a huge presence and to restore order. Hundreds more. I want you to rethink this and get back to me as soon as possible.' 15 minutes later he called back to advise that the number of police was being increased to 600.

This just about floored me, that an ex-lawyer turned pollie with no policing experience, had had to step in and effectively take over the strategic decision making of the NSW Police for the effective resourcing of a major public disorder event."

Thankfully, police then quickly became more proactive, in three more nights restored order, rounded up the main troublemakers, and 'returned to barracks'. It was an unpleasant event but hardly a 'riot'.

The internal review of police performance at Macquarie Fields was conducted with a view to learning and improving, rather than blaming and scapegoating. Out of the former process came the new Public Order and Riot Squad.

Back to Cronulla

On the question of the daytime event at Cronulla itself, we have examined both the literature and interviewed key community leaders at the time. Whilst we concede that it remains a contested notion, a range of views used descriptors for Cronulla as a 'party', a 'demonstration', a 'disturbance' to a 'mobile breach of the peace' but only the scholars and media commentators have stuck to a 'riot'. Let's look at some of these interpretations:

Was it just a party? In what was probably an unintentionally light-hearted academic contribution, Judy Lattas, somewhat unconvincingly argued that the Cronulla troubles were all just one big party getting out of hand and nothing more sinister.

> "...a party turning 'ugly' is an expected outcome of youthful male recreation. A fight or bust up is looked forward to with pleasure as a valued aspect of the experience of leisure, conceived and enjoyed as an opportunity of letting go".[95]

Judy Lattas argues that the broader interpretations of appalling behaviour before, during and after the 'riot' are misconceived and it all boiled down mostly to a really good time just getting out of hand:

> "As it turned out, fuelled by alcohol and the pleasurable prospect of 'letting go', the day became unreasonable and intolerant; aggressive and violent. In the perception of my informants, its party-time progress from happy camaraderie to ugly brawl followed a recognisable social script. The bad behaviour of the rioters and the chanters had more to do with the recreational culture of hegemonic masculinity, they understand, than it did with any 'criminal'/ 'lout' exception in Australia."[96]

Or just a demonstration? One of the first articles written about the Cronulla event was by Ryan Barclay and Peter West published in *People and Place* in 2006.[97] They called it a 'demonstration'. In doing so, they attempted, perhaps clumsily or even naively, to describe the idyllic nature of the average Australian to newcomers and beach sharing: *"Thus Australians seem to have a talent for being inclusive and welcome strangers to their shore".*[98]

In a generic pitch to what occurs almost every day peacefully on our beaches:

> "...the range of behaviour on the beach is wide. People do not, as a rule, care very much about the religious beliefs, opinions, or other aspects of those lying near them. The beach in Australia is a public domain open to use by everyone. Nobody owns the beach; it is a space shared by those who turn up."

This might apply generally to Sydney beaches but would not have been so

---

[95] J. Lattas, p. 331.
[96] J. Lattas, p. 331.
[97] R. Barclay and P. West, 'Racism or Patriotism? An eyewitness account of the Cronulla demonstration of 11 December 2005', *People and Place*, Vol.14, No.1, 2006, pp. 75-85.
[98] Barclay and West, p. 75.

accurate in the simmering discontent at Cronulla leading up to the troubles in late 2005. Barclay and West also provide a good account of a collection of people at Cronulla, responding to incivility and misogyny, meeting in protest, it building to a demonstration, alcohol being added in, which then shifted many in the crowd from patriotic fervour to racist pursuit: *"Little by little, the crowd became an angry mob"*.[99]

If the TV news footage of Sunday 11 December 2005, had been a long presentation of the day, rather than a very short, edited version of its worst aspects, then the event would have seemed far more like a protest to 'save our beach', and a demonstration in favour of 'Aussieness', but then with alcohol flowing in the summer sun, a large vocal mob encouraged the relatively few to become violent. And despite the excesses at the end, it was mostly for most attendees a demonstration, not a riot. This interpretation reflects similar views expressed by former MP for Cronulla Malcolm Kerr, when we interviewed him in December 2020:

"...people were demonstrating...there was very little property damage, very little physical harm compared to what was happening at the same time in Paris for days actually".

Maybe just a disturbance: In February 2021, we interviewed former local Cronulla police officer and long serving lifeguard, Lee Howell and he also distanced himself from the events being described as a riot:

"...because this never happens...I think that word was grabbed out of the sky and said, 'A riot'. And we just said, 'That's not a riot. That's a disturbance'".

A breach of the peace: In early December 2020, we interviewed former Supt. John Richardson who at the time of the Cronulla events was the Commander of the Campsie Local Area Command which covered Lakemba and Punchbowl, two areas of significance regarding the revenge attacks. The former Superintendent was quite dismissive of the notion that what had occurred was a riot:

"I've seen riots and I've seen them in Paris...in London, and...in America...That was no riot in Cronulla. It was a disturbance of the peace that got a bit out of hand".

---

[99] Barclay and West, p. 80.

A riot then?

It is our contention, that based on a reasonable assessment of what happened at Cronulla during the daylight hours of 11 December 2005, when compared to both scholarship and international experience, a clearly unpleasant and confronting affray and breaches of the peace occurred, which did not reach a threshold of seriousness as to warrant it being described as a riot. The 'revenge attacks' had a far greater level of physical violence, assaults, injuries and property damage en-mass, which might have warranted the term 'riot', but only a limited amount of this actually occurred at Cronulla.

However, given the universality of the use of the term 'Cronulla Riots' by the media at the time, its continued comprehensive use by scholars and academics, and its ubiquitousness as a descriptor of those confronting events, we have elected to proceed with using the term throughout this book.

18

Did the Media cause the Riots?

"...the mass media provide a delivery system for image events that explode 'in the public's consciousness to transform the way people view their world"'.[100]

The visual image of the Cronulla Riots

An indelible and graphic image for us all regarding the Cronulla Riots, was formed on the evening of Sunday the 11th of December, 2005 when all four TV news channels broadcast shocking scenes of young, inebriated, Caucasian males chanting racist slogans, searching for 'Arabs' and assaulting them and damaging property. It was nasty, it was ugly, and possibly reflected an end to what we had all understood and admired as a tolerant and respectful multi-cultural Australia.

These visual images have left a mark upon our memories of what happened that day all those years ago, and revealed for all to witness, the racist and violent way in which some amongst us might descend if provoked. But are the images a fair and accurate record of what occurred and an impartial unbiased presentation of what became known as a truly racist community on the south side of Sydney? Or are they a selection of carefully picked editor's narrow views through filtered lenses of the events and mood over an entire day to sensationalise evening news?

The contrast between what police observed in managing and responding to the crowd throughout the whole day, and what they watched on the evening news, seemed a complete disconnect.

---

[100] K.M. DeLuca, and J. Peoples, 'From Public Sphere to Public Screen: Democracy, Activism, and the 'Violence" of Seattle'', *Critical Studies in Media Communication*, Vol.19, No.2, June 2002, pp.125-151, see p. 138.

Did the Media cause the Riots?

Before the evening news TV broadcast, police were satisfied that the event on North Cronulla Beach had becalmed, and with people going home, Police Command pulled about 150 of the police on duty back into the command post on the first floor of the North Cronulla Surf Club. The strategy was to make it look to the crowd like the event was over and everyone was going home. It worked. The police were fed and ready for immediate redeployment should they be needed. A number of police, taking a well-earned rest in front of the Club's TV, were rather surprised at the skewed journalism on the 6pm news broadcasts showing only a series of violent snippets strung together in quick succession with sensationalist voice-overs by news presenters, making it look like the whole 5000 strong crowd at Cronulla had acted like this the entire day.

In actual fact, the far greater proportion of the day was taken up with people milling around, BBQ's cooking, a surf boat launch by North Cronulla Surf Club and patriotic singing and waving of flags more like a typical Australia Day at Cronulla. The far greater majority of the crowd were just there rubbernecking and did not participate in any incident. The violent footage was real, the isolated incidents themselves were disgraceful, but the angled, close-up and selective editing was deceiving in our view.

For police on duty that day, including their commanders, this disconnect between the evening broadcast to millions of viewers, with the reality of what actually happened during the greater proportion of the entire day, is one of their lasting memories. Yes, 5,000 people turned up, many of whom chanted racially offensive slogans, and a small few did take their protest to xenophobic violence. But just a mere 100 out of 5,000 were eventually arrested, charged and processed through the courts. Isolated incidents of 'shock & awe' imagery of violence and racism were strung together in quick succession by TV news cutting rooms to make it look like the entire crowd behaved in this atrocious manner for the entire day. This was just not the case, but it suited the agenda, justified the intense media hype in the build-up prior to the event, and was great for ratings.

There were literally hundreds of hungry journalists there on the day eagerly waiting for something to occur, so they could get at least some imagery and report back to their just as eagerly awaiting editors. The disappointed looks on journo's faces for most of the day was palpable, as the whole event was looking like a complete flop instead of the racist scoop they were hoping for, until things heated up in the afternoon and a few sporadic acts of violence did occur, which was captured by a multitude of waiting cameras from numerous angles, and strung together for the evening news. But the actual reality is, most of the 5,000 turned up to watch people watching, to drink, to party and to chant but not to undertake offensive and criminal acts. However, from the TV coverage that night with careful editorial precision, and the feigned outrage of the presenters, it certainly did seem like the whole mass of demonstrators had embarked on a massive racist bender against Arabic looking people. No wonder, the young impressionable Lebanese men of Lakemba felt aggrieved, disrespected and in need of protecting not a beach, but their valour.

Goodwin recalls his reaction to the TV news of that day:

> *"The footage was real footage and accurately captured what a small number of ratbags had done that day but did not capture that almost all who attended had not criminalised the event. They were loud, they were memorable, they drank, they chanted and cheered and then went home. Only the few shown on TV did some unforgivable things which etched in the minds of many.*
>
> *What was not portrayed and certainly not explained in the Newsreader narrative was that the few minutes of worrisome footage had been obtained over the course of an entire day of mostly peaceful gathering and protest, punctuated by short bursts of the few acting in a fit of xenophobic violence. But that would not have made for a good story".*

Malcolm Kerr, the MP for Cronulla at the time, best summed it up during our interview with him: *"The media coverage, the optics were out of proportion to what had actually happened".*[101]

However, did this edited and angled TV footage cause, or contribute to the revenge attacks? We submit, how could it have not? This extraordinary 'parallel universe' presentation and graphic video footage by the TV newsrooms on the day, must to a large degree explain social commentators and scholars, and even many amongst the media itself, forming an unmovable opinion of Sutherland and Cronulla being xenophobic enclaves. However, in our view, it underpins the need for a wider inquiry of exploring more generally the role the media played in contributing to the riots.

---

[101] M. Kerr, Transcript of Interview, December 10, 2020.

What is the 'media'?

In order to properly discuss the media's contribution, we need to define what we mean by media. What is meant by 'the media' in this context? Did some elements of 'the media' report the conflict and others contribute to it? These are not easy questions to answer but are important to consider.

The word 'media' is used far too freely and a catch all for any journalistic, tabloid, TV, or radio anchor commentary. Some unpacking of the threads of this term is needed to get a gist of what role separate elements of the media may have played in doing more than just reporting the news, but actually contributing to its creation.

For many, the term 'media', is best understood in its traditional guise, as the plural of medium through which written, filmed or spoken news content, is disseminated unilaterally to a substantial audience who read, watch or listen to it. Each medium of newspapers, TV news, or radio programmes when drawn together are universally known by the moniker, 'media'. Not surprisingly, the tabloids, TV news and 'Shock Jock' radio announcers all contributed to the mass communication of opinionated messaging leading up to and during the Cronulla Riots. These three easily fit the bill of what is normally understood by 'media'.

More difficult, is how or where to place in the midst of this, the relatively (then) newcomer of mass communication by text message via mobile phones. As this means of communication played a much greater role in projecting messages of defiance, than any other kind of medium at the time, where it sits in any medium continuum is an important question. If texts are not traditional media, and are not social media, then where do they fit?

Definitions of 'social media' *"typically exclude other 'new media', such as e-mail and text messaging"*, which are normally *"not included in typological lists of social media"*.[102] Whilst texts and e-mails may not be classified as social media, they do share one very important thing in common. Unlike traditional media, they are both interactive exchange-based forms of content communication. 'New media' normally encompasses anything digitally disseminated, which can include both interactive content like texts, or emails, or more traditionally non-interactive produced content such as

---

[102] C. T. Carr, and R. A. Hayes, 'Social Media: Defining, Developing, and Divining', *Atlantic Journal of Communication,* 23:1, pp. 46-65, see p. 48.

podcasts and online newspapers.[103]

Our purpose here is a lot narrower than casting a wide net on better understanding the changing nature of news, information and social exchange through and from various communication media. We are simply concerned, given the profound impact of texting during the Cronulla Riots, that this is properly regarded as a form of communication medium, along with the more conventional notions of disseminating 'news'. We will give it the moniker 'new media' as that seems to be the most appropriate communication pigeonhole for it at the time of late 2005.

The 'media' did it! Really?

It is a little amusing that some social commentators in almost the same sentence can decry the racist Sutherland Shire, but then lament that the good folks of the Shire were panicked into a vigilante response stirred up by White Supremacists and Shock Jock journalism.[104]

The idea that otherwise quiet law abiding citizens rose in racist violent anger because they were all 'morally panicked' by media commentators is questionable on two grounds. Firstly, it assumes that there was no simmering inter-tribal groundswell of discontent which erupted and secondly, considerably overstates the influence of media reporting on human behaviour.

That is not to say, that the media did not contribute adversely, did not add fuel to the fire, did not encourage offensive text messaging, or had no role at all in stoking the fires of discontent. They did all this and more. However, it is a big call to claim that the locals and the visitors were innocent as it was all the fault of the media!

Our point is that there were such deep unresolved inter-tribal resentments, that it is a stretch to suggest or imply that it was mostly media driven. People do not just turn up in the thousands like human automatons to protest because Alan Jones, The Daily Telegraph or mass text messaging told

---

[103] See for example, J. Cote, *'What is New Media?'*, Southern New Hampshire University, February 24, 2020, www.snhu.edu.
[104] S. Poynting, "Thugs' and 'grubs' at Cronulla From media beat-ups to beating up migrants', in *Outrageous! Moral panics in Australia*, ACYS Publishing, 2007, pp. 158-170.

them to do so. There must have been something within, something already brewing, something stirring the emotions, to result in such behaviour.

That said, many elements of the media were unhelpful, did fan the flames of discontent, and could hardly argue they were just reporting an opinionated slant on news. Whilst the ingredients for conflict had simmered for an extensive period, inter-tribal angst was certainly fuelled by provocative talk back, disgraceful vigilante text messaging and selective video feeds:

> "The popular media, notably tabloid newspapers and talk back radio, spent the following week [after the attack on the Cronulla lifeguards on Dec 4, 2005] exaggerating the numbers involved, the brutality of the attack, the extent of injuries and the frequency of such events, and racializing all these aspects to allege an inherent criminality and deviant masculinity of Lebanese-Australian men".[105]

The police investigators on Strike Force Neil also sought to explain why the attack on the lifeguard exploded into riot, whereas other earlier incidents had not:

> "The difference between this incident [the riot on 11 Dec 2005] and others and how it led to riotous behaviour was arguably, the colourful, exaggerated and inaccurate way it was described over the following days".[106]

There are four elements of media we will consider relative to the Cronulla Riots: TV news footage, mass text messaging, *The Daily Telegraph* newspaper and finally, Alan Jones, the then 2GB morning breakfast radio 'Shock Jock' broadcaster.

The TV Footage

It is hard to imagine that the TV News footage across all channels on the evening of Sunday 11th of December 2005 did not have a pervasive influence on what people thought, said, and did following the 'reporting' of that event.

Unfortunately, almost all the footage was typical of "It's Good News Week"[107] style of media reporting which highlights the 'shock and awe'

---

[105] S. Poynting, "Thugs' and 'Grubs' at Cronulla', p. 159.
[106] Strike Force Neil Report, p. 27.
[107] J. King, *'It's Good News Week'*, song released in 1965 by British band, Hedgehoppers Anonymous.

element of visual confrontation, and ignores or considerably downplays, any leavening or mitigating angles and circumstances. The TV 'coverage' of the Cronulla Riot was a classic example of angled video and selective reporting designed to maximise viewer interest and draw out negative feelings and responses. It worked. Anyone who saw the images still remembers them. Anyone watching them even now is appalled by the same images. But was it the real news? Truth and what were or are actual irrefutable facts are always contextual, dependent on the wider circumstances for the full picture and a more accurate determination of what happened, than what is usually presented or asserted anywhere, let alone during a superficial nightly TV News coverage. This is of course, a much deeper and broader philosophical question than one we are able to explore in this book. Suffice it to say, that being presented a version of facts or truth on TV may not necessarily be a wholly factual or truthful depiction when subjected to a broader situational scrutiny. This is in our view, very pertinent when it comes to considering the TV news of the evening of 11 December 2005.

As one scholarly article pointed out in respect of the 1999 World Trade Organisation (WTO) protests and violence at Seattle USA that:

> "By definition, the news is about what is new, what is out of the ordinary. The news is attracted to disturbers of order and deviation from routine. As the new adage goes 'if it bleeds, it leads'. Aside from bloodshed, nothing fits these parameters more precisely than symbolic protest violence and uncivil disobedience".[108]

The impact of images 'witnessed' by viewers can be quite profound and can cause quick disparaging judgments on behaviour without necessarily seeking or considering that there may well be a fuller picture or a wider context.

It is exceedingly difficult, if not impossible, to have a meaningful dialogue on an important issue when words are drowned out with the cacophonic impact of visual images projected over and over on TV screens, as newsrooms reach out for the sensory impact of winning and keeping audiences in the battle for ratings and commercial advertising revenue.

> "TV trades in a discourse dominated by images not words, a visual rhetoric...the visual bias of TV works against those deploying

---

[108] K. M. DeLuca and J. Peoples, 'From Public Sphere to Public Screen: Democracy, Activism, and the "Violence" of Seattle', p.138.

traditional, word-based forms of argument".[109]

This was certainly the case, in our view, of scholars who saw the images and then wrote at length in their own academic ratings war of published papers of just how shocking it all had been. Little of their words challenged the meaning of the images as perhaps suggesting more than what at first appeared.

An interesting comparison of the contrasting impact of 'official' video footage with that of the written word has been provided:

> "...*people's emotional reactions to events and their collective memories [are] different from the dissemination of information by texts...TV news images... have a degree of relative autonomy in the sense that the images themselves can potentially speak about the issue...images constrain the range of plausible interpretations*".[110]

We argue that the TV news footage broadcast during the evening of the 11th of December 2005 settled there and then, what had happened without any need or expressed desire for wordsmithing an alternative interpretation based on context and circumstance. These 'irrefutable visual facts' offended and angered social commentators, political leaders, and many locals alike. However, the 'facts' also deeply offended a core number of young aggressive male Lebanese Australians. Along with serial texting which had helped initiate the first riot and fired up an angry group of Lebanese 'visitors', this footage helped provoke violent and terrifying acts of revenge against anyone, or anything, that was regarded as a "them" and not an "us". Unfortunately, these 'Arabic Supremacists' were never outed for being as such, although much has been written about the role played by White Supremacists stirring up text message driven trouble in the first place.

Once again, the footage of itself did not cause young Lebanese males to respond quickly, aggressively, and violently. There had been simmering tribal tensions for years which underpinned the reaction in late December 2005, but as with most human simmering, it takes a "Flashpoint"[111] to ignite.

---

[109] DeLuca and Peoples, pp.132 and 136.
[110] G. Tang, 'Mobilization by images: TV screen and mediated instant grievances in the Umbrella Movement', *Chinese Journal of Communication*, 2015, Vol.8, No.4, pp. 338-355, see pp. 338 and 340.
[111] G. den Heyer, *Police Response to Riots*, in Chapter 2, 'What Constitutes a Riot', 2.5.2; 'The Flashpoints Model', *Springer Nature*, Switzerland AG 2020, see pp. 29-31.

If the 'attack' on the lifeguard was the ignition of simmering kindling leading to the fire of the Cronulla riot, then so too it could be argued, that the TV news coverage of that same event, was the ignition of simmering kindling leading to the revenge attacks.

Despite the angled TV footage perhaps as few as 200 out of a crowd of 5000 behaved as presented on the news:

> "It began as a street party, as if Australia Day arrived early...at about 10 o'clock there was...about...a thousand people there already...there was lots of alcohol...there was a barbecue going-just, it didn't look like everyone was there to fight. Like, everyone was sort of there, like, to celebrate".[112]

However, the footage doesn't lie, and it does look like everyone is falling over themselves to assault anyone who was an Arabic "them" and did not look like a Caucasian "us".

Despite the relative paucity of those actually participating in violence on the first day, it was the presentation of it being quite otherwise that must, in our view, have adversely affected the already simmering minds of young, offended Lebanese Muslim men. This TV coverage, of course, did not contribute in any way to the initial 'riot', but it did, in our view, contribute in a substantive way to the revenge attacks. Just as social commentators and academics sitting at home were horrified at what they observed as a wholesale racist White Australia enclave, so too were the young Lebanese Australian males watching and seething with unquenched anger. They reacted in violence with baseball bats and knives, as did the scholars in due course, with their pens and quills. The reactions of both were disproportionate and misinformed.

Mass Text Messaging

In our view, it was the combination of massive numbers of text messages, and their aggressively offensive content, which had the single most significant impact of any medium in drawing on enough discontent in young Caucasian and Lebanese males to encourage and even organise protest and violence.

Without this modern version of telephony, the inter-tribal tension which had

---

[112] J. Lattas, 'Cruising: "Moral Panic" and the Cronulla Riot', *The Australian Journal of Anthropology*, 2007, 18:3, pp. 320-335, see pp. 323 and 331.

simmered for years at Cronulla, may well have never morphed from insults and scuffles to more serious fear and violence.

However, with the technological 'advancement' of the phone from land line to wireless handset for voice, and then rather incredibly, to being able to project the printed word, the possibilities for profoundly disseminating these tensions, as a clarion call to many to converge at an angry point had arrived. It is almost impossible to imagine the Cronulla riot and revenge attacks happening as they did, without the serial text messaging to tens of thousands of mobile phone users.

Historical context

To put the 'new media' of texting properly in the context and circumstances of its time in December 2005, compared to the much later ballooning influence of 'social media', Facebook was launched in February 2004[113] with just 650 users, but by December 2005 had an incredible growth to 6 million users but still a miniscule coverage compared to the ubiquitous platform it was soon to become. Twitter was not established until March 2006[114], WhatsApp in May 2009[115], and Instagram not until October 2010.[116] So, in late 2005, apart from a very nascent Facebook and early internet search engines, the extent of comprehensive user content driven interactive media was basically email over the internet, or texting via a mobile phone.

In December 2005, the capability of mobile phones to transmit text messages was just 12 years old and as a universally used means of communication was then less than 5 years old.[117] In the year 2000, approximately 362M text messages were sent, whereas during the financial year 1 July 2005 to 30 June 2006, this had exponentially ballooned to 1.2B text messages in just that one single year.[118]

We now simply take for granted the profusion and universality of social

---

[113] S. Barr, 'When did Facebook Start? The story behind the company that took over the world', *Independent*, August 23, 2018.
[114] N. Carlson, 'The Real History of Twitter', *Business Insider Australia,* April 14, 2011.
[115] A. Pahwa, 'The History of WhatsApp',www.feedough.com. October 3, 2019.
[116] D. Blystone, 'The Story of Instagram: The Rise of the #1 Photo-Sharing App (FB)', www.investopedia.com, May 19, 2019.
[117] C. Gayomali, 'The text message turns 20: A brief history of SMS', *The Week* December 3, 2012.
[118] J. Cahir, 'Traces of Trust: A study of text messages in everyday life', *PhD Dissertation* 2010, University of Western Sydney, p.1.

media platforms to transmit messages, images and video, but back in late 2005, only texting and emailing were available, and even these were relatively new phenomena, as can be seen from the table below:

New and Social Media	Date introduced
Email universally used	1990s
Mobile phone texting	1993
Ubiquitous use of SMS texting	2000
Facebook	Feb 2004
Cronulla Riots texting and emailing	Dec 2005
Twitter	Mar 2006
Whats App	May 2009
Instagram	Oct 2010

By late 2005, millions of mobile phone users had enmeshed themselves in this wonderful and rapid new form of communicating instantaneously by the written word. Emails had already become used extensively but it was the transmission of short instant messages on handheld mobile phones which really did revolutionise the speed and manner in which people communicated.

Mainstream media outlets played some part to a larger or lesser degree in informing, motivating or even provoking the initiation of riot and retaliation in response at Cronulla in December 2005. However, we believe, it was the comprehensive, omnipresent, and inflammatory text messages on mobile phones, in their thousands, that did more than any other form of medium to fan the fires of discontent.

In times gone by, it would have been pamphlets, public oratory and the word of mouth which inspired people to act upon grievances. Then came radio broadcasts and finally TV video coverage. In some ways, texting became the modern technological version of the paper pamphlet. The printing press, ink, paper, and hand delivery now replaced by the phone, its words and the 'send' button, but the power of the printed word had come full circle. Printed words, not voice, not images, but words, had shown again the power of their motivating capacity.

Cronulla in late 2005, was not the first example of this new power of text messages to incite demonstration and protest. It happened in Manila in mid-January 2001 when approximately one million protestors gathered on one of Manila's major highways to demand the resignation of the Philippines' President Joseph Estrada, on the grounds of egregious corruption. Most accounts of the subsequent overthrow of the president point to the "*crucial importance of the cell phone in the rapid mobilisation of demonstrators*".[119] As with Cronulla, those who protested in Manila, were already simmering with resentment, and texting marshalled them to action but didn't of itself cause them to protest. Likewise at Cronulla, the angry demonstrations at Manila, would have not happened without the organising potential of the humble text message.

For text messaging to succeed as a 'clarion call' to protest, three essential ingredients must be present: pre-existing anger or fear, persuasive content, and pervasive distribution.

Pre-existing anger

People simply do not rise in anger because a text message tells them to. There must be a reason for provocative messaging having such an impact in people's consciousnesses that many converge at a highly promoted point to protest and demand action. This was so at both Manila and Cronulla.

In Manila, months of testimony in their Congress of presidential corruption, and widespread TV, print and radio coverage of that testimony delivered enough pre-existing anger for texting to light the fuse of a peaceful coup.

At Cronulla, years of acrimonious inter-tribal tensions simmered below the surface. Incivility, disrespect, and a challenge for turf, were all there well before any text messages were sent. People were angry and had savoured that anger until a degree of coverage of the life saver incident provided enough emotional gunpowder for the SMS keg to be exploded. Folks then were called up and responded to the draft in their thousands.

Likewise, young Lebanese males from Lakemba and Canterbury-Bankstown were also angry at being expected to comply with local rituals concerning the use of the beach and the interaction with its users.

Both sides of the "us" and "them" divide were angry enough to well hear the messages of division and action from the words, not the voice, of the modern phone.

---

[119] V.L. Rafael, 'The Cell Phone and the Crowd: Messianic Politics in the Contemporary Philippines', *Public Culture* 2003 15(3); pp.399-425, see p. 401.

Persuasive content

The SMS messages disseminated by both Caucasians and Lebanese, drew on xenophobia and a desire for revenge, to encourage protest and violence. Many were quite offensive but in drawing out the anger of already angry people they were very effective.[120]

Some examples of the texts circulated at the time are set out in the table below:

Caucasian	Lebanese
"Aussies...this Sunday every fucking Aussie in the Shire get down to North Cronulla to help support Leb and wog bashing day"	"All lebo/wog brothers. Sunday midday. Must be at North Cronulla Park. These skippy aussies want war. Bring your guns and knives and lets show them how we do it"
"Every fucking aussie. Go to Cronulla Beach Sunday for some Leb and wog bashing Aussie Pride ok"	"O fight each aussie. Yulleh. Lets get hectic and turn gods country into wogs country. Habib will be cookin victory kebabs after all. Tell your cousins"
"Bring your mates and let's show them that this is our beach and they are never welcome...let's kill these boys"	"We fear no ozy pigs"
"Who said Gallipoli wouldn't happen again! Rock up 2 Cronulla this Sunday...u can witness Aussies beaten Turks on the beach"	"Get the Aussie dogs"

At the time there were strong suggestions that White Supremacists had sent out some of the more offensive messages and if so, then some in return must have been sent by Arabic Supremacists.

Pervasive distribution

Strike Force Neil during its investigation of police performance before and during the Cronulla Riots accessed a treasure trove of mass text messages sent via mobile phone telecommunications carriers. It found *"that over 270,000 individual text messages were transmitted inciting a racially motivated confrontation at North Cronulla on 11th December 2005"*.[121]

This was certainly a 'pervasive distribution', and unquestionably let a lot of

---

[120] See Strike Force Neil, Volume One, p.35; *The Daily Telegraph,* 'Second beach brawl', December 8, 2005; *The Daily Telegraph,* 'A line in the sand', 10 December 10, 2005.

[121] Strike Force Neil, Volume One, p.35.

people know about a protest event at which, if so inclined, they would have probably felt encouraged to attend.

What is particularly interesting in the case of the 'Cronulla Troubles' is that text messaging in Australia which had until then been traditionally and almost exclusively person to person, now morphed into chain text messages where group message lists were used to spread the clarion call for protest as far and wide as possible.[122]

Did mass texting cause mass panic?

This is an important question to consider. However, it assumes human automatons reacted to the messages only, rather than their dramatic ability at marshalling pre-existing discontent. People were marshalled not morally panicked. This is a particularly important difference.[123]

New police powers to seize phones

The new police powers enacted by the NSW Parliament on 15 December 2005, gave police the power to seize mobile phones and examine them for text messages likely to incite riot or public disorder.

Law enforcement and riot control is almost entirely a state government jurisdiction, but the regulation and authorisation of access to the servers enabling telecommunications devices to send and record messages is a Commonwealth responsibility. The NSW police could use their new state powers to inspect and seize mobile phones, but they were not able to access the servers to detect wider offences and offenders.

This power had been provided by an earlier amendment to Commonwealth legislation through the *Telecommunications (Interception) Amendment (Stored Communications) Act 2004* which was used by both police as a law enforcement tool and by Strike Force Neil in examining just how many racialised and troublesome text messages had been transmitted.[124]

When just a few days after the troubles began, police boarded a bus, checked phones, and arrested an offender, the message it gave was palpably effective; police and the government would no longer tolerate mobile phones being

---

[122] J. Cahir, 'Traces of Trust', pp. 67-68.
[123] G. Goggin, 'SMS Riot: Transmitting Race on a Sydney Beach, December 2005', *Journal.media-culture.org.au* Volume 9, Issue1, March 1, 2006.
[124] J. Cahir, 'Balancing Trust and Anxiety in a Culture of Fear: Text Messaging and Riots', *SAGE Open* April-June 2013; pp.1-13, see p.2.

used as a modern form of pamphleteering to incite riot and discontent. It very quickly had an impact as text messaging dramatically fell away, police restored order, and the troublesome few returned to their homes and their tribes.

This was probably the first time that text messaging was regulated and subjected to police scrutiny, as a means of detecting incitement to riot and violence, and as a means, at the same time, of quelling it.

The Daily Telegraph

The Daily Telegraph (DT), much like Alan Jones, was predictably 'shocked' as a tabloid usually is when reporting 'shocking news'. Also, predictably, it and its stable of reporters and headline crafting sub-editors, soaked up and broadcast as much as it could of their indignation leading up to Cronulla 2005.

However, these 'stories' were not causative ones, just indignant ones, with one clear exception. In one article, delivered twice in two consecutive days, on the 9th and 10th of December 2005, the DT gave extraordinary coverage of the Maroubra Beach based Bra Boys surfer gang leader, Koby Abberton, effectively daring young Lebanese men to visit Maroubra and show just how tough they were. They did show up, and local cars and property were trashed with baseball bats and residents left in fear. The causality between this publication and the revenge attacks, must on any assessment be considered strong. As Michael Daley MP for Maroubra said in our interview with him: *"It appears that it was perceived as a challenge and the challenge was accepted"*.[125]

Alan Jones' exhortations about the attack on the lifeguards being an attack on the very essence of what it meant to be an Australian, combined with the DT talking the story up as much as possible, certainly had the issues surrounding Cronulla at the forefront of many people's minds.

Despite this newspaper being at times a provocative headline screaming broad sheet, at least in the lead up to the riot, rather than afterwards, it is unlikely its coverage alone motivated the young males of the Shire to rise and protest. Although at the same time, it needs to be said, the Daily

---

[125] M. Daley, Transcript of Interview, February 17, 2021.

Did the Media cause the Riots?

Telegraph like Jones, hardly did much to discourage Cronulla locals from 'taking their beach back'.

Some examples:

Date	Headline	Story summary	Possible impact
7th December 2005	Gangs turn Cronulla beach into war zone	Young females '*assaulted and harassed*', abused, asked if virgins ...by thugs of Middle Eastern descent'.	A blunt reminder of the Skaf brothers' violent attacks on young Caucasian women.
8th December 2005	Second beach brawl Police call for calm as locals plot revenge	'*Racial tension exploded last night with a brawl near the scene where two lifeguards were attacked.*' ' *a text message circulated... urging locals...to take revenge* '	Communal apprehension increased. Some may have embraced vigilantism.
9th December 2005	Not on our beach Cronulla police vow to defend Australian way	'*Police... warning to ethnic gangs and...vigilantes...they will use the full force of the law in defence of our summer lifestyle*'.	Discouragement of trouble and that police would be out in force and ready to act.
9th December 2005	Caught in the middle Parents fear for safety of children	Shopkeepers not surprised by the outbreak of violence which happens every summer.	Local negative perceptions of visitors reinforced.
9th December 2005	A beast surfaces- battle of the beach Racial tensions across Sydney's beaches have exposed a dark undercurrent of intolerance and violence	"*The reason why it's not happening at Maroubra is because of the Bra Boys....If you want to go to beaches and act tough in groups you better be able to back it up. If these fellas come out to Maroubra and start something, they know it's going to be on, so they stay away*".	This was probably the DT at its most irresponsible, in effectively broadcasting a public dare from the Bra Boys leader that young Lebanese males were too scared to turn up. They weren't.

Date	Headline	Story summary	Possible impact
10th December 2005	A Line in the sand Cronulla is a suburb under siege	Locals think: "*the wogs…hate us…*[and]…*tomorrow…residents…will…defend their beach against the threat of Middle Eastern gangs*". The beach is for everyone, but the Lebanese visitors do not respect local rules. Even toddlers have to cover up for fear of being '*branded little tarts*'. Allegedly drawing on the huge Skaf Brothers prison sentences for violent rapes, visitors had said to some young local women, "You're not worth 55 years".	A very provocative piece, just a day before the riots. Locals may have been encouraged to protest, and the visitors, effectively being accused of misogyny, gang rapes and quasi-paedophilia would have been angrier still.

Was Alan Jones to blame?

For those not from Sydney, Alan Jones was a leading 'Shock Jock' morning host on radio station 2GB.

On a simple reading of the words used in many of Alan Jones' excoriating exhortations on behalf of Caucasian Australia, it could be argued that he contributed to the Cronulla Riots. However, we argue that this is unsustainable.

As we discuss in further detail below, Alan Jones was almost entirely preaching to an audience who were mostly seeking a confirmation of their already held views, rather than a convincing case for changing them. They were simply not brought to an outraged state by their favourite radio host's provocative radio messages, as it was a mantra they enjoyed hearing and nodded in agreement as they listened.

In other words, the audience who might have been provoked into protest or just turning up, were simply not listening. In December 2005, Jones had an audience of seniors who much like the two old men, Statler and Waldorf, in the Muppets, liked to cheer or groan on from the sidelines, but not actually turn up anywhere to do anything about it. And they did not turn up at Cronulla. The crowd at Cronulla were relatively young 16 to 35 year olds, and were not of the Alan Jones radio demographic of 50+ year old seniors.

However, on any reasonable reckoning, the language and narrative used by Jones over the several days preceding the riots were unhelpful and provocative at best, and at worst, may have fanned the flames of already brewing discontent. However, it is simply not possible to draw a direct causal link between what Jones and listeners said on air and individuals committing criminal acts.

So far as we are aware, no-one brought a unique defence before the courts and argued: "Alan Jones made me do it"! That is why we argue that at most it can be stated that Jones may have contributed to some of the ingredients which incited riot, but we cannot say definitively that he did so.

Jones was somewhat confrontive in stirring up the passions of anyone who wanted to protect Australian values, Aussie Icons like Lifeguards, and our flag, and was receptive to the notion that Lebanese gangsters were unwelcome on our beaches. Jones was doing here what Jones does best: beat the chest, stir up indignation, draw the crowd to his notion of what is right, just, and good, and exhort all to do something about it.

Unsurprisingly, some of Jones' commentary brought attention and complaint.

The Australian Communications and Media Authority (ACMA)

A useful point of analysis on Alan Jones for the purposes of this discussion is the consideration of complaints made against him in early 2006 to the Australian Communications and Media Authority (ACMA).

The ACMA is an independent statutory authority set up under Commonwealth legislation and is charged with regulating media services in Australia against appropriate Codes of Conduct and relevant legislation. Although very unlikely, a possible outcome of upholding a complaint against a provider of media services is to put at risk their licence to operate.

In early 2006, several complaints were made to the ACMA that Jones had by a series of broadcasts between the 5th and 9th of December 2005 *'encouraged violence and incited hatred against or vilified people of Lebanese background"*. Some were upheld and some were not.

The Cronulla Riots

The 2GB radio licence was never seriously at risk.

It is useful to examine a selection of the commentary of Jones and some of his listeners on those days.

Date	Broadcast	Finding
5th December 2005	**Jones**: *"I'll tell you what type of grubs this lot were. This lot were Middle Eastern grubs"*	Did not vilify or encourage hatred on ethnic grounds. Perpetrators criticised for their behaviour not their ethnicity.
6th December 2005	**Caller**: *"...the next step is vigilantes..."*. **Jones**: *"Yeah, good on you"*. **Caller**: *"Shoot one, the rest will run"*. **Jones**: *[laughing]*.	Listeners would give more weight to the broadcaster than a listener ringing in. Laughter did not indicate approval but closure of the discussion.
7th December 2005	**Jones**: *"...these people are... Lebanese gangs"*. **Jones reading a letter**; *"The only language the Middle Eastern youth understand is a good hiding...my suggestion is to invite the biker gangs"*.	Despite reading listener's letters this constituted vilification of Lebanese visitors to the beach. Endorsing biker gangs was likely to encourage violence.
8th December 2005	**Jones**: *"We don't have Anglo-Saxon kids out there raping women in Western Sydney...the gangs are of one ethnic composition"*. **Jones reading an email**: *"It's not just a few Middle Eastern bastards, it's thousands. Cronulla...it's been taken over by this scum"*.	Likely to vilify people of Middle Eastern background on the basis of ethnicity.

Date	Broadcast	Finding
8th December 2005	**Jones** quoted several quite offensive text messages then circulating calling for a: "*Leb and wog bashing day*" "*Now, it's got pretty nasty when you start talking like this... That's gotta be stopped... Boys, don't get down there and come at this nonsense, this will only make things worse*".	On balance the broadcast did not encourage violence, the messages were not endorsed, and Jones had mitigated their effect by clear statements. However, "*...the use of the quotes was ill-judged* [But]*... on balance... an ordinary listener would* [not] *have considered the quotes in their contexts as likely to... encourage violence*".
9th December 2005	**Jones**: "*Last weekend gangs bashed up two lifesavers*". **Jones**: "*...there are behavioural standards that have to be met... you don't start shouting abuse at other people... You don't start calling them filthy names... these people don't meet behavioural standards*". **Jones**: "*You simply don't just gather your mates, no matter what your ethnic background, barge down to the beach and intimidate, violate and brutalise people*".	Not likely to incite or perpetuate hatred against or vilify Lebanese people based on ethnicity or nationality. Whilst the program did include "*a number of comments that were capable of giving offence... the program included a number of more moderate remarks*" by both callers and the presenter, the material when considered in the context of the whole program "*was not so strong as to be likely to vilify or incite or perpetuate hatred as required by the Code*".

It is important to point out here, that the role of the ACMA inquiry was not to consider, whether or not there was a causal link between the Alan Jones broadcasts and actual violence, only whether or not they '*encouraged violence*' in breach of the code of conduct it was administering. This is an important distinction:[126]

> "*No 'likely causative link' between the broadcast and 'probable or consequential violence' need be demonstrated. All that must be demonstrated is that the ordinary reasonable listener would regard the broadcast as likely to have one or more of the effects* [of breaching the

---

[126] Australian Government Australian Communications and Media Authority, Investigation Report No. 1485, 'ACMA Investigation Report – *Breakfast with Alan Jones* broadcast by 2GB on 5,6,7,8 and 9 December 2005', p. 18.

code, not actually directly causing violence] ... *Whether or not the events actually transpire is not relevant for ACMA's assessment under the code".*

Who was listening to Jones anyway?

As mentioned earlier, in our view, a reliable assessment of Jones' culpability regarding stirring up the initial 'event' at North Cronulla Beach, is to compare the typical audience to whom Jones then preached to daily, with the 'audience' who turned up to protest. If the two differ markedly, then a fair conclusion is that Jones was not talking to many at all who turned up to protest, riot and/or commit acts of violence.

Was Jones more hype than influential? Perhaps: *"Fifteen years of research and I haven't found Alan Jones to be much more influential with voters than ABC Radio or the SMH. He is only powerful because politicians think he is".*[127]

Even if he did preach to a younger audience, Jones' reach compared to those of the print and TV media was relatively insignificant. The comparison is telling.

In early 2006, just months after the Cronulla riots, Jones commanded top place with 16% of the Sydney breakfast radio market, or about 182,000 listeners in Sydney which whilst impressive:

> *"...the number of his listeners is dwarfed by the readership of the main newspapers and the audience of television channels. The highest rating television shows during prime time receive upwards of 600,000 viewers in Sydney. The top rating news program, National Nine News Sunday, had 552,000 viewers in Sydney for the last week of March 2006...Similarly, the two largest Sydney newspapers are read by close to a million people".*[128]

Put simply, Jones did not then command the influence and media coverage the hype around him would suggest. His media coverage when compared to all other forms of media was simply too small to suggest anything like a pervasive influence on human behaviour.

> *"Jones' audience was primarily over 50 and a large percentage of that were over 65. In 2006, 37% of Australians were in the*

---

[127] R. Huntley, referred to in M. McKenzie-Murray, 'The Power of Alan Jones', *The Saturday Paper,* October 13, 2018.

[128] C. Hamilton, 'Who listens to Alan Jones', The Australia Institute Webpaper, June 2006, pp. 3-4.

14-34 age category but made up only 7% of Jones' audience".[129]

More importantly, Jones' style of alt-right demagogic conservative intolerance was preaching to an audience who already held these views or approaches and were not tuning in to be convinced of changing their political hue:

> "More to the point, they tend to be conservative. They share his populist, right-wing views. They bask in his outrage. They listen to have their opinions confirmed rather than challenged...the majority of Sydneysiders never listen to him".[130]

Jones certainly expressed provocative umbrage at the time, but he did so to an audience who wanted to hear it, to have their views reinforced not altered. The audience was old relative to the Cronulla Beach turnout, it did express outrage on his talkback programme but then went nowhere near the beach to put any of that outrage into action. Put simply, Alan Jones entrenched in the minds of his 'seniors' of the righteousness of his cause but they then did nothing about it.

Did the media do it?

So, in conclusion to the question: "Did the media cause or contribute to the Cronulla riots"?, we have shown, that there is not a simple answer. It is both yes partially and no not really. We submit the gathering at Cronulla was mostly driven by mass text messaging, which was a relatively new phenomenon at that time. And what about the 'Revenge Attacks'? Again, yes, to a certain degree, but only a partial yes. In both cases, whilst the media drummed away in the background like white-noise, somewhat fanning the already existing flames of tension, the real cause was the existing simmering hatred between the 'us' and 'them' tribes - the beach locals versus the outside visitors - over things like offensive conduct, incivility, disrespect, the way people 'should' behave at the beach and who 'owned' the public domain, which was ultimately ignited by a flashpoint incident, that being the assault of the lifeguards at Cronulla. An analysis of these contributing factors forms the basis of the next several chapters.

---

[129] C. Hamilton, 'Who listens to Alan Jones', p. 5.
[130] M. Lallo, 'Alan Jones is not as powerful as politicians think', *The Sydney Morning Herald*, October 8, 2018.

19

Was it motivated by racism?

> *"What is race, exactly? Science tells us that there is no genetic or scientific basis for it. Instead its largely a made up label, used to define and separate us…race is misconceived".*[131]

At the time of the Cronulla Riots, the behaviour of a large drunken crowd and the excesses of some among them, was widely attributed to an innate racist attitude of Caucasians against anyone of Middle Eastern appearance. The violent acts in revenge were not so attributed in reverse, by either social commentators or otherwise serious academics. We challenge this inconsistency:

> *"It bemuses me that some absolve non-white people of racism. 'It's literally impossible to be racist to a white person'. 'Racism against white people doesn't exist' … 'minorities can't be racist because they have no power to act on such antagonism' …Racism is individual, not just institutional. As individuals we all have the power to hurt one another".*[132]

The brush of racism has been applied liberally and so often, that it has writ large both an image and an imagined reality, across the memory and consciousness of what happened, or more accurately, what might have happened, at Cronulla in late 2005 and into early 2006. Given this, and that we contend that this needs to be challenged, it is appropriate that we first consider what the words 'race' and 'racism' actually mean.

---

[131] E. Kolbert, 'Skin Deep', *National Geographic,* Washington, Vol.233, Iss.4 (Apr 2018), pp.1-7, see pp. 1 and 4.
[132] M.I. Gao, 'Who can be "Racist"? *The Harvard Crimson,* August 10, 2018, www.thecrimson.com.

What is race?

Using 'race' as a descriptor of difference, thereby ensuring belonging and exclusion, remains a key platform upon which groups of humans tribalise each other, either into an "us" which look like us, or into a "them" who look different to us. But upon what scientific basis can an 'Other' be identified by something as crude as skin colour, or religious belief, or cultural mores?

By June 2000 *"Craig Venter, a pioneer of DNA sequencing, observed, 'the concept of race has no genetic or scientific basis'"*.[133] The Human Genome Project, laid to rest the fallacious claim that we are genetically different and can be racially assigned by physical appearance.

However, despite the results of that Project, many will still discern *"the racial pedigree of different humans through the simple act of looking at them"*.[134] Humans have virtually identical chromosomal makeup across the world except for minor 'mutations' which took account of sunlight:

> *"Across the world today, skin colour is highly variable. Much of the difference correlates with latitude. Near the Equator lots of sunlight makes dark skin a useful shield against ultraviolet radiation; toward the poles, where the problem is too little sun, paler skin promotes the production of vitamin D...*
>
> *...Science tells us that the visible differences between peoples are accidents of history. They reflect how our ancestors dealt with sun exposure, and not much else".*[135]

One may well ask, if there are no races then how can 'race' continue to be an omnipresent means of labelling and discriminating? How can one be a 'racist' if the term 'race' is in fact, "fake" scientific news?

Even as far back as 1994, scholars had already come to the view that 'race' really was a social construct rather than a scientific one:

> *"Race has no scientific basis as a term for the relationship between skin colour, physical features and gene pool on the one hand, and social and cultural behaviour on the other...*
>
> *...so, any use of racial categories must take its justifications from other*

---

[133] E. Kolbert, 'Skin Deep', p. 1.
[134] F. Armstrong-Fumeroa, "'Even the Most Careless Observer': Race and Visual Discernment in Physical Anthropology from Samuel Morton to Kennewick Man', *American Studies*, Vol.53, No.2, 2014, pp. 5-29, see p.11.
[135] E. Kolbert, 'Skin Deep', pp. 3-4.

sources than biology... 'race' has primarily social meaning".[136]

At Cronulla there were the 'Whites and the Caucasians' lined up against the 'Arabs and the Lebanese'. It is interesting, that despite the lack of scientific basis for 'race', many people who should know better have had their discriminatory actions and words against a group of 'Others' not labelled as 'colourist' or even 'tribalistic' but 'racist' on the basis that 'race' does still exist! This is perplexing to a degree but only to the extent that the pejorative term is usually only applied when a tribalistic action or word is given on an unfair, offensive, or discriminatory basis.

> "To the victims of racism, its small consolation to say that the category has no scientific basis".[137]

Convenient social and ethnic classification of tribal communities according to 'race' may serve a purpose of distinguishing one group from another, rather than using this process to necessarily discriminate. So, it is now timely to consider how and under what circumstances 'race' moves to racism.

What is racism?

'Racism' is a term used more broadly than just signifying pejorative, disparaging or discriminatory actions, or words, directed at someone or a group of people simply because of their skin colour. However, it is a useful starting point: *"Racism is any attitude, action, or institutional structure or social policy that subordinates persons or groups because of their colour".*[138]

However, this is a somewhat narrower definition than one provided by Ramon Grosfoguel from the University of California, Berkley, with a more expansive definition in 2016:

> "Racism can be marked by colour, ethnicity, language, culture and/ or religion. Although since colonial times colour racism has been the dominant marker of racism in most parts of the world... ".[139]

---

[136] A. Jakubowicz et al. *Racism, Ethnicity and the Media,* 1994, Allen & Unwin, p.28.
[137] E. Kolbert, 'Skin Deep', p. 4.
[138] D. W. Sue, *Overcoming Our Racism: The Journey to Liberation,* 2003, John Wiley and Sons, p. 31.
[139] R. Grosfoguel, 'What is Racism?', *Journal of World-Systems Research,* Vol.22, Issue 1, pp. 9-15, see pp. 10-11.

What is bigotry?

At Cronulla, the conflict emanated from simmering disquiet between local Caucasians and visiting Lebanese. There are enough distinguishing skin and bodily features between the two to allow a racial Whites against Arabs narrative. But somewhat more was in play than "they do not look like us".

The texts sent by Cronulla locals, by non-local White Supremacists and by Lebanese males to stir up tribal angst and response against the 'Other' certainly drew on religion, ethnicity and culture to rile and encourage discontent by "us" against "them".

It would seem that a bigot can be a non-racist, but all racists are bigots:

> "Bigotry is prejudice against an individual or group of people based on real or perceived characteristics; in the case of race, **bigotry most often manifests itself as white prejudice against people of colour.** A bigot is an individual who harbors negative attitudes and emotions towards another individual or group".[140]

Islamophobia, religiophobia, misogyny, ethnophobia, or even incestophobia, to name a few intolerant conditions, which result in jaundiced or disparaging words or actions by an "us" against the 'Other', or racial prejudice itself against a "them", are all on the above definition, varying strands of bigotry. At Cronulla and beyond, there were enough examples and reporting of actual and alleged bigotry for the 'event' and the label to endure in our consciousness to this day.

What is Islamophobia?

A fear of Islam and its assumed teachings of hatred of the West, and comfort if not encouragement of harming Caucasian Christians, underpins a fear of Islam and its Muslim adherents.

The attacks around the world in the early to mid-2000s in the USA, the UK and Indonesia, combined with the Charlie Hebdo atrocity in Paris, and the depredations of the ISIS Caliphate, have certainly instilled a fear in the West by both governments and the citizens they represent, that Islam is both an enemy and something to fear.

---

[140] C.A. Gallagher and C. D. Lippard, *Race and Racism in the United States*, p.114.

Not surprisingly, this has attracted defenders and critics in both the West and the Arab world: *"We contend that foremost among folk demons of the contemporary 'West' is the Muslim Other".*[141]

Maligning Muslims as a danger to the West, as universally harbouring resentment of Christians or 'Western Liberalism', or one step away from doing or encouraging acts of violence, would satisfy any broad definition of Islamophobia.

Interestingly, the notion of Islamophobia standing on its own as a disparaging form of bigotry has generally fallen away to be regarded as a form of religious or cultural racism:

> *"If 'race' is a fiction created when certain ethnic or cultural practices attach to social advantage or disadvantage, it is hard to see religious identity as...distinct from 'race'. For good reason then, racialisation is increasingly used to explain Islamophobia as a form of racism'.*[142]

However, what about 'Christophobia' or 'Westophobia'? If a fear of the Muslim 'Other' was in play at Cronulla, then surely so was a fear of the Christian or Western 'Other'. Why one and not the other? The dearth of academic discourse in such an equal-handed approach to our own troubling events at and beyond Cronulla, is an unsatisfactory outcome of one-sided scholarship on the issue.

No races but plenty of racism

Interestingly, the Human Genome Project found that there is no such thing as race but as the term 'racist' rather than 'colourist' prevails to describe discrimination based on colour, religion, ethnicity or cultural mores, it is a term which none the less prevails.

Whilst the tribal protagonists during the Cronulla riots had clear differentiating markers of religious beliefs, cultural mores, appearance, and skin colour, they were not scientifically of different races. However,

---

[141] S. Poynting and L. Briskman, 'Terror Incognito: Black Flags, Plastic Swords and Other Weapons of Mass Disruption in Australia', in *What is Islamophobia? Racism, Social Movements and the State,* Pluto Press, 2017, p.138.

[142] N. Massoumi, T. Mills, and D. Miller, 'Islamophobia, Social Movements and the State: For a Movement-centred Approach', in *What is Islamophobia?* Pluto Press, 2017, p.5.

whilst the term 'race' may have no real scientific meaning, the recognition of these markers to distinguish, penalise and discriminate on that basis, by one tribe against the 'Other', means that the term used to describe that process: 'racism', does indeed have considerable social scientific meaning.

Anti-non-conformists not racists

We explore in chapter 22, in the context of the Cronulla Riots, the ground breaking theory of human conflict provided by the political sociologist Karen Stenner, which supports our claim that the conflict was far more about an '*Intolerance to Difference*' than an intolerance of physical appearance. After carrying out extensive field research in the United States, Professor Stenner concluded that most people are not intrinsically racist, or bigoted, or politically deviant, just extremely sensitive to those who are not "us".[143] And that intolerance is only manifested and expressed in words and actions, when a perceived or actual threat emerges from "them" towards "us".

Stenner argued that upon perceiving a threat, what might then be said or acted out by an "us" in response, may per se seem, sound, or appear as racist, but may in fact not be driven or inspired by base racist sentiments, but by a human desire for sameness and a need to shun difference. This potentially rewrites the theory of racist behaviour, to something much more benevolent than it being always regarded as a forum for tribal colour-based supremacy. This will be a challenge to many.

The myth and reality of racism at Cronulla

There is no doubt that some of the chants, chest emblazoned messages, clarion calling texts, and various calls to arms, from both Cronulla Caucasians and Lakemba Lebanese, would have satisfied any reasonable or broad definition of what constituted racism.

Here are some examples:

Caucasian	Lebanese
"Fuck off Lebs"	*"Get the Aussie dogs"*
"Middle Eastern Grubs"	*"We fear no ozy pigs"*

---

[143] K. Stenner, *The Authoritarian Dynamic,* Cambridge University Press, 2005.

Caucasian	Lebanese
"Go to Cronulla Beach for some Leb and wog bashing"	"These skippy aussies want war. Bring your guns and knives"

To the extent that these offensive messages demonstrate a smearing disparagement of the 'Other', for no better reason than *'they are not us'*, *'they don't look like us'* or *'they don't believe what we believe'*, they all satisfy a definition of racist behaviour. They suggest bigotry, misogyny, xenophobia, and an intolerant collection of taunts designed to abuse, harm, or incite the 'Other'. Each tribe in its pursuit of its "us" pitted against their "them", was as bad as the other. Tribalism was in full disparaging and violent display at Cronulla and beyond. In the case of both Cronulla and Lakemba, racism was clearly prevalent and expressed by both tribes.

However, despite the competitive tribalism at work at Cronulla with both Caucasians and Lebanese giving as much as they got, the narrative for Cronulla has almost entirely focussed on 'White racism' and virtually ignored the racist and bigoted behaviour of young Lebanese men in the lead-up and in revenge. This is an extraordinarily subjective academic and commentator imagining, in creating a false narrative of who was to blame and who was to remain as the 'innocents'. This false narrative remains alive even to this day. It remains, 'Fake News' as it assumes that only white people can be racist.

> "We argue that the definition 'racism = White supremacy' is logically flawed, demonstrates reverse racism, is disempowering for individuals from all racial groups who strive for racial equality, and absolves those who do not".[144]

Young Lebanese men claimed that they acted in response to significant provocation, but their response could not be classified as any less racist or bigoted as the initial provocation itself.

The actions of the Caucasian few were committed in the full glare of sunlight, before all the assembled media ready for maximum image damage, in which only the media specialises. Many far more violent acts were committed by Arabic males, with very few of these inadvertently caught in grainy images on business camera systems. The attacks were done under cover of

---

[144] P. Sawrikar, and I. Katz, "'Only white people can be racist': What does power have to do with prejudice?', *Cosmopolitan Civil Societies: An Interdisciplinary Journal*, January, 2010, Vol. 2, Issue 1, pp. 80-98, see p. 80.

darkness, without warning, and certainly not packaged up for that day's TV news coverage. They still remain mostly unseen and unacknowledged.

Some facts

The number charged with offences against total population numbers is an interesting and useful exercise in assessing the credulity of a 'racist Shire'.

The data from the 2006 Census makes for a sobering comparison of the two tribal areas; Cronulla vs Lakemba or Sutherland Shire vs Canterbury Bankstown and the wider narrative of what the Cronulla riots still might mean for these two divergent areas of Sydney.

Category	Cronulla	Lakemba	Sutherland	Canterbury / Bankstown
Population	16,754	14,468	205,000	300,452

Let us assume that the estimate of 5,000 who attended the Cronulla 'protest' before it descended into something more confronting, is a correct one. Even if every one of the 5,000 who turned up engaged in racist behaviour, that does not make for a 'racist Shire' or a 'racist Cronulla' based on 5,000 out of 205,000 or even just 16,000! That perhaps no more than two, maybe three hundred, behaved criminally and violently on the day tests the assertion somewhat of a suburb riddled with xenophobes. This is greatly exacerbated by the fact that a large number of attendees on the day were actually not even residents of Cronulla or the wider Sutherland Shire.

Likewise, there were approximately one hundred Lebanese revenge attackers processed through the courts after the Cronulla riots, roughly equal in number to those Caucasian offenders also processed.

It is unlikely that the total number of revenge attackers would have exceeded more than maybe a few hundred. A few hundred violent and racist Lebanese out of 300,000 in Canterbury Bankstown, or even out of 14,000 at Lakemba, would not go anywhere near to justifying the calling or academically imagining of those locations as a 'racist Lakemba' or a 'racist Canterbury Bankstown'. And nor should it have! However, this is exactly what has happened in reverse to Cronulla and the Sutherland Shire. This is an absurd racialised topographic disparagement which can no longer be sustained.

If the imagining is a correct one, then where were the thousands of Cronulla locals being paraded through the courts to give evidence to the academic and broader claims of a sick and decayed racist community? They were not paraded, because there were only a relatively few who committed offences.

Likewise, perhaps no more than 200 Arabic males were involved in attacking cars at Maroubra and committing acts of violence on innocent Caucasians across parts of Sydney. Conversely, this violent spree which swept a whole city up into a state of fear, had no impact on the long-term narrative for Lakemba and Canterbury Bankstown. And nor should it have.

Reverse racism

In some ways, scholars, commentators, and the broader community have allowed a reverse racism to take place in maligning a white part of Sydney but not an Arabic one. However, the reality is that given the few that were involved, the speed with which it all happened and subsided, and that Sydney has lived in peace since late 2005, ought to allow the false imagining of Cronulla to die a justified death. But the scholars will not allow that to happen any time soon.

Let us canvass a few examples from the 'academic' discourse to get a better understanding of the racialised misfit between what they say as scholars happened, and what really happened.

It was 'mass racist violence'

Writing in a journal called *'Race and Class'* perhaps compelled academic Scott Poynton to overreach, even in the abstract before the article proper when he referred to: *"The outbreak of mass racist violence against young men of 'Middle Eastern appearance' on Cronulla beach"*.[145]

This does invite dismissal as somewhat exaggerated, as does his sweeping assertion that it was the whole *"frenzied mob of 5,000 'white' Australians... attacking anyone of 'Middle Eastern appearance' that they could find near...Cronulla beach"*.[146]

Like most 'scholars' he struggles with the notion that precursor cultural and ethnic conflict on Cronulla beach fuelled the events of late 2005. Almost incredulously, he dismisses the claim of one author that *"locals had taken 'a lot of shit' from Muslim youths"* by reaching for the scholar's sanctuary: *"On*

---
[145] S. Poynting, 'What caused the Cronulla Riot?', *Race and Class*, 48 (1), 85-92.
[146] S. Poynting, 'What caused the Cronulla riot?, p.85.

the basis of what research – urban myth digested from afar".[147]

He even referred to the claims of young local women of being targeted for inappropriate behaviour as 'folklore'. Despite that dismissive confidence, a well-constructed academic interview schedule, conducted even now, would elicit in detail the 'shit' which locals put up with and which eventually caused a strong reaction.

It was a pogrom

Perhaps the most extreme version of the denialism by scholars and commentators of the equally racist revenge attackers was the labelling of the initial riot by Caucasians as a 'pogrom' against innocent and downtrodden Lebanese. Surely this is an academic *'bridge too far'*?

A pogrom has had awful historical relevance to the discrimination, violence and murder committed against Jewish individuals and whole communities in Russia and Europe from the late 19th Century through to well into the 20th Century. It is a single word used to describe violent acts committed on a minority usually with the sanction of the state and its law enforcement personnel.

It is in this context that two well-known genocide scholars accepted a brief to write an essay in 2009 for a publication on various 'scholarly' perceptions of the Cronulla riots.

Dirk Moses and Geoffrey Levey tried valiantly but unconvincingly to portray 'The Jewish Question' of 20th Century Europe, as possibly now, 'The Muslim Question' of the 21st Century.[148] In a real stretch, Levey and Moses argued that the Cronulla Riot was a pogrom against 'Muslims and Arabs':

> "Significant differences can be discerned between the extent of violence in Russian and American pogroms in the late 19th and early 20th centuries and the Cronulla incident. The former often claimed hundreds of lives at a time, with significant property damage while no-one was killed or even seriously injured at Cronulla...
>
> ...[However], the passions aroused on Sydney beaches, and the other features of Cronulla, then, do bear a disturbing resemblance to a

---

[147] Poynting, p. 87.
[148] G. Levey, and D. Moses, 'The Muslims are our misfortune!', in *Lines in the sand*, Chapter six, pp. 95-110.

pogrom".[149]

And Scott Poynton hardly needed any encouragement with his take on events:

> "the Cronulla riot was...in the nature of a pogrom: a violent attack by members of a dominant ethnic group against a minority, in order to put them in their place".[150]

Cronulla in late 2005 was clearly on any reasonable assessment not a pogrom and must be regarded as being at the very low end of historical global inter-ethnic clashes. Kristallnacht (or the Night of Broken Glass) in Berlin on the 9th and 10th of November 1938 was definitely a pogrom, but Cronulla Beach in Sydney on 11th of December 2005 was definitely not.

Despite the clear absurdity of comparing the Sutherland Shire with Nazi Germany, it was in a book of essays published in 2009 which explored scholarly interpretations of the Cronulla Riots where:

> "Levey and Moses...draw a powerful and provocative parallel with anti-Semitism. They compare the 'Muslim question' in contemporary Australia with the 'Jewish question' in Nazi Germany, as the creation of a dangerous, unassimilable Other which needs to be dealt with".[151]

Bob Carr and John Howard did it!

The heading might seem ludicrous but then this is what Scott Poynton had to say in 2009:

> "In reality, Labor Governments for three terms of office under Bob Carr had led the charge to racialise crime and perpetuate the populist ethnic targeting of high-profile zero tolerance gestures. This, as much as the federal government's manipulation of xenophobia over the same period, from the 'Middle Eastern' boat people to the 'war on terror' contributed to the intercommunal conflict at Cronulla."[152]

An interesting perspective, seeing how Bob Carr retired in July 2005, six months prior to the Cronulla Riots!

We will now consider two related notions concerning the alleged denial of

---

[149] Levey and Moses, p. 100.
[150] Poynting, p.85.
[151] Greg Noble (ed), *Lines in the Sand*, 2009, p. 73.
[152] S. Poynting, 'Scouring the Shire', *Lines in the sand*, 2009, Chapter three, pp. 44-57, see p. 53.

racism by Whites at Cronulla, and a broader concern of apparently allowing the passage of time to 'cleanse' our racist selves.

Racist denialism and forgetfulness

We have endeavoured to argue throughout this book that the central causes of the conflict at Cronulla were incivility, disrespect, tribalism, territory and an 'intolerance of difference' towards the 'Other', rather than a base outburst of unbridled deep-seated racism.

However, some scholars perpetuate a myth that the contrary was in play with our continued *"disavowal of race'* and by doing so we all allow our '*racism...to flourish"*[153]

Rather than rejoicing that participants and community members on both sides, could years later, lament the events and appreciate inter-tribal peace and harmony, one scholar sees this as an act of racist denialism by effluxion of time:

> *"The...disavowal* [of racism] *is embedded in what I call 'the narrative of pastness'...Here the riots are read as an historical anomaly, as belonging to yesterday...While the desire to move on is understandable, something is lost when the racism of that time has not been sufficiently acknowledged. Prematurely 'cleansing' and leaving the past behind comes at the expense of collectively owning what went on".*[154]

And with full one-sided colour blindness in place this academic then finished with a flourish:

> *"...racism expressed in the Cronulla Riots toward Arabic-speaking Australians has been **disavowed, disowned and distanced.** I ask, what does this collective forgetting suggest about contemporary patterns of racism in Australia".*[155]

If that was not enough, the rest of the country has apparently, dismissed the Shire as uniquely *"white, bogan and parochial"* thereby, enabling us all to collectively absolve ourselves of our full racist responsibilities:

---

[153] S. Perera, 'Race terror, Sydney, 2005'. *Borderlands* e-journal 5, No. 1, p. 14.
[154] A. Wise, (2017) 'The Long Reach of the Cronulla Riots: Denying Racism, Forgetting Cronulla', *Journal of International Studies*, 38:3, pp. 255-270, see p. 262.
[155] A. Wise, 'The Long Reach of the Riots', p. 255.

> "By fetishising the Shire as an exceptional place of white racists, it excuses the rest of Sydney, indeed Australia, from reflecting on their own attitudes and finding racism there".[156]

This kind of one-sided racial assessment of the Cronulla riots, and indeed the rest of Caucasian Australia, perpetuates a myth of Lebanese innocence and Caucasian guilt and underpins much of the flawed imagining of the inter-tribal conflict like the following:

> "The Cronulla riot was a blatant manifestation of Islamophobia- a form of the so-called 'new racism'- in the national public space. The rioters and their sponsors racialised the Muslim Other on the grounds of both religion and culture".[157]

Mild not wild racism

There have been a host of alternative theories as to what might have motivated a large crowd to congregate one warm Sunday in late 2005 and express in colourful and at times quite racist language their thoughts on unwelcome Lebanese visitors.

Some of those theories range from the **bizarre** to the **ridiculous** and finally to the **unsustainable**.

Incestophobia

Bizarre, in that according to an academic from the Australian National University, it was allegedly a revulsion by Caucasians of Lebanese cousin marriages that motivated a level of incestophobia, which combined with their own surfer culture of homo-erotic bonding, led to a rejection culturally and sexually of the Lebanese 'Other':

> "The exchange of insults preceding, and subsequent to, the Cronulla riot provided a set of circumstances in which ambivalences within, and between, a range of fraternal groups raised anxieties regarding incestophobia and homoerotic bonding to a pitch that was able to be expunged only through physical confrontations of 11 and 12 December 2005".[158]

---

[156] A. Wise, p. 260.
[157] R. Itaoui, and K. Dunn, 'Media Representations of Racism and Spatial Mobility: Young Muslim (Un)belonging in a Post-Cronulla Riot Sutherland', *Journal of Intercultural Studies*, 2017, Vol. 38, No.3, pp. 315-332, see p. 316.
[158] A. Redmond, 'Surfies versus Westies: Kinship, Mateship and Sexuality in the Cronulla Riot', *The Australian Journal of Anthropology*, 2007, 18:3, pp. 336-350, see p. 347.

The downtrodden Shire

Ridiculous, in that one scholar claimed it was the sense of disenfranchisement of the downtrodden of the Shire which led them to rise up and demand to be counted and matter.

> "...many white Australians, who previously had felt themselves to be entitled members of the Australian state, experience an increasing disenfranchisement. Resorting to nationalism as a way of asserting their membership of the nation-state, the Cronulla riots were a manifestation of the frustrations of many white Australians".[159]

Ridiculous because Cronulla and the Sutherland Shire are probably one of the wealthiest, most educated and environmentally attractive parts of the whole country let alone just Sydney.[160] It is hardly the place to look for the out of luck and angry searching for someone to blame, as one might amongst Donald Trump's 'deplorables'[161] or even Boris Johnson's 'Brexiteers'.[162]

But this academic was not quite done:[163]

> "We can now understand that the white rioters at Cronulla were motivated by disappointment in the role of that state in protecting and nurturing them as privileged citizens. Central were the changes to industrial relations legislation [by]...the Howard Government...in 1996 [to]...the Workplace Relations Act...[and] on 2 December 2005... the passing ...of WorkChoices".

In other words, industrial legislation passed nine years before the riots, and the Work Choices legislation passed by the Commonwealth Parliament in December 2005 (the same month as the riots), assented to on 14 December 2005 (four days after the initial event), and which did not take effect until

---

[159] J. Stratton, 'Non-citizens in the exclusionary state: Citizenship, mitigated exclusion, and the Cronulla riots', *Continuum: Journal of Media and Cultural Studies* Vol. 25, No.3, June 2011, pp. 299-316, see p. 299.
[160] M. Norquay and D. Drozdzewski, 'Stereotyoing the Shire: Assigning White Privilege to Place and Identity', *Journal of Intercultural Studies*, 2017, Vol. 38, No.1, pp. 88-107, see pp. 89 and 104.
[161] For a description of 'deplorables' see H. Clinton, Interview on Israel's Channel 2, September 8, 2016.
[162] J. Gabbatiss, 'Brexit strongly linked to xenophobia, scientists conclude', *The Independent,* November 27, 2017; M. Goodwin and O. Heath, 'Brexit vote explained: poverty, low skills and lack of opportunities', Report from the Joseph Rowntree Foundation, August 31, 2016.
[163] J. Stratton, p. 313.

late March 2006 some weeks after the riots had come and gone, had in some way caused or contributed to the Cronulla Riots. The timing alone of the second, and the lack of proximity of the first, makes this a ridiculous assertion.

A Muslim woman's view

In Part 4 'Reflections from the field' we reported on 12 interviews we conducted with MPs, community leaders and police, who were at the vanguard of events in late 2005. One of those interviews was conducted with Mecca Laalaa who in 2006, as a then 19-year-old, became the first Muslim woman to wear the 'Burkini' whilst training at Cronulla as a new lifeguard.

Mecca Laalaa, as a child, spent every weekend at Cronulla Beach and not once experienced any racialised treatment at the hands of Caucasian locals: *"I was born in Sydney...I grew up on the beach"*.

When asked why the conflict has not returned:

> **Laalaa:** *"I think people are learning how to deal with differences. And I think we've been given the tools to [do that]"*.

When asked whether or not Caucasian and Lebanese men were driven by racism, her response provides the fitting last words on the matter:

> **Laalaa:** *"No. There's always an underlying issue, whether it's an anger problem, whether it's feeling unsatisfied in your life. I wouldn't say racism is at the forefront of somebody's life"*.[164]

---

[164] M. Laalaa, Transcript of Interview, December 14, 2020.

20

Why Did it Happen?

"It's hard to launch surfboards from a beach where other people want to play soccer or play soccer where other people are hanging out to go into the surf"[165]

Making sense of it all

The events at and beyond Cronulla in late 2005, 'shocked and awed' the people of Sydney into an initial apprehension of their personal and communal safety, and then a reflection that perhaps our peaceful multicultural society could not be taken for granted. We have earlier outlined in detail the precursor simmering tensions between rival groups for the spatial and cultural control of the beach, how that ignited into conflict, and the manner in which police quickly restored peace to the streets, suburbs and beaches of Sydney.

The conflict, its unexpected occurrence in an otherwise relatively tranquil and tolerant Sydney, continues to raise questions which have, in our view, never really been satisfactorily answered. How did Sydney come to this? Why did it occur but never return? Was it really a racist event or was something else underpinning the conflict? To endeavour to answer these broader and deeper questions about the conflict, we drew on scholarly research to better explain human behaviour, tribalism, identity and intolerance of the 'Other', as a means of better understanding what happened, than just what a descriptor of the events and the policing in response might indicate.

---

[165] A. Jakubowicz, 'Masculinity, culture and urban power: the Cronulla conflicts and their amplification in popular media', in Chapter 10, *Lines in the Sand* ed., Greg Noble, The Institute of Criminology, Series 28, Sydney 2009, pp. 169-184, see p.182.

What happened and how police dealt with it, are of course critically important aspects to the Cronulla Riots, but here we endeavour to make meaning of those events by drawing on our notions of human nature in times of conflict. In doing so, we have presented the case that the events cannot be so easily dismissed as racist in riot and not so in revenge. If not one, then it can't be the other. And perhaps, neither tribe was so motivated, despite what the chants, the tattoos, the texts and the attacks might suggest. This will challenge many to see Cronulla in a different light.

Belonging and identity are very important aspects to appreciating what underpinned this conflict, as is the human need to tribalise into groups, and self-validate with stigmatising labels of "them" and "us". This more than anything else, in our view, provides the basis for a much deeper understanding of what happened at Cronulla and beyond all those years ago.

Belonging

He was a young male. He was a white Caucasian. He was a local Shire lad. He stood on Cronulla beach wearing an impossible to miss statement of territorial claim of space and identity: *"We Grew Here! You Flew Here!"*

In some ways, this catchy slogan became the advertising motif for what the Cronulla riots were allegedly about: That the "us" of the Shire had greater claim to territorialising the beach against the lesser claimant of the visiting "them".

These six words almost immortalise much of which underpinned the conflict given just how much the man and his chesty narrative were filmed and photographed. Whilst it did make for great copy, there is plenty to challenge in the claim itself, quite apart from the fact that many other issues were at play in driving the conflict.

But let us first look at this 'in your face' bald and bold claim of territorial entitlement. What are the limitations or inaccuracies on the validity of its assertion?

Firstly, grew where?

The young man emblazoned with *'We Grew Here! You Flew Here!'* is effectively asserting that as members of the Lebanese community were allegedly not born here, they were accordingly, less entitled to use and enjoy a beach 'owned' by locals who had been born and bred on its shores.

Assuming for argument's sake, that the claim of territorial entitlement to the beach can be grounded upon place of birth and upbringing, the rest of the claim is almost certainly a false one.

Except for a minority of the young Middle Eastern males frequenting Cronulla Beach in late 2005, most of the Arabic 'visitors' actually *'Grew Here'*. Most of their parents would have been born in Lebanon and to escape civil war, migrated in large number to the 'Lucky Country' in the 1970s. Perhaps as many as 70% of those who participated in the reprisals were born here in Australia.

The irony of all this 'we were born here but you were not' argument, is that at some historically distant point, there was no human presence at all on our huge continent and all of us, including the Indigenous, the Anglo Celts and the Lebanese, all descended ultimately from migration.

No-one can claim in Australia that they have a greater entitlement to possession because they 'grew here' and others did not! It is simply contrary to our historical record. No community just 'grew here'. We all came here from across the seas at some point in the past, either distant or recent!

Thousands of years ago the seas north of Australia were significantly lower than they are now but a measure of island hopping was still required by our first settlers:

> *"About 45,000 years ago, they [our first settlers] somehow crossed the open sea and landed in Australia – a continent hitherto untouched by humans".*[166]

This has been confirmed by research conducted by the Australian National University which concluded that it was island hopping water crossings which led to the first settlements on mainland Australia.[167]

---

[166] Y. N. Harari, *Sapiens: A Brief History of Humankind*, Vintage, 2011, p. 45.
[167] S. Kealy, J. Louys and S. O'Connor, 'Least-cost pathway models indicate northern human dispersal from Sunda to Sahul', *Journal of Human Evolution*, Vol. 125, December 2018, pp. 59-70.

As our First Australians arrived probably by small boat from Asia around 40-50,000 years ago, and the Anglo-Celtic communities of Sydney were originally settled by convict ship, and our Lebanese migrants arrived by plane, perhaps a more accurate chest emblazonment might have read as follows: *"You boated here. We sailed here, and You flew here."*

Not as catchy, but more accurate, far less grounded in a geographical entitlement, and less offensive. And it changes an aggressive claim of spatial domain, to one of historical interest only, which elicits more of a 'so what?' feel to its sentiment.

Interestingly, and despite the evidence that our indigenous communities were migrants too:

> *"...this proprietorial white-settler slogan was countered in Koori networks by the quip '**We growed here, You rowed here**', drawing attention to the strategic amnesia of the White postcolonial "custodians" as well as the hollow basis of their originary claims".*[168]

Anthropologically inaccurate, but sociologically understandable, given the subliminal case for a superior assertion of spatial possession, which the 'We grew here' slogan suggests.

Secondly, restricting movement for whom?

By asserting or resisting the claim for spatial domain at the beach, both locals and visitors were endeavouring to control and restrict the movement of the 'other'. The claim of territorial entitlement advocated by Cronulla locals was an important ingredient in the simmering tensions which led to the conflict.

It is an unusual occurrence for individual vigilante action by citizens to assert domain over 'their' territory to the exclusion of citizens from somewhere else. The power to lockdown and exclude is one almost entirely exercised by the law enforcement arm of the state and not by aggrieved individuals. Apart from the Cronulla riot and during the Covid 19 pandemic, this power has rarely been used in any comprehensive way. In the case of Cronulla locals, how could they sustain the case for territorial entitlement to the

---

[168] A. Taylor, 'Australian bodies, Australia sands', *Lines in the sand*, 2009, Chapter seven, pp.111-126, see p. 122.

beach and its surrounds? Even if the claim of overseas birth were entirely true for visitors to the beach, then so what? Thankfully, where you're born or what might be your cultural heritage has never been a basis upon which Australian governments regulate access to space, and nor should it be the basis for vigilante territorial entitlement.

We just take for granted, that relative to the rest of the world, we are genuinely free (most of the time), and that must and does include the right to travel and use public space where and when we please, no matter from whence we, or our forebears came.

As Noble and Poynting have argued: *"Access to public spaces and freedom to move are seen as fundamental to a democratic state."*[169]

Along the same lines, Itaoui and Dunn asserted in 2017 that: *"In a highly mobile world, the ability to access, move between, and inhabit space is fundamental to citizenship and belonging."*[170]

The claim of entitlement to space based solely on place of birth or where one's forbears were born, is simply an unsustainable one.

Thirdly, who and what is the 'other'?

The universal notion of human 'Otherness' and our need and desire to attain identity, is succinctly and sadly summed up in those confronting words of *'We Grew Here! You Flew Here!'*.

In other words, this chest adorned work of art, so graphically displayed that day, is a statement of identity, belonging and inclusion on the one hand, and Otherness and exclusion on the other. This all goes to the heart of what happened at Cronulla Beach in December 2005 and the weeks that followed.

It has been easy for countless commentators and even academics to simplify the whole Cronulla 'transaction' as an unexpected racial outburst of an otherwise calm and tolerant multi-cultural Australia. This somewhat

---

[169] G. Noble and S. Poynting (2010). 'White lines: the intercultural politics of everyday movement in social spaces', *Journal of Intercultural Studies*, Vol. 31 (5) pp.489-505, see p.496.

[170] R. Itaoui and K. Dunn, 'Media Representations of Racism and Spatial Mobility: Young Muslim (Un)belonging in a Post-Cronulla Riot Sutherland', *Journal of Intercultural Studies*, 2017, Vol. 38, No.3, pp. 315-332, see p.316.

superficial approach simply looks at the offensive words and actions of some of the 'Anglos' on the day of the riot, and the actions of some of the 'Lebs' during revenge attacks which followed and conclude that it was all race based on both sides.

But was it unambiguously race-based, or religious, or cultural, or about something else altogether? Was it more about how they formed their own group sense of individual belonging, the label this might be given to identify the group, and the consequent joy of excluding 'Others' from the group?

An analysis of these concepts and questions, and how they might better explain the Cronulla 'transaction' forms the basis of the next chapter.

21

Tribalism and Identity: Belonging and Otherness

> *"We are going to have to guard against a crude sort of nationalism, or ethnic identity or tribalism, that is built around an us and a them... the future... is going to be defined by what we have in common, as opposed to those things that separate us and ultimately lead us into conflict".*[171]

What is tribalism?

A detailed consideration of just what is tribalism, identity and belonging, and their corollaries of exclusion and Otherness, will go a long way, to enable an appreciation of what was really underpinning the adverse human interaction during the Cronulla Riots.

What drives the need or desire for us to form groups, claim a reassuring sense of an "us" and a "them" by leveraging off the group for identity and belongingness, and to label the "them" as not being part of "us" or amongst the "we", and therefore, pleasurably excluded as "Others"?

Amy Chua in her excellent work on political tribes, describes what can happen once we have tribalized and then feel the need to exclude others:[172]

> *"Humans are tribal. We need to belong to groups. We crave bonds and attachments, which is why we love clubs, teams, fraternities, family. But the tribal instinct is not just an instinct to belong. It is an instinct to exclude...*

---

[171] Former US President Barack Obama, 'Obama warns against "a crude sort of nationalism" taking root in the US', *The Washington Post,* November 16, 2016.
[172] A. Chua, 'Political Tribes', Bloomsbury Publishing, 2018, p. 1.

> *Some tribes are sources of joy and salvation; some are the hideous product of hate mongering by opportunistic power seekers. But once people belong to a group, their identities become oddly bound with it. They will seek to benefit their group mates even when they personally gain nothing. They will penalise outsiders, seemingly gratuitously. They will sacrifice, and even kill and die, for their groups".*

The human inclination to group, and then to exclude, has been graphically illustrated in literature such as the fictional account of William Golding's 1954 *"Lord of the Flies"* and its follow-on movie of the same name in 1963. Even Aristotle weighed in over two thousand years ago when he described us all as social beings who need to associate with one another for our own and group good.

> *"Man is by nature a social animal".*[173]

And eminent modern-day philosopher, Kwame Anthony Appiah, developed his own notion on grouping:[174]

> *"We're clannish creatures... we prefer our own kind and we're easily persuaded to take against outsiders.*
>
> *...we humans ascribe a great deal of significance to the distinction between those who share our identities and those who don't, the insiders and the outsiders".*

Tribalism and identity

The associating with what we regard as like-minded people gives us a sense of value, belonging, place, identity, and empowerment. And this sense of who we are, and where we fit in, is considerably enhanced by the pleasure of exclusion of those who do not belong, are different to "us" and are just not welcome. The happening of "belonging" and its consequent, but parallel "Otherness" are the two essential ingredients of tribal dynamics and inter-tribal conflict.

> *"...every identity comes with labels...identities matter to people... because having an identity can give you a sense of how you fit into the*

---

[173] Aristotle, *Politics*.
[174] K.A. Appiah, *The Lies that Bind Rethinking Identity*, Profile Books, 2018, pp. 30-31.

> *social world. Every identity makes it possible...for you to speak as one "I" among some "us": to belong to some "we"".*[175]

An identity can both protect and serve, as well as harm and hinder, depending on what identity in what circumstance. For example, being a keen and vocal follower of a soccer team in Australia is very unlikely to result in a violent outcome for a fan before, during, or after the game.[176] However, the same could not be said of the United Kingdom.[177]

We all have multiple social identities throughout our lives, and usually many at the same time, which reflect our comfort, if not need, to group into say, religious, political, professional, or sporting tribes. Without these critical ingredients of human nature, we would live in a quite different world and the Cronulla Riots may well have not happened.

Judy Lattas summed up succinctly the application of belonging and Otherness: *"The ugliness of the moment* [Cronulla] *lay in the reckless release of a widely shared, but routinely buried, aversion to and distrust of the Other".*[178]

The reason why race is such a simplistic explanation for what happened in late 2005, is that the two primary 'tribes' in conflict, the Anglo-Celtic Shire and the Southwest Sydney Lebanese, had much more to distinguish themselves from one another, than just what skin colour they carried. Language, religion, clothing, culture, dietary habits, and ethnicity, all played a part in defining entry or exclusion from either group.

Whilst there is ample record of 'Nulla boys' looking for 'Lebs' to bash, and the middle eastern violent responses being aimed at 'white people', it is way too glib to just dismiss this as a straightforward outburst of unbridled racism.

Tribalism at play in our ethnic communities is not much different to what is

---

[175] K.A. Appiah, pp. 9-10.
[176] The violence at an Edensor Park soccer match in Sydney's Southwest in March 2005 between rival Croatian and Serbian teams had far more to do with long inter-ethnic hatred of one another, than anything to do with soccer. See 'Firebombs, shots fuel soccer violence', *Sydney Morning Herald*, March 16, 2005.
[177] A. Roadburg, 'Factors Precipitating Fan Violence: A Comparison of Professional Soccer in Britain and North America', *British Journal of Sociology*, Vol. 31, No. 2 (June 1980), pp. 265-276.
[178] J. Lattas, 'Cruising: 'Moral Panic' and the Cronulla Riot', The Australian Journal of Anthropology, 2007, 18:3, pp. 320-335, see p.332.

entrenched in politics, religion, sport, and the workplace.

Who was the "us" and who was the "them"?

Tribes need a label to identify to what, and to whom they belong, and 'Otherness' also compels a label of disparagement, to identify what the belonging is not, and what and who to exclude. The disparagement label makes the group feel better about itself and why excluding the 'Other' is a noble deed in protecting the group.

It is this coalescing of belongingness, and its consequential essentiality of the labelling of "them" and "us", which fuels, and then ignites a 'clash of identities'. And the clash, when it occurs, might be racial, or cultural, or religious, or political, or sporting, or none of the above.

Tribalism rules

Tribalism, belonging, identity and 'Otherness' provide a compelling narrative to explain conflict, violence and animosity between competing groups at particular points in time. However, these things should not be overplayed as sources of human misery as they have also been the source of great cooperation and human achievement, although sometimes after a period of troubling interaction. Witness to this would be the Civil Rights movement in the USA, an acceptance and later support for Homophobia legislation in the developed world, and in Australia, the strong majority vote in late 2017 in favour of same-sex marriage.

It should never be forgotten that despite the turbulence, tribalism and 'Otherness' of Redfern, Macquarie Fields and Cronulla, we are a relatively very peaceful community. Most of the time we live amicably in civil society and when the tribes clash, we should not lament too much that this means the end of a tolerant Australia that most of us love and respect.

'Otherness' and the temptation to exclude, can and often has led to sweeping reforms, peace, and improvements between different tribes, as they all realise how much better in the end we are when we cooperate for a much greater good. Peace in our community does not occasionally break out but is the norm.

But in Cronulla and beyond in late 2005 it was not, and a primary reason was of identity as each tribe lived out its notion of what needed to be done to ensure it was protected and the 'Other' excluded.

However, as already noted, just being tribal or belonging to a tribe does not of itself cause inter-tribal conflict. Something more is needed to take that sense of belonging from just an "us" to an indignant and even angry reaction to an excluded "them".

In exploring explanations for what took the 'Anglos' and the 'Lebs' from simply belonging to their own "us" into attacking the excluded "them", we argue that it was not deep-seated racism driving the conflict but a discomfort with the differences between them and an absence of sameness on the beach. This 'intolerance to difference' manifested itself when perceived incivility and disrespect occurred on the beach causing the "us" to claim that the "them" were not entitled to the beach or the flag or what it meant to be an 'Aussie'. And the expression of much of this manifested intolerance certainly appeared racist or bigoted even if not causally driven by it.

All these notions which we believe coalesced to ignite the long simmering tensions between the "us" and the "them" at Cronulla Beach will now be explored in the next several chapters and why it was almost entirely between men.

22

Difference-ism not race-ism

> *"...much intolerance of different races, beliefs, and behaviours is driven primarily...not by animosity toward any specific target...but rather by a fundamental and overwhelming desire to establish and defend some collective sense of oneness and sameness".*[179]

Tribalism and difference

Much of the process of group forming manifests itself into harmless but manageable collections of comfort forming, *"sameness"* around the things which interest and matter to all the individuals forming whatever particular "us" it may be from time to time.

At Cronulla there were and still are multiple ethnic, religious, and political groups, which apart from late 2005, live in relative harmony. What changed? What shifted a relatively quiet interaction of even perhaps just simmering tensions to a full-blown conflict?

Why then does this almost constant grouping of us all into multiple identities and mutual acceptance of what is meant by "us" and "them" only rarely result in the "us" and the "them" transforming their differences on inclusion and exclusion into disagreement, dissension and sometimes violence? What are the triggers which fire up these intemperate reactions?

---

[179] K. Stenner, *The Authoritarian Dynamic*, Cambridge University Press 2005, p. 276.

The superficial approach: disparage, do not analyse

Most scholars have surprisingly, in their explanations for Cronulla, sought to apply simple but effective stigmatising labels: racism, islamophobia, incestophobia, partying, masculinity, and even homo-erotic bonding to just name a few.

For this discussion, we need to dig a little deeper than just label those manifestations of intolerance, and ask what caused those manifestations?

Did the mostly young men of the Shire and the entirely young men of Lakemba, just decide to embark on a racist bender because they were simply racist, or even Islamophobic or Christopohbic, or maybe even ethnophobic, or was there something else underpinning that behaviour?

In 2005, just months prior to the Cronulla Riots, the political psychologist, Karen Stenner, published a ground-breaking answer to the fundamental question of generic human conflict:

What are the root causes of intolerance?

In an extraordinary and confronting finding from exhaustive field research, Stenner found that what may seem on the surface as simply racist, bigoted, or morally deviant actions or words, may in fact be motivated far more by a shunning of difference:

> *"I have argued that a good deal of what we call racial intolerance is not even primarily about race, let alone blacks, let alone African Americans and their purported shortcomings.* **Ultimately, my contention is that much of what we think of racism, likewise political and moral intolerance, is more helpfully understood as "difference-ism".** *This is a strong and no doubt controversial claim"*.[180]

To the academics and social commentators who see Cronulla as an example of Whiteness engaging in unbridled and shameful racism against the Arab 'Other', Stenner's work would be regarded as heretical. However, science and not unbridled emotion is what should drive 'informed' conclusions on this.

It is still "them" and "us".

Stenner still settles on the universal notion of an "us" against a "them" as

---

[180] K. Stenner, *The Authoritarian Dynamic*, p. 276.

the driving force behind tribal conflict:

> "...the entire defensive arsenal is fuelled by the need to identify, glorify, privilege, and reward "us" and whatever beliefs and behaviours make us "us", and to differentiate, denigrate, disadvantage, and punish "them", and whatever beliefs and behaviours make them "them"..."[181]

But what if the "them" became part of "us".

In an almost déjà vu account of the Cronulla riots, Stenner, by highlighting the intolerance of difference per se, and the higher priority of the group protection of "us-ness" has inadvertently put into place the historical context of the cultural battles for the beach over nearly 50 years at Cronulla:

> "...should a new and even more different "them" make those who were formerly "them" look more like "us", then the formerly "them" should no longer be denigrated and punished, but instead come to share in the rewards of being "us"..."[182]

In other words, the Sharpies, the Westies, the Greeks, and the Italians, who once fought for spatial domain on Cronulla beach, eventually, with the sands of time, became more of an "us" than a "them", and a predisposition for local intolerance dissipated.[183] If Stenner is right, then this should go a long way to explaining why little noticeable conflict between the "us" and the "them" has occurred at Cronulla in all the years since late 2005.

Difference-ists not race-ists

Stenner wanted to test the change in manifestations of intolerance with a credible claim that NASA had confirmed the existence of alien life form *"who are very different from us in ways we are not yet able to imagine"*. She found a significant reduction in expressions of racial intolerance from those with a predisposition towards it in other circumstances:

> 'Clearly, to those relentlessly monitoring sameness and difference, black people seem more like "us" than "them" once there are green men afoot, and as such, are lavished with all the glory and rewards

---

[181] K. Stenner, *The Authoritarian Dynamic*, pp. 277-278.
[182] K. Stenner, p. 278.
[183] C. Evers, 'Locals Only!', *Everyday Multicultural Conference Proceedings*, Macquarie University September 28-29, 2006, pp. 1-9.

authoritarians reserve for "us". Thus, in the "aliens" condition, authoritarians actually express great affection for African Americans, and distaste for Nazis and the Ku Klux Klan, and far more than do libertarians, who seem to grow more intolerant (and punitive) when confronting the prospect of alien encounters. **These findings simply cannot be sensible unless much of what we call racial intolerance is primarily about difference more than race'.**[184]

This fascinating process of absolutely no behavioural change in glorifying "us" against "them" but a huge change in just who is the "us" and who is the "them" augurs surprisingly well for finding harmony between different tribes. It turns on its head the conventional multicultural approach of celebrating diversity and strongly suggests that the best way to attain peace and harmony is to search and highlight sameness and oneness rather than difference. This will be a challenge to many.

Stenner concluded that her "alien" experimental findings allowed her to make a confronting finding: that racism was far more driven by an intolerance of difference rather than an intolerance of colour or creed.

Intolerant to difference not just intolerant

Stenner found that many, if not most of us, have a predisposition to being intolerant to difference. She found that folks might be intolerant but never need, or bother to express that intolerance, until they feel their group's values and ways of doing things are under threat.

When a threat appears, in Stenner's view, people react in intolerant ways: morally, racially, or politically.

At the heart of her theory and one which provides a possible solid explanation for the one-offness of Cronulla, is that if a threat does not appear then no intolerance is manifested. Likewise, if a current threat recedes then so do the expressions of intolerance. This does not mean that folks who might comfortably say and do quite racist and bigoted things, are no longer going to engage in this kind of behaviour. What it does mean is that we are unlikely to hear from them unless and until a perceived threat re-emerges.

If this theory is sound, then it explains the long-term relative break out of

---

[184] K. Stenner, p. 280.

peace between the tribes at Cronulla. It does not mean, of course, that each of the "them" are now in a tolerant and loving embrace of the different 'Other'. Rather, it means that they each have no need to make any public expressions or actions to the contrary. The trigger for intolerance having passed, there is no impulse, need, or wish for any manifestations of that intolerance.

If there is any better explanation for what happened during and since the Cronulla Riots, then we are yet to hear of it. Stenner called her theoretical explanation as: *"The Authoritarian Dynamic"*.

The authoritarian dynamic

Stenner's seminal work on human intolerance defies the traditional knee jerk response of scholars, commentators, and the community, to stigmatise offensive behaviour with readily recognisable labels.

> *"Individuals possess fairly stable predispositions to intolerance of difference, that is, varying levels of willingness to 'put up with' differing people, ideas, and behaviours".*[185]

Stenner argued that her model of human intolerant behaviour had two fundamental interactions which underpin intolerant behaviour:

Firstly, a predisposition to being intolerant to difference or a perceived lack of sameness.

Secondly, the emergence of a threat to values, sense of order, 'appropriate' behaviour or simply a challenge to "us" by "them". This 'threat' to how "we" see things as working triggers an intolerant reaction.

Stenner regarded such things as expressions of racial, political, or moral intolerance as simply manifestations of a triggered discomfort towards anything different rather than something which might seem and be consequently labelled as simply 'racist' or 'deviant' or 'politically unacceptable'. That of course, does not mean that a manifestation was not racist, just that the cause of it emerging after a threat trigger, may not be a racist one.

Many Anglos and Lebanese in late 2005 certainly spoke, chanted, and

---

[185] K. Stenner, pp. 2 and 6.

behaved in a racist and religiophobic way but then stopped. Why? Stenner's work provides a plausible explanation.

If we apply Stenner's work to the Cronulla 'conflict' then we might be able to conclude that the two tribes were far less racist, bigoted or ethnophobic for the sake of it, as some would like to suggest, and far more motivated to behave as they did, because of a threat provided by the 'Other' as to how the beach should be used.

What was the 'threat' to sameness at Cronulla Beach?

Perhaps the most significant assertion we make in this book is that 'visitors' and locals engaged in disrespectful verbal interactions with one another, and visitors to the beach challenged the local behavioural code of how the beach ought to be used and shared.

Disrespectful language, and the towel versus the soccer ball, provided the trigger which threatened the 'sameness' we expect at the beach. The acculturated uniformity of how all of "us" use and enjoy the beach was challenged by the "them" with an alternative approach on how "they" believed it ought to be used and enjoyed by "them". This created a difference threat from the "them", and the "us" reacted in a demonstrably intolerant way, as did the "them" in revenge.

That is, the "them" were seen and regarded by the "us" as not behaving in a civil and courteous way on the beach according to what the "us" thought was an established and well understood ritual. This and little else is the fulcrum around which hinges most of what occurred in and around Cronulla all those years ago and will be explored in more detail in the next chapter.

What is an authoritarian?

Stenner used the term 'authoritarian' as the opposite of 'libertarian' with the former seeking group sameness and the latter non-groupie individualism:

> *"...authoritarianism is an individual predisposition concerned with the appropriate balance between group authority and uniformity, on the one hand, and individual autonomy and diversity, on the other".*[186]

This means that a challenge to the ways things 'ought to be' in the eyes of

---

[186] K. Stenner, p. 14.

an authoritarian results in intolerant manifestations which will be expressed depending on each circumstance. To most libertarians, tolerant academics and reasonably minded people in the broader community, the person expressing or acting out these intolerances would be labelled and possible permanently categorised as racist, or religiophobic, or homophobic, or at least culturally insensitive, depending on what reaction may have surfaced in each circumstance.

However, Stenner argues that these adverse and confronting responses are the products of an intolerant predisposition not the predisposition itself. That is, what might be generically regarded as intolerant behaviour will be neither seen nor heard, if there is no challenge or 'threat' to how the "us" sees things as working.

This means that those who use any opportunity to express intolerant views despite any present threat to 'sameness' are probably not 'authoritarian' but simply racist or homophobic or morally repugnant all the time. These kinds of people do not need a 'catalyst' to live out an intolerant predisposition and simply live and breathe their intolerance despite any prevailing 'threat' or challenging circumstance. At Cronulla there were a small number of White Supremacists who turned up to fan the flames of difference and discontent. They are and remain simply racist and bigoted individuals and thankfully, were a small minority of participants.

The failure by almost all academics and social commentators to adequately distinguish between the intolerant per se, and those who have a predisposition to intolerance, has left a gaping hole in the effective analysis of the 'Cronulla transaction'. Stenner's work does not excuse the offensive and intolerant actions by the Anglos and Lebanese in late 2005, but it does explain why it happened and why it has not happened again.

Threats to our wish for sameness

People do not lose a predisposition to intolerance, but they will quickly lose any desire to act intolerantly if a threat recedes or fails to materialise. Stenner described the process of how something becomes a threat which triggers an intolerant response:

> "...threats...to some system of oneness and sameness that makes "us" an "us": some demarcation of people, authorities, institutions, values,

> *and norms that for some folks at some point defines who "we" are, and what "we" believe in... In diverse and complex modern societies, the things that make us one and the same are common authority and shared values."*[187]

Stenner found in her field research that expressions of racial, moral, or political intolerance were all 'kindred spirits' connected and initiated as *"elements of a kind of defensive stance, concerned with minimising difference and promoting uniformity"*.[188]

> *"Conditions of societal threat...dramatically magnify the impact of authoritarianism on intolerant attitudes. Most notably, great variance in public opinion at the time, high levels of protest demonstrations...all vastly increase the propensity of authoritarian respondents to express racist, intolerant, and punitive attitudes".*[189]

This finding that intolerance is manifested to a much greater degree when protest and varying public opinion takes the stage, lends credence to claims that the emotive and divisive language used at the time by radio 'Shock Jocks' and tabloid newspapers, certainly stirred up a righteous 'moral panic' regarding allegedly 'rude' Lebanese visitors to the beach. However, two things were still essential for the conflict to burst forth: a predisposition to being intolerant to anything different and a breach of group values or desire for oneness. At Cronulla both tribes satisfied both litmus tests for intolerance to manifest.

Stenner found that authoritarians were:

> *"...relentless boundary maintainers, norm enforcers, and cheerleaders for authority whose classic defensive stances are activated by the experience or perception of threat to those boundaries, norms and authorities...authoritarians are oriented to collective rather than individual conditions".*[190]

And in what could have been an accurate sociological prediction and subsequent explanation of the Cronulla outburst and subsidence:

> *"Authoritarian fears are alleviated by defence of the collective...order:*

---

[187] K. Stenner, p.17.
[188] K. Stenner, p.25.
[189] K. Stenner, p.31.
[190] K. Stenner, p.32.

> *positive differentiation of the in-group and discrimination against out-groups, obedience to authorities, conformity to rules and norms, and intolerance and punishment of those who fail to obey and conform...*

> *...authoritarianism may be thought of as a reasonably stable individual predisposition that expresses itself to varying degrees under different environmental conditions. It is activated under conditions of collective threat, and yields...racism and intolerance in response to those threats to the collective.* ***This account allows for both an enduring individual predisposition and attitudes and behaviours that surge and subside under different environmental conditions".***

It should be made quite clear that the predisposition to intolerance of difference and the catalyst for intolerant actions applies equally to both the Anglos and Lebanese at Cronulla. The catalyst for riot and revenge almost came out of the blue after years of simmering but presumably manageable testy interactions at the beach:

> *"...this dynamic process – in which contemporaneous threats activate latent predispositions – explains the kind of intolerance that seems to 'come out of nowhere', that can spring up tolerant and intolerant cultures alike, producing sudden changes in behaviour that cannot be accounted for by slowly changing cultural traditions".*[191]

Multicultural conviviality vs intolerance to difference

That the 'Cronulla Troubles' were a placid affair compared to the great riots and genuine pogroms which have happened and continue to happen around the world, is far more a testament to our tolerant diversified society than a burial of it.

However, Stenner's work does throw up challenges for many who may like to imagine an infectious Australian society of universal embracement of diversity. If tolerance is better understood as the opposite of intolerance, then perhaps the notion ought to be regarded as more pejorative than laudable. If intolerance is analogous to 'not putting up with' then surely, tolerance is more akin to 'putting up with' than anything approaching a universal embrace. Putting up with a diversified multicultural society is

---

[191] K. Stenner, p. 136.

nothing like absorbing and living it, as some ethnic professionals, social commentators and academics would have us imagine. The notion that inter-personal and inter-tribal conviviality in a diversified society, might function and even prosper alongside the occasional expressions of xenophobic and racist attitudes, explains far more the value of Stenner's work, than might the superficial alternative of simply pretending that an absence of riot at Cronulla for many years, must mean that love and not hate has blossomed at the Shire.

> "...the concept of conviviality does not entail 'the absence of racism or the triumph of tolerance'. Indeed, [in] various ways...convivial relationships produce and co-exist with racist and xenophobic attitudes".[192]

It is quite possible, indeed in our view, quite probable, that the convivial calm between the tribes at Cronulla beach may still allow an interpretation of a successful multicultural society, whilst at the same time acknowledging below the surface, inter-tribal intolerance to difference and unuttered racist attitudes from all who is an "us" towards all who is a "them".

However, far from lamenting the decline of our notion of societal diversity and tolerance, we should celebrate it, and respect the human condition which seeks order, sameness and an unthreatening environment. And recognising this trait in most of us, provides a greater opportunity for peaceful co-existence than might otherwise be the case. If we all work towards an enhanced awareness of the benefits of highlighting our common communal interests, then perhaps we can witness a much larger group of "us" and "we" working together in greater harmony than the opposite. This we suggest is why having seen battle unfold between the tribes of Cronulla and Lakemba, peace was sought, found and has endured:

> "This perspective suggests that redefining the boundaries of "us" and "them" by creating a common in-group identity... is a fruitful approach to dealing with those who are intolerant of difference, reducing bias and minimising intergroup conflict".[193]

The challenge here, however, for the multiculturalists, is that achieving this

---

[192] K. Tyler, 'The suburban paradox of conviviality and racism in postcolonial Britain', *Journal of Ethnic and Migration Studies*, (2017), 43:11, pp.1890-1906, see p.1891.
[193] K. Stenner, p.281.

kind of harmonious existence draws on a group defending *"some oneness, not someone"*.[194]

Labelling the 'racists'

The initial and subsequent labelling of the Cronulla riots as an inebriated, White, racist, and bigoted bender, not only excuses the 'revenge' attacks from any such disparaging label but does not provide a satisfactory explanation for the conflict.

Much of what was said and done at Cronulla and beyond in late 2005 by both Anglos and Lebanese would satisfy a definition of racism or bigotry or ethnophobia. However, why did the participants act in this way? It is way too simplistic to suggest as many academics and social commentators have; that racist behaviour was driven by racists!

Karen Stenner provided that deeper consideration with her field-tested theory known as The Authoritarian Dynamic. Most individuals have a predisposition to being intolerant to difference and react when that difference appears to threaten the group notion of how things should work.

As will be seen in greater detail in the next chapter the threat which did emerge, and which triggered mutual manifestations of racial, religious, and ethnic intolerance was disrespect in verbal exchanges and a clash of how each should behave and use the beach. This was enough to cause the riots, but not enough for the tensions and underlying predispositions to being intolerant to difference, to perpetuate conflict.

In other words, the Anglos and the Lebanese may have had an underlying predisposition to being intolerant of each other, but are not per se racist, bigoted, or morally deviant towards the other. But should a threat emerge again from one towards the other, on what is considered inappropriate behaviour at the beach, then manifestations of racism, bigotry and generic intolerance are likely to reappear from either the "us" or the "them" or both. Thankfully over many years this has not happened.

We will now examine in greater detail in the next chapter what made disrespect and incivility on the beach, a trigger for an aggressive response from the competing tribes at Cronulla beach. How these factors created

---

[194] K. Stenner, p. 281.

a threat environment, which then fuelled an 'intolerance to difference' response, provides a compelling interpretation of what really caused the Cronulla Riots.

23

A Threat Emerges: Incivility on the Beach

> *"...the necessity of civility is imperative... When men shout and shriek or call names, we witness the end of rational thought process if not the beginning of blows and combat".*[195]

Civility and incivility

Given that incivility and disrespect played critical roles in triggering intolerance at Cronulla, it is useful to consider how they are defined.

> *"Civility is a social norm and a standard 'of behaviour... based on widely shared beliefs* [about] *how individual group members ought to behave in a given situation'. Put differently, 'A norm of civility defines the kinds of behaviour that persons can rightly expect from others'".*[196]

What is difficult in providing a universally agreeable definition of civility, is that what is appropriate in one setting might be considered rude in another. However, much of what was said by young Lebanese men of a sexual nature to young bikini clad Anglo women, in any context or setting would be regarded as uncivil, rude, and disrespectful.

Likewise, this would also be clearly the case if the contra had applied, with Cronulla males visiting Lakemba and using similar sexually predatory

---

[195] US Chief Justice Warren E. Burger addressing a meeting of the American Bar Association, May 18, 1871, 'The Necessity for Civility', *Litigation*, Vol. 1, No.1 (Winter 1975), p. 8.
[196] K. H. Jamieson et al, 'The Political Uses and Abuses of Civility and Incivility', *Oxford Books Online*, Oxford University Press, 2018.

language towards young Muslim women.

In any context, anywhere, if such confronting demeaning language were used by men towards any women, either burka or bikini clad, it would be regarded as uncivil, rude, and disrespectful. If young Caucasian men, regularly visiting Lakemba, had been so offensive as to have done this, it would have almost certainly resulted in an even angrier and more violent response from young Muslim men than what occurred from Cronulla males in reverse.

In this vein, but to a lesser degree, the disparaging remarks of some Anglos regarding an inability to swim or being unwelcome in respect of the Lebanese visitors, would have been interpreted as uncivil and rude.

Accordingly,

> *"Everyday incivility can be thought of as commonplace actions and interactions that are perceived to be rude or inconsiderate".*[197]

Why be rude?

It is probably universal that an uncivil verbal interaction is going to elicit strong emotive responses. The ruder and more insulting the greater the aggressive response. So why be rude?

> *"Insults and invective are a powerful means of differentiating an in-group from an out-group, an opponent from an ally".*

> *"Precisely because it evokes a strong emotional response, incivility is also a strategic tool in the arsenal of individuals seeking dramatic social or political change".*

> *"...invective can serve as an assertion of identity and power by those who are being marginalized by a majority community".*[198]

It could be argued, that at Cronulla all these factors were in play for both the conflicted tribes. If being rude defines belonging and exclusion, then the corollary of that must be that being civil, embraces a broader sense of inclusion and fellowship.

---

[197] T. Phillips and P. Smith, 2003. 'Everyday incivility: Towards a benchmark', *Sociological Review*, 51 (1): pp. 85-108, see p.85.
[198] K.H. Jamieson et al., p. 5.

In 1992 Phillip Selznick argued that civility has two important strands. Firstly, it encompasses the behaviour we expect of a citizen and secondly, it has an assuaging effect on potential conflict:

> "He defines the norms of civility as impersonal, rational, inclusive but he also points out that, as a norm of behaviour toward nonintimates and even strangers, it is, 'cool, not hot; detached, not involved'".[199]

Markus in interpreting this work of Selznick argued that:

> "Being 'detached, not involved', civility on its own does not generate an interest in the interests of others. At its best, it allows us to deal with these interests in a 'civilised' way, without recourse to hostility or violence".[200]

This then leads to an intersection of civility with respect:

> "Civility...concerns in a 'society of strangers' the recognition of the other as a bearer of basic and inalienable rights; it demands forms of conduct that respect these rights...and allows others to exercise them. It involves toleration of views different from one's own, a respect for the right of others to arrange their lives-within the limits of legality-according to their own convictions and values, and a readiness to find a modus vivendi in which these various convictions and plans of life can coexist".[201]

We can now clearly see that on all these definitional fronts, the Cronulla tribal interaction was uncivil and disrespectful. But civility and respect are not quite the same things.

What is respect?

As we would expect, there are multiple notions of respect:

- One notion of respect is to claim a universal expectation of every human being to be treated with dignity, thoughtfulness and courtesy despite whatever values, colour, or creed. This idea is that **respect is a right** and fits squarely with the belief that all of us are of equal value and equally

---

[199] M. M. Markus, 'Decent society and'/or civil society?' *Social Research*; Winter 2001; 68, 4 pp. 1011-1030, see p.1019.
[200] M. M. Markus, p. 1021.
[201] M. M. Markus, p. 1021.

entitled to proper regard and consideration.

- Another is that respect centres around an admiration and esteem given by others to another after engaging in commendable behaviour. This idea is that **respect is earned.**

- Finally, to ensure a peaceful and harmonious community, **respect needs to be mutual.** This aspect to respect requires a level of reciprocity between dual givers and receivers of thoughtful interaction.

Andrew Millie in 2016 outlined the challenge of the first and second notions of respect interacting: *"...there is a potential tension between respect being due to all persons (our rights) and respect having to be earned (our responsibilities)".*[202]

However, the overriding essentiality of respect is its mutuality. This above all other notions of respect is the most relevant to the Cronulla troubles:

> *"Respect is only possible if...different ways of living...are mutually recognised...It is also a cosmopolitan approach, which...can be regarded as 'an orientation, a willingness to engage with the Other'. One does not have to agree with the Other but has to at least be willing to engage...characterised by '...genuine acceptance of, connection with, and respect and space for the cultural other, and...the possibility of a togetherness in difference'".*[203]

Millie suggests we just need to respect each other and rejoice in difference, whereas Stenner argued the opposite: that we need to avoid difference as a vehicle to achieve peace and harmony amongst different groups in the community. One notion assumes we just owe a duty of respect to our fellow citizens, whereas the other does not take it for granted.

At Cronulla, many of the locals complained of a simmering tension caused by disrespectful interactions at the hands of Arabic visitors and their failure to use the beach 'as everyone else does'.

---

[202] A. Millie, *Philosophical criminology*, Bristol University Press, 2016, Chapter 7, 'Respect', pp. 99-109, see p. 101.
[203] A. Millie, p.103.

The beach: there to share

Ryan Barclay and Peter West in a paper published shortly after the riots, attempted to describe how Australians on the beach usually relate one to the other:

> "...the range of behaviour on the beach is wide. People do not, as a rule, care very much about the religious beliefs, opinions, or other aspects of those lying near them. The beach in Australia is a public domain open to use by everyone. Nobody owns the beach; it is a space shared by those who turn up".[204]

If we accept that this is the norm for our beaches, then the beach itself, and even the people on them, is almost never either a place, or a vehicle for expressing tribalism, belonging or exclusion. For almost all the time, our beaches are microcosm of a tolerant multicultural Australia.

Barclay and West share the view that the precursor to Cronulla Beach becoming exactly that: a place and a vehicle for expressing belonging and exclusion, was the increasingly misogynist and aggressive incivility of young males of Lebanese ethnicity. They seem to suggest that a lot of this was absorbed with gritted teeth until an overreach with an attack on lifesavers. This in their view, altered the dynamic to one of being or not being Australian. This might explain flag displays by several locals as an expression of their Australianness and belonging to the beach tribe. Barclay and West also provide a good account of a collection of people, building to a demonstration, then alcohol being added which shifted many in the crowd from patriotic fervour to racist pursuit: *'Little by little, the crowd became an angry mob'*.[205]

The Cronulla local perspective

Andrew Lattas (2007), unlike most academics, conducted interviews with a range of mostly Cronulla locals, and almost universally was told that the 'riot' was generated by incivility and a failure to respect fellow users of the

---

[204] R. Barclay and P. West, 'Racism or Patriotism? An eyewitness account of the Cronulla demonstration of 11 December 2005', *People and Place*, Vol.14, No.1, 2006, pp. 75-85.
[205] R. Barclay and P. West, p. 80.

beach and the beach itself, and not racism.[206]

However, at least one interviewee did concede that chants of 'wogs go home' did have 'a racial aspect'.[207]

One interviewee claimed: *"this was not about race but just manners"*.[208]

A common thread through the interviews was a Cronulla local perspective of 'visitors' to 'their' beach not fitting into the peaceful, sharing, relaxed co-existence of Australianness at the beach.

> *"The new migrants do not allow people to be at peace with themselves, with the beach, the sun and the need for solitude. They disturb a tranquil world. Time and again the theme of respect came up in interviews as what the riot was really about".*[209]

Interestingly, Lattas found that both locals and

> *"visitors from an ethnic background were not happy with the media's portrayal of both the riot and the suburb as racist. They* [both claimed] *...that Middle Eastern youths had a lot to answer for and that this was being glossed over".*[210]

Lattas also referred to the cultural clash of different interpretations of how beach space should be used. As one local put it:

> *"They just take up so much of the space...they come down and...maybe there's twenty or thirty of them in a family. And it's a space thing...I wouldn't have thought it was a race thing."*[211]

Playing soccer, taking large families to the beach and projecting ethnic difference were all hardly enough to have precipitated the events of late 2005, but may have had a contributing irritating factor to locals who preferred to see 'their' beach and its space used in a different way. This combined with insults and disrespect to local women, and an Aussie icon, the lifeguard, precipitated a reaction which Lattas describes as follows:

---

[206] A. Lattas, '"They Always Seem to be Angry": The Cronulla Riot and the Civilising Pleasures of the Sun', *The Australian Journal of Anthropology*, 2007, 18:3, pp. 300-319.
[207] A. Lattas, p. 313.
[208] A. Lattas, p. 304.
[209] A. Lattas, p. 306.
[210] A. Lattas, p. 310.
[211] A. Lattas, p. 310.

> *"The riot was ultimately a defense of civil society, of the informal regimes of moral order that Australians had now to rely on given what many residents criticised as absent and inadequate state policing and a state government biased towards minorities at the expense of the rights of the majority."*[212]

This may have been how some locals felt in interviews well after the events, but it still belies an unreasonable expectation of police resolving incivility, disrespect and culturally awkward use of beach space and naively suggests government was ignoring their plight by being focussed elsewhere.

Bad manners

Greg Noble (2009) believed that racism, as either an instigator or a consequence of what happened on Cronulla Beach, was a far too simple and dismissive social construct:

> *"... a theme that emerged in the weeks before and after the riots was a concern over the appalling behaviour of (some) Australians, demonstrating, it was claimed, a lack of respect and a decline in standards of public behaviour."*[213]

In somewhat of a stretch, Noble packs all the behaviour of pre-cursor insults, the inebriated reactions on the beach and the violent responses as all 'criticism of bad behaviour'.[214] And again, in dismissing local angst towards sexist, misogynist visitors as: *"The preoccupation with bad manners imposes a singular moral universe that reflects the dominant culture".*[215]

Perhaps only an academic could argue that one.

Manners are certainly culturally, socially, geographically and religiously influenced, but as discussed above, some of the things said to the young women at Cronulla Beach, over a sustained period, would probably have upset any group of women anywhere, as would some of the commentary directed at the Lebanese men in response. However, there is certainly a case for Noble to argue in respect of taking and using beach space, rather than

---

[212] A. Lattas, p. 306.
[213] G. Noble, '"Where the bloody hell are we?" Multicultural manners in a world of hyperdiversity', in *Lines in the Sand,* ed., Noble, G. Institute of Criminology Press, Sydney, 2009, pp. 1-22, pp. 5-6.
[214] G. Noble, p. 6.
[215] G. Noble, p. 10.

implying an excuse for misogyny:

> "There is a tension, then, between the way in which manners are a form of social lubricant which works productively to give people a sense of social order and enable cohabitation, and the way manners are used to police marginalised groups, moral deviance and social inequality".[216]

Finally, Noble succinctly sums up the larger question of whether the 'riot' could be classed as racially inspired or was simply a clash of different notions of civil behaviour and good manners:

> "...concerns with forms of social conduct that allow people to get along in local spaces also involve larger questions of racialised perceptions of order".[217]

Enforced togetherness: How we are meant to behave

Amanda Wise also in 2009, provided an excellent essay on how the different cultural expectations of Western and Middle-Eastern approaches to the civil use of 'enforced togetherness' in such public places as shopping centres and the beach contributed to the unrest at Cronulla:

> "Cultural norms involving specific rituals and codes for the management of such situations are embodied in our habitus which reproduces these rituals at the pre-conscious level".[218]

Our learned and ingrained habits: 'habitus'

'Habitus' is an interesting term, coined by the eminent French sociologist, Pierre Bourdieu and refers to:

> "...the physical embodiment of cultural capital, to the deeply ingrained habits, skills, and dispositions that we possess due to our life experiences...In the right situations, our habitus allows us to

---

[216] G. Noble, p. 13.
[217] G. Noble, p. 14.
[218] A. Wise, '"It's just an attitude that you feel": Inter-ethnic habitus before the Cronulla riots', in *Lines in the Sand*, 2009, Chapter eight, pp. 127-145, see p. 131.

successfully navigate social environments".[219]

Wise argued that the quite different approaches to what were 'ingrained habits' on the beach by Anglos and Lebanese led to conflict:

> "Extending the notion of habitus to the discomforts experienced in the crowded public beach suggests that certain behaviours are noticed more where the actors involved are differently embodied and where codes and ritual norms are not shared".[220]

The long build up to December 2005, was to a large extent the increasingly strident masculine preening from and towards Lebanese 'visitors', but also involved a clash on the beach between the quiet claiming of space by the towel and the body of Anglos, and the boisterous challenge of that space by Lebanese soccer games. This clash was cultural and not racial and its gradual percolation into a conscious and unconscious local irritant certainly added fuel to the fire created by the 'battle of the life-guards'.

In our view, it was primarily incivility, as perceived by Shire locals, in the way it breached their notions of how individuals ought to ritually behave in the 'enforced togetherness' of a crowded beach, which eventually ignited the Cronulla riots:

> "In a highly individualised Western context, civility requires that strangers maintain a separateness in crowded places. Rituals for the maintenance of self-containment in public places involve what Goffman calls 'civil inattention', which refers to those micro-rituals employed to achieve a sense of staying unknown in public places. It represents a 'competence to refuse relations without creating non-persons'".[221]

Polite inattention of the Other: How civil society works

Like Bourdieu, Erving Goffman, also one of the great sociologists of the 20th century, argued that to achieve constructive communal sharing in crowded public places, we need to dance a kind of careful ritualised inter-acknowledgement of each other, without actually interacting or formally

---

[219] W. Longhofer and D. Winchester, *'Habitus Social Theory re-wired'*, Routledge, 2016.
[220] A. Wise, pp. 131-132.
[221] A. Wise, p. 132.

connecting. This is what he meant by "civil inattention".²²²

As Wise put it: *"This management of strangeness is a normalised non-relation designed to maintain a sense of apartness in a context of enforced togetherness".²²³*

This kind of sociological analysis of how we are coded and acculturated as to how to 'behave' in public goes a long way to providing a theoretical underpinning of the human clashes on Cronulla beach:

> *"These rituals...help explain some of the irritation at soccer on the crowded beach. When young men enter the "zone" of other users...it is experienced by Anglos as an act of incivility...*
>
> *...Despite the crowded space, the layout and codes of organisation which help sustain unobstructed movement, and rituals which manage the civil non-relation with other users, maintain the myth of 'freedom' and a sense of 'aloneness in a crowd', and produces a feeling of relaxation and comfort...*
>
> *...boisterousness on the beach is experienced as intrusive; without the ritual of civil inattention, this is experienced as an act of incivility".²²⁴*

Much was and continues to be written about the 'White trash of the Shire' rising up in an orgy of '*mass racist violence*' which, given the relative calm and peace since late 2005 at Cronulla beach, make this kind of explanation of what happened, that much harder to sustain.

A somewhat simpler but more sustainable explanation is required:

> *"Western bodies often feel uncomfortable in crowded spaces because their culturally attuned sense of interpersonal distance is much greater than other cultures. Personal space is 'an extension of the self's presence in space, and violation of this space by another is felt to be like the violation of the body itself'. So physically, habitually, and historically engrained is this spatial and bodily order, that the disorder can produce a sense of bodily threat and a sense of shock,* **especially when there is no accompanying apology or acknowledgement of transgression.***'²²⁵*

---

²²² E. Goffman, (1963) *Behaviour in Public Places,* Free Press/Macmillan, New York.
²²³ A. Wise, p. 132.
²²⁴ A. Wise, pp. 132 and 135.
²²⁵ A. Wise, p. 133.

Finally, Wise gives a withering message to all those quick to conclude that 'Something is rotten in the state of Cronulla'.[226]

> "Such encounters produce a sense of dis-ease. Many commentators dismissed Anglo beach users irritated at young men playing soccer in their midst as prejudiced, however this irritation had as much to do with subconscious expectations about how public spaces such as the beach should be used and shared, about the kinds of bodies one might expect and how they should move as a cluster".[227]

Clashing behavioural codes: conflicting habitus

Clifton Evers drew on the notion of subconscious coding, to explain a clash of 'habitus' between two groups of mostly men with quite different ritualised approaches on how to behave in a crowded public space, such as a beach:

> "The unwritten rules of this local area could seem strange and frightening because they're rules made by others. Ideas about where you walk, swim, surf, how you dress, what kind of games you play and food you eat on Cronulla Beach have evolved to fit a particularly Anglo-Australian view of the world. Inexperienced beachgoers and people from other backgrounds transgress the beach rules, often unintentionally, because these practices are unfamiliar".[228]

Evers then succinctly sums up the coded clash:

> "The problem was that the Lebanese Australian blokes' own rules and values were already deeply ingrained in their flesh, so they didn't want to become the same as the locals. In fact, **they couldn't learn the script and would never be able to belong.** The rules and values that they'd grown up with had become a part of their flesh, meaning that they would have been damned hard to shake even **if they had wanted to**".[229]

Whilst the ritualised coding we all become acculturated with by adulthood

---

[226] A play on the words spoken by Marcellus in Hamlet, 'Something is rotten in the state of Denmark', W. Shakespeare, *Hamlet*, Act 1, Scene IV.
[227] A. Wise, p. 133.
[228] C. Ever, 'Locals Only', *Everyday Multiculturalism Conference*, Proceedings, Macquarie University, September 28-29 2006, edited by Selvaraj Velayutham and Amanda Wise (2007) pp. 1-9, see p. 3.
[229] C. Evers, 'Locals Only', p. 6.

explains to a substantial degree the underlying reasons for 'cultural clash', and the constant and inexorable increase in local irritability, it took a lot more than loud music and kicking soccer balls in the wrong place to have lit a local fuse. However, this did provide a 'code clash' platform, upon what would sit offensive discourse and assaults upon a sacred cow: The Life Guard. The threat developed and lit the fuse for all those Anglos and Lebanese with a predisposition to react intolerantly to difference.

24

Claiming Territory: "It's our Beach!"

> *"Our construction of 'Others' are...intimately linked to our construction of places...the apparently innocent spatiality of social life...become filled with politics and ideology".[230]*

Spatialising tribalism

What is unusual but not unique, is that the 'clash of identities' played out at Cronulla beach in late 2005 was grounded in geography, as much as the more generic concepts of belonging and exclusion.

Tribalism often does not depend upon, nor in any way require, a spatial domain. Loyalty to a political party, a religion, or a football team, does not require a specific geographic point to confirm identity. However, at Cronulla, the various tribal groupings in play, were very much about who was entitled, because of a particular identity, to freely use and dominate the beach space.

Noble and Poynting described this as:

> *"...the spatial regulation of cultural difference: such spaces become landscapes of social exclusion because they define who belongs and who does not".[231]*

And who has the domain over a public space in the event of inter-identity rivalry will be determined by the 'dominant group'.

---

[230] K. Durrheim, and J. Dixon, 'The role of place and metaphor in racial exclusion: South Africa's beaches as sites of shifting racialisation', *Ethnic and Racial Studies* Vol. 24, No.3, May 2001, pp.433-450, see pp. 433-434.

[231] G. Noble and S. Poynting, (2010). 'White lines: the intercultural politics of everyday movement in social spaces', see p. 496.

Due and Riggs described the sociological phenomena as follows: [232]

> "...dominant group members...have an image of what that space "ought" to look like, in terms of who gets to occupy that space, and under what conditions. As such, notions of "undesirability" rather than "inferiority" become important
>
> ... a dominant group may not necessarily consider a certain racial group to be inferior, they may nonetheless consider them to be undesirable, and therefore not want them occupying "their" space, unless it is under certain terms".

They then argue that the central motivating issue becomes one of space and not race, but that this is also tied up closely with how the dominant group pictures national identity and spatial domain:

> "This means that the problem becomes a spatial-national one rather than one of racism, in which discourses of belonging and nationalism imply a positioning of a minority group into the national space according to how and where the dominant group wants them to fit".[233]

Tribal battles through religion, politics, and cultural difference, can be quite aggressively pursued without the need for a spatially driven flag raising ceremony. In other words, exclusion is not always a territorial process, but it was at Cronulla.

> "Belonging in space, indeed was one of the core issues at the heart of the Cronulla riot – where tensions around the 'right to territory' was written in the sand of the beach, and on the bodies of the rioters, who felt entitled to regulate access to 'their' territory"'[234]

Localism, masculine bonding, and spatial claim

Clifton Evers has a relatively gentler and a somewhat more anthropologically accurate assessment of male bonding, friendship, and the protection of local space as a major cause of the Cronulla riot:

---

[232] C. Due, and D. W. Riggs, '"We Grew Here You Flew Here": Claims to "Home" in the Cronulla Riots', *Colloquy*, 16, pp. 210-228, see p. 215; see also: H. Hage, *White Nations: Fantasies of White Supremacy in a Multicultural Society*, Pluto Press, 1998.
[233] C. Due and D.W. Riggs, p. 215.
[234] R. Itaoui, K. Dunn, 'Media Representations of Racism and Spatial Mobility', p. 316.

> "My focus is on explaining how the masculine bonding that localism fosters led to some– surfers - a key group at–Cronulla - participating in the violence that took place, even though some of them may not have intended to be racist. The bonding I discuss is a form of mateship that functions as a type of care. It's a way of doing care that doesn't exempt violence, so it can become ugly at times."[235]

Conflict between visitors and locals at Cronulla has been going for decades, and by 2005, was nothing new except for the change in profile of the 'visitors'.

> "In the 1960s 'sharpies' would arrive at Cronulla via the South-West train-line. They were from inland suburbs. Their hair was spiked on top and long at the back, and they wore pinstriped pants, black shirts, and suede shoes. Surfers used to recruit each other and converge on Cronulla station where they would throw stones at, or beat up, the sharpies. But the sharpies gave as good as they got".[236]

This is almost déjà vu.

> "Over the last few years it's been the Lebanese-Australian men's turn. They travel to Cronulla in cars and on trains, and also favour particular sports, food, and ways of dressing. Even their bodily posture is read for its cultural coding: how they stand, walk, and sit. What's radically different is that racial, ethnic and cultural differences have become the easiest markers of difference".[237]

What emerges here in this analysis is that local rules and mores of behaviour and space sharing were set by locals and informally enforced against all visitors no matter what colour or creed. This would be a revelation to many who imagine that White Cronulla in December 2005 unleashed pent up unbridled racist violence. If only it were that historically simple.

Wendy Shaw remembered in 2009 growing up in Cronulla in the 1970s and recalled a time of locals protecting their beach against all visitors *"regardless of where they had come from"*:

> "...the Shire's surf culture included a form of beach apartheid which

---

[235] C. Evers, 'Locals Only!', *Everyday Multicultural Conference Proceedings*, Macquarie University, September 28-29 2006, pp.1-9, see p.1.
[236] C. Evers, 'Locals Only', p. 3.
[237] C. Evers, 'Locals Only', p. 3.

although not overtly racialised, was territorial: you were either one of us, or you were against us. The train, which terminated at Cronulla, brought carriage-loads of visitors who came to spend a day at "our" beaches. Many of the teenagers and young adults who visited were marked with "difference", and therefore fair game to their surfie counterparts. "We", as in "surfies" (males with female supporters) particularly hated "westies" (people from Western Sydney) and the groups of youths who came in from other suburbs, to go to the cinema or beach by train, were labelled "westies" or "bankies" (that is, from Bankstown), regardless of where they had come from".[238]

Racialising the tribal and spatial conflict at Cronulla in late 2005 is convenient for some but challengeable, given the history at that place of tribal and cultural conflict, around the beach space going back to the 1960s. First, the Sharpies, then the Westies and finally, the Lebs. And long before the Anglo/Lebanese 'battle' of 2005 was the Eastern Beach versus Western Sydney conflicts of the 1970s:

"Particularly vulnerable were the visually obvious "westies": anyone sporting untanned skin, a distinctive haircut (especially one lacking sun-bleached "rats tails") and/or tattoos, risked ridicule".[239]

Claiming the beach

Both tribes during the Cronulla 'troubles', in their own space would have felt comfortable and secure, one tribe in Sutherland Shire, and the other in South-West Sydney. But the beach is an attractive place to be with friends, family, and mates and unsurprisingly, tribes from the western reaches of Sydney have sought space on our beaches over a long period of time. The contrast in the mores and accepted rules of tribal membership almost compel resentment and conflict when the two would uncomfortably interact on the beach.

The conflict at Cronulla was as much about tribal lore, cultural difference and the 'taking' and 'protecting' of space as is any other explanation. Once

---

[238] W. Shaw, 'Riotous Sydney take three (Cronulla) Confessions of a beach survivor', in *Lines in the Sand,* Institute of Criminology Press, 2009, Chapter four, pp. 58-71, see p. 65.
[239] W. Shaw, p. 65.

a visiting group is seen as an 'Other', then the seeds are planted initially for resentment, then response and finally retribution.

The concept of enforcing belonging and shunning 'Otherness', in the case of Cronulla centred around space and territory, as the defining place of tribal angst:

> *"Localism is a process of dominating a territory and policing its cultural laws. It works with the same logic as nationalism, in that it creates an us and them situation, in which the them is never as good or as right as we are".*[240]

The "us" excluding the "them" from the beach and the flag

The conflict at Cronulla was underpinned by tribalism, exclusion, and spatiality. White Christian Anglo-Celtics who projected a bronzed Aussie masculinity, were always going to coalesce very differently than Arabic Muslim Lebanese, who projected a quite contrasting cultural, ethnic, and religious paradigm. However, neither were, nor are, right or wrong, simply different, and each tribe gravitated in somewhat contrasting directions.

The defining identities of each were also what determined their notion of belonging, as well as 'Otherness' and the basis upon which inclusion or exclusion were stipulated.

What makes Cronulla a fascinating case study in inter-tribal conflict is that the conflict itself was centred around the claim of one tribe over another to a spatial domain: the beach. And in laying claim to that spatial domain, some locals, some talk back radio shock jocks, and some White Supremacists, asserted an Australian identity which allegedly one tribe had over the other: the Aussie flag as well as an Aussie beach.

---

[240] C. Evers, 'Locals Only!', p. 2.

25

Claiming the Aussie Identity: "It's our Flag"

"[For] some people the flag... represents the best of American ideals... [But] in certain contexts, say flown from the back of a big pick-up truck with tinted windows, flags are intimidating, even scary... [and] ... 'asserting the flag...always comes at somebody's expense. Because... nationalism is always about who's an insider and who's an outsider'".[241]

Only 'Aussies' welcome!

Leading up to, during and beyond the initial 'riot', there was an attempt by a vocal few, to claim the Australian identity as belonging to Shire locals and not those who lived elsewhere in Sydney, especially those of Middle Eastern appearance. This was a quantum shift of belonging and 'Otherness', from *"you don't belong on our beach"*, to *"you are not Australian"*. This was certainly a significant change from the previous 'battles for the beach' which have been waged at Cronulla for over 60 years.

The claim of being the truly Australian identity by posting or wearing the flag, projecting 'patriotic' slogans, and being a surf life saver, thankfully, in the end, was as ephemeral as the assertion of primacy over the beach space.

Despite this, some exaggerated academic commentary maintains a myth that every single riot day attendee was asserting this rather new, limited, and reactionary view to what it meant to be Australian.

"By holding the Australian flag, the Anglo-Australians (Sutherland

---

[241] A. Venugopal, 'The American Flag: Symbol of Beauty or intimidation?', *WNYC News*, June 14, 2018.

Shire boys/Cronulla residents) claimed their exclusive territorial rights over the Cronulla space".[242]

This is historically, academically, and sociologically misleading.

There is no question that several Cronulla locals hoisted the Australian flag, or draped themselves with it, or painted our flag on their bodies, or wrote or chanted 'Aussie' themes. However, even a most cursory examination of the footage will show a large majority were not so adorned. And for those who were, rather than asserting territorialised Whiteness, perhaps they might have been reaching for a vehicle to assert that attacking a lifeguard, or behaving in an uncivil way on the beach, was simply un-Australian.

It is quite different to assert *"This is un-Australian"*, rather than *"I am Australian, and you are not"*. The former is far less offensive than the latter, as the first asserts that certain behaviour is unwelcome for all, whereas the second, both claims and rejects an entitlement to an emblematic patriotism.

We should not pretend that some offensive messages did not transpire leading up to, during and after the conflict. Perhaps the two most infamous messages are as follows: *"Every fucking aussie. Go to Cronulla Beach Sunday for some Leb and wog bashing Aussie Pride ok".*

And that was followed with: *"All lebo/wog brothers. Sunday midday. Must be at North Cronulla Park. These skippy aussies want war. Bring ur guns and knives and lets show them how we do it".*

In this digital age it takes only a small number of violent White, or Muslim supremacists, to stir up a whole lot of trouble with text messaging campaigns like these. The Cronulla riots were no exception to this. Rather interestingly, if perhaps inadvertently, both clarion calls to commit violence on the Other, assert or imply a level of Australianness.

"These skippy aussies…" more than suggests that there must be other kinds of 'aussies' who are not descendants of Caucasian Europeans. Whereas *"Every…aussie. Go to Cronulla for some bashing Aussie Pride"*, makes it pretty clear that the author of that message felt it was all about Australianness versus non-Australianness.

But it is a long stretch to claim that anyone who turned up as a result, was

---

[242] N. A. Kabir, 'The Cronulla riots: Muslims' place in the white imaginary spatiality', *Cont Islam* (2015) 9, pp. 271-290, see p. 275.

either claiming, or seeking to claim, a monopoly over the Australian identity. The issue and the trouble this generated at the time, compels a consideration of the quantum difference between patriotism and nationalism, and how both interact with national identity.

What is it to be, or claim to be, of a national identity? For example, what does it mean to be American, or un-American, or Chinese or un-Chinese, or Australian, or un-Australian? These are not easy questions to answer, and simply flag draping for the cameras, is not enough anywhere, anytime, to purloin a national identity for your "us" against their "them". However, all jurisdictions from time to time assert that an 'Other' within, does not quite measure up to a pre-conceived notion of 'nationess'.

Let us look at these three jurisdictions in turn to get a broader picture on this important issue and then draw parallels for Cronulla and the claim of 'Aussieness'.

The United States

The experience of US American Somali Muslim Congressman Ilan Omar on this issue is worth recounting. The then newly elected Democrat Rep. in 2018, took no time to position herself as a strong critic of Israel and the level of support it gained from US congressman. Interestingly, she questioned and was then in turn questioned herself, in respect of both her loyalty to the US and her Americanness.

Rep. Omar in challenging the role and influence of the Israel lobby in the US was accused of accusing the 'Other' of being un-American and who in turn herself was accused of being un-American by virtue of her faith. No wonder Rep. Omar responded:

> "I am told every day that I am anti-American if I am not pro-Israel. I find that to be problematic and I am not alone. My Americanness is questioned by the President and the GOP on a daily basis, yet my colleagues remain silent. I know what it means to be American, and no one will tell me otherwise".[243]

You can almost hear all the Cronulla participants and 'visitors' saying then

---

[243] D. Paul, 'Top Democrat demands another apology from Rep. Ilhan Omar, accusing her of "a vile anti-semitic slur"', *The Washington Post,* March 4, 2019.

and now: *"I know what it means to be Australian, and no-one will tell me otherwise".*

Chelsea Clinton, the daughter of Bill and Hillary Clinton, added fuel to the fire by criticising Omar and then signing off her missive as '*an American*' as if Omar was no longer, at least on this issue, a fully-fledged American.[244] No wonder Mitch McConell the US GOP Senate minority leader got into grief when arguing that Republican voting restriction initiatives were not designed to curtail African American voters supporting the Democratic Party: *"African American voters are voting in just as high a percentage as Americans".*[245]

China

The treatment of Xinjiang Uyghur Muslims in Western China by the Chinese Government puts into stark contrast the relatively minor challenges to our multicultural model which occurred during the Cronulla Riots.

China established in 2017, a Soviet era style of Gulags across Xinjiang province for its Turkic Muslim inhabitants, with an estimated 1200 camps imprisoning perhaps as many as one million people. Initially, the Chinese Government denied the existence of the camps, but with strong satellite and local evidence to the contrary, eventually admitted that they were *"vocational education and employment training centres*' designed to address 'extremism".

> *"It is believed that the PRC has so far locked up over 10 per cent of the adult Muslim population of Xinjiang".*[246]

If social and academic commentators still think that the inebriated few at Cronulla were engaging in Islamophobia then perhaps this account will temper their disparagement of the Sutherland Shire:

> *"Muslim-majority regions are being assigned detention quotas, resulting in the internment of large swathes of Muslim populations without due process. Rather than representing court-sanctioned*

---

[244] C. Clinton, @ChelseaClinton, February 11, 2019.
[245] K. Johnson, 'Mitch McConnell says Black people vote just as much as "Americans"', *USA Today,* January 20, 2022.
[246] J. Milward, '"Re-educating" Xinjiang's Muslims' *The New York Review of Books,* February 7, 2019, p.38.

> *criminal punishments, official documents portray re-education in terms akin to free medical treatment of a dangerous religious ideology... the state has been framing the Uyghur population almost as a biological threat to society, which must be contained through physical separation, surveillance and detention".[247]*

There has been unrest in Xinjiang and racial and religious conflict between the Han dominant Chinese Government and the minority Uyghur Muslims.

> *"The Chinese Communist Party's mass internment and coercive indoctrination of Muslim minorities is intended to forcibly remake their identity.*
>
> *...The party now increasingly finds Islamic faith and even non-Han ethnic culture to be inimical to the goal of homogeneous Chinese identity".[248]*

This is an aggressive agenda pursued from Beijing to transform China from an imperialist plural and religiously tolerant society, to one which knows only one ethnic and national identity. It is reshaping what it means to be Chinese and that means not being a Muslim, and being an ethnic Han, or as close as one can get to that after 're-education'.

As practising the Muslim faith and living the cultural life of an ethnic Uyghur are now regarded as un-Chinese, steps have been taken by the Chinese government to eradicate both: *"Distinctive Uyghur religious and other cultural practices are increasingly circumscribed or legally banned. School instruction in the Uyghur language... has been eliminated".[249]*

This appalling episode of religious and ethnic cleansing in China, makes a wholesale mockery of any claim that the level of racial, religious and ethnic intolerance displayed by Anglos and Lebanese at Cronulla bordered on the end of our pluralist multicultural society as we then had known it.

Our relatively peaceful Sydney since late 2005, and comparisons with US White Supremacists, and China Han Supremacists[250], more than suggests

---

[247] A. Zenz, "'Thoroughly reforming them towards a healthy heart attitude": China's political re-education campaign in Xinjiang', *Central Asian Survey,* 2019, Vol.38, No.1, pp. 102-128, p. 103.
[248] J. Milward, *The New York Review of Books,* February 7, 2019, p. 41.
[249] J. Milward, *The New York Review of Books,* February 7, 2019, p. 41.
[250] See C. Campbell, *'The Han Supremacy',* Time, July 19/July 26, 2021, pp. 39-43.

that despite Cronulla, we are in fact a relatively tolerant multicultural community.

Australianness

However, in late 2005 there was an attempt by a minority of shire locals to claim both the Australian identity and Muslim un-Australian 'Otherness'. Thankfully, neither prevailed.

'Australianness' is an intangible, subjective and ethereal term which can and does mean many different things to different people. When asked, people typically reference some of the following notions:[251]

- Egalitarian and democratic values
- Concepts of mateship and a 'fair go'
- Tolerance
- A relaxed easy-going lifestyle
- Equality for all
- Freedom of speech
- Multiculturism
- A willingness to go to war for Australia

Draping a flag, or chanting 'Waltzing Matilda', does not seem to have got a mention.

Despite that, there was an attempt by some to emblemise the surfer, the life saver, and the beach towel, tied into displaying the flag and singing renditions of our formal or informal national anthems, as a tribal definition and claim of Australianness.

Some of the process of this flag draping claim of Australianness, must be seen well beyond the associated beach myth. Something far more sinister in both Australia and overseas had provided an underpinning of later moral panic of what local Muslims had done and might do in their own backyards.

Amelia Johns in 2008 argued that the September 11 and Bali bombing attacks were followed by:

---

[251] For various references to scholarship on this see: N. Kabir, 'What does it mean to be un-Australian? Views of Australian Muslim students in 2006', *People and Place*, Vol.15, No.1, 2007, pp. 62-79, see p. 63 and footnotes 7-10 on p.78.

> "...creation of the good Australian and the un-Australian as categories that construe community relations in terms of social war ("you are either with us or against us")...formalising the Arab Muslim as the primary other in Australia today, their very presence in the national community conceived as a security risk..."[252]

It is not much to expect that these attacks by Muslim extremists targeting mostly Caucasian Christian victims, might have played on the minds of some folk in Sutherland Shire and influenced their behaviour. If so, their reactions were muted to a day of inebriated offensive behaviour, rather than what could have been a more violent and lingering response.

It is still one thing to 'reclaim the beach' and quite another, to act out a *"paranoid nationalism"*[253] to defend not just local spatial domain, but also the very essence of what it meant to be Australian, against either a real or imagined 'Other'. Given the short-lived transient nature of the rollicking chants, anthem singing, flag draping and violence, it is unlikely that such White Supremacist agendas took hold at Cronulla despite the 'best laid plans' of some offensive few.

What is it to be an 'Australian' or 'un-Australian'?

Interestingly, the terms Australian and un-Australian are not polar opposites. As one Muslim interviewee said in a 2006 study of Muslim students: *"...you could be Australian and un-Australian at the same time"*.[254]

Another student summed up quite succinctly the unsustainability of the Cronulla case prosecuted by a few in late 2005 of the un-Australianness of the Lebanese visitors: *"It's such a multicultural country, you can't really say 'Oh, like it's just white people are Australian', because we're just as much Australian as they are"*.[255]

Being un-Australian relates far more to attitude, views, or behaviour at a point in time rather than a disparaging badge of not being an Australian.

---

[252] A. Johns, 'White tribe: Echoes of the Anzac myth in Cronulla', *Continuum: Journal of Media and Cultural Studies*, Vol.22, No.1, February 2008, pp. 3-16, p. 5.
[253] A. John, p. 5 referring to G. Hage, 1998. *White nation: Fantasies of white supremacy in a multicultural nation.*
[254] N. Kabir, 'What does it mean to be un-Australian?', p. 70.
[255] N. Kabir, p. 68.

In other words, one can quite easily be an Australian and mostly exude Australianness but on occasion say or behave in an un-Australian way. This is opinionated, subjective and pejorative. It is far more a vehicle for the "we" and "us" in distancing itself from, or in justifying the exclusion of the 'Other'.

In what might be a surprise to the Shire locals, a majority of the 60 Muslim students interviewed in that 2006 study, thought that the actions of both sides at Cronulla was 'un-Australian'.[256]

In 2010, some five years after the dust had settled on the Cronulla riots, several academics undertook a detailed study of the pro-riot and anti-riot groups in claiming the true Australian identity:

> "...despite the strenuous efforts of the rioters to portray their actions as expressive of an Australian identity, they were dismissed by critics as failing to reflect the true Australian identity...
>
> ...If we accept that the rioters were acting simply as Australians then we partially limit the applicability of the Australian identity to their Muslim victims and to non-Muslim Australian critics of their actions..."[257]

To these academics: *"The Cronulla riots offer a powerful example of the way that two different groups in conflict contest the meaning of national identity".*

It needs to be pointed out for clarity that these scholars defined the competing groups not as the actual participants in either riot or revenge, but as those who sought to defend or oppose the 'Other' by use of what they termed 'strategic rhetoric'. And in developing this theme they come to some interesting conclusions:

> "Australian identity is defined by the two groups either as a multicultural or a predominantly European identity. **The opponents of the riots** embrace the first definition and tend to not share the perception of Australian in general as racist...
>
> ...**The supporters of the riots** tend to define Australian identity as predominantly white European and see the Cronulla riots...as collective

---

[256] N. Kabir, pp. 70 and 72.
[257] A. Bliuc et al., 'Manipulating national identity: the strategic use of rhetoric by supporters and opponents of the "Cronulla riots" in Australia', *Ethnic and Racial Studies*, 35:12, pp. 2174-2194, see p. 2178.

action in line with attitudes that are widely shared in the Australian society".[258]

And as for the few flag draped Cronulla locals desperately seeking to purloin a monopoly on the Australian identity, to justify and underpin excessive protection of 'their' beach, these scholars provide a confronting analogy by substituting 'British' for 'Australian':

> *"When a British observer objects to a British racist group marching under the Union Jack and expects other fair-minded Britons to share their opposition...we have the...platform for a debate about the contested content of British national identity".*

The draping of our flag over the body of Shire locals, as they contested the spatial occupation rights of Lebanese visitors, with racist taunts, slogans and national anthem singing, certainly did provide a 'platform for debate' about the 'contested content' of Australian national identity.

Before concluding this discussion, it is valuable to consider the wider application of the true meaning of both nationalism and patriotism, and what this might have meant for the Cronulla protagonists in reaching for their claim or version of what was meant by an Australian identity.

Nationalism versus patriotism

The public displays of the Australian flag on fences and on male chests leading up to, during and after the Cronulla riots, might for some have added to an exclusionary narrative, that as Lebanese Australians weren't locally born Anglo-Celtic Australians, then they were not Australians, did not belong under the comforting drape of our National symbol and could effectively 'bugger off' from the beach.

For the more tolerant, the display of the flag could unfortunately now be interpreted not as a display of national pride, but in a public statement of racist intolerance.

Prior to the Cronulla riots the Australian flag had been a universally unifying symbol and motif but in a few short days at the end of 2005 became for some, something a lot less pleasant.

---

[258] A. Bliuc et al., p. 2188.

White supremacists were certainly out and about stirring up racial discontent and using the flag as a vehicle to create as much anger as possible. Their motive was a nationalist one, which sought to draw overreacting young men of the Shire, into their much broader desire for an intolerant white dominated Christian society. This is quite different to being, feeling and displaying patriotism for a country you feel might not be living up to expectations.

The President of France, Emmanuel Macron, at the 100th Anniversary of the end of World War 1 on the 11th of November 2018, gave a poignant and moving articulation of the fundamental difference between the two:

> *"Nationalism is a betrayal of patriotism. By saying 'Our interests first, who cares about the others', we erase what a nation holds dearest, what gives life, what gives it grace and what is essential: its moral values".*

So when our own then new Prime Minister, Scott Morrison, himself a product of the Shire, proudly boasted at the start of his first cabinet meeting in August 2018, that he had issued Aussie flag lapel pins to all ministers, and pointing to his own firmly clipped to his suit, and claimed: *"I've worn one of these for years as it shows what side I am on. I am on the side of Australia",* was he dog whistling to nationalism, or was he just emphasising his understandable proud patriotism?

This is what former US President Barak Obama had to say on the issue:

> *"Following the attacks of 9/11, I had taken to wearing an American flag lapel pin, feeling that it was one small way to express national solidarity...Then...I quietly set my own pin aside...a reminder to myself that the substance of patriotism mattered far more than a symbol.*
>
> *When asked...I told the truth...saying that I didn't think the presence or absence of a token you could buy in a dime store measured one's love of country".*[259]

Although it must be added, that the photographs which accompany Obama's memoir include no fewer than twenty two photos of him suitably adorned with a US Flag pin firmly clipped to his navy blue suit lapel. And twenty of these were during his Presidency. Perhaps he was into flag clips after 9/11 as an Illinois State Senator, but dropped the idea sometime after becoming

---

[259] B. Obama, *A Promised Land*, Penguin, Random House, 2020, p. 132.

a US Senator in 2004, only to take it up again with a vengeance after being elected President in 2008. Who knows? All we can glean from this is that his narrative tells one story and his photos quite another.

Furthermore, near the end of his large memorial tome, he shares his personal experience of being attacked by Donald Trump for not really being born in the US despite demonstrable proof to the contrary. He mentions that he had not passed on to his wife Michelle, that *"polls were showing that roughly 40 per cent of Republicans were now convinced* [he] *hadn't been born in America...* [as] *she saw the whole circus for what it was: a variation on the press' obsession with flag pins..."*.[260]

As for our more local version of 'fake patriotism', the former NSW ALP MP Alan Ashton, summed it up well in September 2018: *"Australians are generally wary of this type of faux patriotism. I always wonder why someone would put an Australian flag on a pole in their yard! What other flag would you put up"*.[261]

The Australian flag certainly figured strongly in the Shire leading up to and after the Cronulla riots. Were these 'locals', who participated in 'showing off' our flag, making a nationalist and racist statement of exclusion towards the 'Other', or simply stating in a blunt way that incivility, disrespect and failure to amicably occupy space on the beach, were un-Australian and unwelcome. One is confrontingly offensive, and the other a call for help. It is not possible to properly discern what underpinned and motivated the desire for flag bearing, but it is clear, that all were about a statement of group belonging, exclusion and 'Otherness'.

We might be all Australian, but we can also at the same time be un-Australian as many at Cronulla beach and beyond demonstrated all those years ago.

---

[260] B. Obama, *A Promised Land*, p. 675.
[261] Personal communication with Alan Ashton.

26

Why was it Mostly Men?

"Violence is fundamentally male... Women never track down their entire families and kill them... Unlike men, women kill male partners after years of suffering physical violence, after they have exhausted all available sources of assistance...".[262]

Men are more violent than women. However, the tribalising desire to form into comfort forming groups, predispositions to intolerance and intolerant responses to threats to group values are all gender neutral.[263]

In other words, men and women want to equally form into tribes, they are equally predisposed to being intolerant and react just as intolerantly as the other when threats emerge to group values and order.

However, males and females part company when intolerant acts and words veer towards physical and even violent confrontation.

The footage and still photos of the Cronulla riots and the simple arrests figures at the time, show that it was almost entirely males who were protesting, chanting, drinking, yelling, rioting, committing violent acts or acts of offensive behaviour. The females in attendance as the riot first simmered and took off were very few. And interestingly, in revenge, it was entirely young Arabic males and zero females.

Men are simply more violent, more aggressive, and more prone to a physical

---

[262] M. Daly and M. Wilson, *Homicide*, New York, 1988; N. Boyd, *The Beast Within Why Men are Violent*, Greystone Books, 2000, pp. 3 and 40.

[263] As advised by Karen Stenner in a personal communication October 23, 2019: "There's no significant relationship between sex and authoritarian predisposition".

response to a perceived slight or insult than women generally the world over.

This is especially so with respect to adolescent males and young men, as many pass through a 'rite of passage' from the turbulent challenges of puberty, through to an eventual calm and socially acceptable maturation. In this process many young men compete for their own and their tribe's place of value, validation, and identity.

Not surprisingly, young men with a natural penchant for aggression and even violence, will from time to time, confront and then engage with individuals or groups with the same propensity and desire, and who are seen as a threat to themselves, their group and their sense of belonging and identity. This as much as anything explains the masculinity of the Cronulla conflict and the almost complete dearth of a feminine aspect to that tribal struggle. This was as much intertwined with the mostly male concept of honour and its defence, giving or responding to notions of offence and insult by demonstrations of physical or aggressive prowess:

> "In honour cultures...one must respond aggressively to insults, aggressions, and challenges or else lose honour...Insulting others when such insults might invite violence helps establish one's reputation for bravery...The result is a high frequency of violent conflict as participants in the culture aggressively compete for respect".[264]

At Cronulla, it was young women who were insulted and 'ogled' by visiting young Lebanese men, but it was male 'Lifeguards' who responded by insulting the 'offenders', who in turn insulted the insulters and then gave them a good thumping for good measure. The public forum for a collective preening of male 'honour' was then complete.

But why was it mostly, if not entirely men? Not only are men more violent than women, they are naturally more aggressive and more likely to riot.[265] Women certainly protest and demonstrate on issues as much as men, but it is men who are far more likely to express themselves aggressively. Why is this so?

---

[264] B. Campbell and J. Manning, *The Rise of Victimhood Culture*, Palgrave Macmillan, 2018, pp. 12-13; see also J.M. Roose, *Political Islam and Masculinity: Muslim Men in Australia*, Palgrave, 2016, pp. 4-5.

[265] See W.A. Santoro, 'Gendered Rioting: A General Strain Theoretical Approach', *Social Forces*, Vol. 93, Issue 1, September 2014, pp. 329-354.

Why are men far more likely to be violent than women? Why is it mostly men who take protest, slights, or provocations to a physical conclusion? Why are men angrier than women?

These are not easy questions to answer, and it is simply beyond the parameters of this book to do the issue justice. However, we considered it a relevant matter to point out, and discuss to a degree, the lop-sided nature of the riot and revenge at Cronulla when it came to gender.

The total lack of Lebanese women in revenge, the relatively few Caucasian women in protest, and their very limited presence in committing violence on the day at Cronulla, does invite a query as to why this was so?

Statistics

It is virtually a universally known and settled fact that across the world, in developed or undeveloped countries, democratic or authoritarian that:

- Gaols are overwhelmingly populated by men and not women.
- There are considerably more prisons housing men rather than women.
- Serious violent crimes are far more likely to be committed by men.
- Any violent crime, physical confrontation or break and enter is far more likely to be committed by a man.
- Men are far more likely to be angry and take that anger to a physical altercation.
- It is young men between 15 and 29 who are most likely to offend.

The actual statistics make for quite sobering reading: *"As at 30 June 2016, there were 3,094 women and 35,745 men in Australian adult correction"*.[266]

Not surprisingly, this extrapolates to the state level in New South Wales on an almost pro rata basis.

> *"As at 30 June 2017 there were 13,149 prisoners in New South Wales of which 12,145 or 92% were male, and 1004 or 8% were female. This translated to a male imprisonment rate of 406 prisoners per 100,000 male adult population, and a female imprisonment rate of just 32 prisoners per 100,000 female adult population".*[267]

These are extraordinary figures.

---

[266] ABS, '4125.0 – Gender Indicators, Australia', September 2017.
[267] ABS, '4517.0 – Prisoners in Australia', 2017.

The actual arrest numbers at Cronulla

There were approximately 200 people charged with criminal offences arising out of either riot or revenge during the Cronulla riots. The numbers charged and processed through the courts for Cronulla offences were almost equal in number between Caucasians and Middle Easterners.

So far as we are aware, only three female Caucasians were involved in violence during the Cronulla Riots, only one of whom was charged and later convicted of assault.[268] Apart from that, it was basically all men both in riot and revenge.

The scholarly literature is filled with theories on the preponderance of male violence and offensive behaviour which mostly centres around the old nature versus nurture debate. That is, are we who we are because of what we were born with, or because of the way we were brought up and the context and environment in which we lived.

The question of whether it is biology, or parenting and environment, or other factors, which have the greater impact on later life tendencies to violence, does make for interesting reading. Some possible explanations:

Lloyd DeMause argued in 2007, that it was far less the biological make up of young males and far more the extent to which they received unconditional parental love which was the greatest determinant of later violence or anti-social behaviour:

> "...when boys grow up with empathy, no matter what the sex of the caretaker(s), they grow up non-violent...If...they are brought up with love and care...they grow up neither violent nor war lovers. But abandoned and abused boys regularly hide their shame and fears behind a defensive fantasy of grandiosity, dominance and violent bravado".[269]

Demause dismissed the notion that it was testosterone levels which distinguished male and female violence levels but embraced the notion that girls rather than boys got the lion's share of unconditional nurturing empathetic parental love.

He even argued that *"boys actually need more love and caretaking than girls as they grow up"* but the reverse was usually the case, as boys were

---

[268] Strike Force Neil Report, Volume One, p. 40.
[269] L. DeMause, 'Why Males Are More Violent', *The Journal of Psychohistory* 35 (1), Summer 2007, pp. 22-33, see pp. 27, 32-33.

expected from quite a young age to toughen up.[270]

Countless scholars and household conversations over decades have dwelled upon the question: Is a bad egg born or made?

Neil Boyd in a fascinating account of the underlying causes of male aggression assessed the claims of the inherited, as opposed to the learned side of the argument, and put the view that both biological and environmental factors influence the propensity for expressions of male aggression.[271]

To support his case for duality, Boyd referred to a Danish study conducted in 1984 to determine any relationship between the criminality of biological and adopted parents and the future criminality of an adopted child. Thankfully, there are far too few cases of violence to enable that kind of causal or correlative study, but the far greater commission of property crimes enabled an assessment on that crime possible.

The study of 14,400 Danish adoptees between 1924 and 1947 found that if no parents had a criminal conviction then just 13% of adopted boys *"had at least one conviction"*. If a biological parent had a conviction but not an adoptive parent, the rate rose to 20%. However, if both sides of the parental line had convictions then the likelihood rose to 25%.

The strong link between the criminality of a biological parent and the criminality of an adopted boy was again confirmed in a study in 1995 in Sweden of 862 men and 913 women adopted between 1930 and 1950. This study found a 3% risk of males committing a crime if no parent had convictions, a 7% risk if no biological conviction but adopted parents did, a 12% risk if biological parents had convictions but not the adopted ones, and an astronomical increase to a 40% risk if both sides of the parental aisle presented adverse histories. In Boyd's view these studies emphatically linked both genetic inheritance and environmental experience with a male's likelihood to commit crime.[272] And in his view the link between inherited genes and later male criminality was too strong to ignore.

Men are on average taller, heavier, and stronger than women.

What some may dispute is studies which demonstrate that on average men have a greater spatial problem-solving skill than women. That is, how to

---

[270] L. DeMause, pp. 24-25.
[271] N. Boyd, *The Beast Within Why Men are Violent*, Greystone Books, 2000.
[272] N. Boyd, pp. 103-105.

move, apply objects and body movements to achieve a desired purpose.

Boyd argued that it is this combination of strength and the spatial ability on how best to aggressively apply it, which makes men far more violently successful than women.[273] But as we know, most adolescent and mature men are not violent. There must be more at play to 'convert' that physical and spatial capability into violent action.

Studies have not conclusively demonstrated a causal link between testosterone and aggression although there is an overwhelmingly convincing correlative link.

A relevant analogy can be drawn from the causal versus correlative link between smoking and lung cancer. The tobacco industry claimed quite successfully for decades and can still claim to some extent now, that it is simply impossible to demonstrate that smoking a single cigarette, or in fact many cigarettes, directly leads to cancer. All that could be shown and all that can be shown now, is that smokers have an astronomically greater statistical likelihood of contracting lung cancer than do or did non-smokers. That is, smoking and lung cancer are correlative links not causal ones. Non-smokers still contract lung cancer but in statistically significant fewer numbers than smokers. On that basis alone, health authorities around the world have counselled and cautioned against the wisdom of smoking.

Likewise, with young pubescent males, it can be shown that at the same time as testosterone is surging like rocket fuel into the body of a teenage male, their homicide and suicide rates rise astronomically *"from 15 (years of age) through to 20 then falls precipitously to age 30* [and] *once men reach 40 years of age violent crime becomes a rarity".*[274]

> *"One explanation for... homicides comes from the realm of biology. Most violence in every society is perpetrated by young males between the ages of 15 and 29".*[275]

When the proportion of 15- to 29-year-old males rises dramatically in a population, so then does the level of homicides. The massive proportional increase of pubescent and young males in the UK, Canada and the USA between 1962 and 1975 following the post WW11 'baby boom', was followed

---

[273] N. Boyd, pp. 23 and 78.
[274] N. Boyd, p. 137.
[275] N. Boyd, p. 142.

by a doubling in that time of the homicide rates in all three countries.[276]

Is the rapid rise of testosterone in a young male's body at the same time as too many of them become aggressive and violent co-incidental, or damning, or just plain interesting?

Whilst many teenage males might be regarded as somewhat aggressive when compared to females of the same age, so few pubescent males commit acts of violence, it is not possible, like tobacco smoking and cancer, to draw a causative link between testosterone and violence. However, it remains convincingly correlative. It is quite likely that the surge of testosterone in adolescent males does not cause violence but provides the potential for it. If so, then we need to look for environmental factors which might trigger that potential.

In other words, were these boys lovingly nurtured, had parents who were empathetic and law-abiding contributors to the community, and had minimal if any exposure to some of the social and familial misery of drugs and domestic violence that too many of our current violent criminals seem to have experienced? If so, then perhaps the trigger for firing the potential which testosterone provides is substantially muted.

On any account, a lot of alcohol was consumed under the sun on the day of the initial Cronulla 'protest'. However, it is reasonable to assume this was one sided, given the revenge attacks were undertaken by Muslims who almost universally do not consume alcohol. However, for what probably greatly contributed to getting the whole Cronulla 'transaction' underway the issue remains of important relevance.

There is a strong link between the excessive consumption of alcohol and violence.[277] Once again, like smoking and cancer, or testosterone and violence, the link is correlative not causal. Many people and many young males often drink to excess, but few then commit acts of violence or simply commence aggressive encounters. Something more is needed to light the fuse.

Drinking excessively lowers an ability to focus or to maturely assess

---

[276] N. Boyd, pp.142-143.
[277] T. Norstrom, and H. Pape, 'Alcohol, suppressed anger and violence', *Addiction*, Sept. 2010, Vol.105 (9), pp.1580-1586; W.A. Pridemore, 'Alcohol and Violence', *Encyclopedia of Criminological Theory*, Sage Publications, 2010; N. Boyd, *The Beast Within*, pp. 155-160.

provocations or slights which without drink might be ignored or dismissed.[278] Equally, those with suppressed anger and frustrations are the least likely to be peaceful after consuming alcohol.[279]

Aggression and violence at Cronulla

The male aggression and violence during the Cronulla riots were somewhat different to the violence which has been the subject of countless studies and to the brief discussion above. At Cronulla, the aggression and violence was collective not individual, although given that so few from each tribe were violent, this 'anomaly' does compel the broader question of what does drive a young male to hurt another individual even in a collective context.

At Cronulla in riot and beyond in revenge, the rise of protest to aggression and then violence, and the immediate violence in provoked response, were not individual acts of hard to explain actions. The whole 'transaction' of aggression and violence from and towards the Shire was a collective act of a tribal "us" against a spurned "them". The Caucasians rose up and the Lebanese responded.

At the initial 'protest' in the sun, most in the 5,000 strong crowd were young men, drinking, chanting, and cheering, but only a small few took that to a violent conclusion. It was tribal in the beginning and the end.

We know from Karen Stenner's field work that many people harbour a predisposition to intolerance but only express or act out that intolerance when a real or imagined threat emerges to "us" from a "them". Few on the day at Cronulla took their intolerant chanting, cheering, and texting to a violent end. Were these few the ones who allowed that predisposition to intolerance to combine suppressed 'angry feelings' with a cocktail of alcohol?

The revenge attacks by a small marauding band of young and aggressive Lebanese was more focussed, more violent, and more troubling than anything unleashed by that band of angry and violent Caucasian heavy drinkers on Cronulla beach. However, this aspect of the riots is almost universally ignored by the academic scholarship.

---

[278] N. Boyd, p. 158.
[279] Norstrom and Pape, p. 1584; N. Boyd, p. 158-159.

Still mostly men

As mentioned, it is simply beyond the remit of this book to get a definitive position on why it is mostly men who commit crime or why it was almost entirely men who behaved offensively, aggressively and then violently at Cronulla and beyond in late 2005.

If it was just differing testosterone levels between the sexes then why are most men calm, peaceful and law-abiding citizens. If it was excessive alcohol consumption, then why do most male heavy drinkers not go on to commit violent offences. If it was just being young and male, we have already shown that there is only a correlative link, not a causal one, between testosterone and aggression. And most adolescents are not violent. But that said, far more violence is committed by men than by women.

However, something more is needed to explain the preponderance of males at the barricades at Cronulla and beyond in riot and revenge, and more generically across the prison population.

A reasonable theory is that those males who are angry, are more likely to have been those who lacked the kind of desirable parenting, love, and empathetic tender care we should all receive in our early years. A predisposition to intolerance, a suppressed sense of unreleased anger, the consumption of alcohol and acting to protect the group, were all factors at Cronulla for mostly men and almost no women.

Whatever the explanation, the purpose here has been to highlight the overwhelming number of males involved in the Cronulla transaction and posit a possibility as to why females were mostly singularly absent when intolerance went physical.

27

Why was it Mostly Lebanese Muslim Men?

"They come from a patriarchal village. They don't go for the greater good ... tribal ... aggressive ... in your face".[280]

"An acculturated disrespect for the law"[281]

We discussed in the last chapter why it was mostly men in riot and revenge during the Cronulla riots, and we canvassed some theories in an endeavour to explain this.

What we want to explore in this chapter, is that not only were the Middle Eastern men attacking in revenge, completely lacking any women participants, but that they were almost entirely if not solely, Lebanese Muslim men. Why was this so?

The Lebanese concession

Lebanese migrants have been settling in Australia since the 1880s, and with their cultural and culinary contributions have made a wonderfully positive impact on our way of life. The settlement of Maronite Christians in Sydney occurred around the Redfern area and explains why, to this day, we still have in that suburb some of Australia's finest Lebanese restaurants.

For decades this gradual migration of mostly Lebanese Christians led to a rich and valuable addition to mainstream Australian life, which included former NSW Governor Dr Marie Bashir, and her husband and former Rugby

---

[280] M. Kennedy, referred to in *'A great divide takes some understanding'*, The Sydney Morning Herald, December 17, 2005.
[281] S. Stanton, Transcript of Interview, February 16, 2021.

Union great Sir Nicholas Shehadie.

Likewise, and in more recent years, we have had enormous contributions from Dr Jamal Rifi and Lakemba local MP Jihad Dib, both Lebanese Australians of Muslim faith.

However, there has been a darker side to the migration of Lebanese nationals to our shores.

Prior to the mid-1970s, the overwhelming majority of Lebanese immigrants were Maronite Christians who settled peaceably, but that all began to change with large numbers of Lebanese Muslim migrants arriving from 1976 onwards under an initiative called the "Lebanese Concession".

The new Liberal Party government of Malcolm Fraser decided to extend a humanitarian visa programme to those suffering under the yoke of civil war in Lebanon. Lebanese Sunni Muslims began arriving in Sydney and settled in the Lakemba area and soon built their well-known Mosque in that suburb. A few years later, Shia Lebanese Muslims began to arrive and settled in Arncliffe where they also built their own Mosque.

However, whilst many Lebanese Muslims have now made incredible contributions to Australian life, politics, commerce and community, and the vast majority are peaceable law-abiding citizens, a menacing minority have disproportionately contributed to major crime and violence in Sydney. Why?

Not a Lebanese enclave

Despite the amount of crime and negative news generated by the Muslim Lebanese community in South West Sydney, this migration programme did not create a Lebanese enclave or ghetto in Sydney, as some may have assumed. This is confirmed by an assessment of ethnic community statistics of the 2006 Census of Canterbury/Bankstown, which encompasses the suburb of Lakemba.

At that time, 300,000 residents lived in Canterbury/Bankstown with only 44,000 claiming to be Muslim or just 15%, whereas 116,000 claimed to be Catholic or Anglican, or a rather more sizable 29%.

On a dive into the 2006 figures for Lakemba, far more Muslims had migrated from Bangladesh and Pakistan than did from Lebanon. These numbers provide a contextual "truth" around the broader "Fake News", that Lebanese Muslims are the dominant religious and ethnic community in Southwest Sydney.

The Lebanese are surrounded by other communities and Lebanese Muslims in turn, are overwhelmed in numbers by Muslims from countries other than Lebanon. Additionally, the total of all of those Muslims are surrounded by Anglo Catholics. Unfortunately, for some wishing to write of a Lebanese ghetto, from which an almost suburban wall of crime sprang, truth does get in the way of the imagining as opposed to the real story. And that real story is that the Lebanese Muslim community in southwest Sydney, is a small minority, but unfortunately a community from whom a disproportionately menacing violent and criminal few are very well known to police.

This was a similar pattern in the 2001 census which had been the most recent one conducted prior to the 2005 Cronulla riots, which found that in the Local Government areas of Bankstown, Canterbury and Auburn, the percentage of first- and second-generation Lebanese was between 10-13%.[282] This is hardly a towering enclave from the Beqaa Valley. This was illuminated by the 2005 study on the same issue by academic Jock Collins:

> "Media portrayals of Lebanese crime have shone a spotlight on suburbs such as Bankstown, Punchbowl and Lakemba as 'no-go' Lebanese enclaves. In fact, Sydney's immigrant settlement is so diverse – coming from some 180 different birthplaces – that our suburbs of immigrant settlement are populated by a great diverse range of ethnicities, with no ghettoes in the sense that we see in the USA or UK".[283]

In other words, the areas amongst, within and surrounding where concentrations of Lebanese Australians live in Sydney are ethnically, culturally, and religiously diverse. They are not monocultural. They are multicultural.

---

[282] J. Collins, 'From Beirut to Bankstown: The Lebanese Diaspora in Multicultural Australia', in Chapter 8, *Lebanese Diaspora History, Racism Belonging, Lebanese*, American University Beirut, 2005, pp. 192-193.

[283] J. Collins, 'From Beirut to Bankstown', p. 192.

The greater preponderance for crime and violence

This then invites a serious question: Why does a relatively low demographic presence in Sydney of Lebanese Muslims result in their relatively very strong presence in serious violent crimes, gang warfare, commercial drug dealing, and the extraordinary commitment of police resources?

In our view, the reasons are threefold.

First, the exceptional transportation and replication of patriarchal village communities based on masculine respect. Second, the Lebanese migration concession drawing on many least likely to peaceably integrate into mainstream law-abiding Australian society. Third, the inter-generational passing of a 'baton' of contempt for police, law and order, and what is required for cooperative civil society.

We will deal with each in turn.

Transposing the Lebanese village

Interestingly, Lebanese Muslim migration into the southwest of Sydney, replicated village life, mores, customs and practices of their community back home in Lebanon. This has been described as *"village chain migration"* and has arguably occurred more so than probably any other ethnic community migration.[284]

This may sound good on paper, to the extent that some have suggested that *"it takes a village* to *raise a child"*[285], but the villages in Lebanon were patriarchal, founded on masculine notions of honour and respect, and with far greater regard for immediate wider family, and a very strong focus on the currency of respect, than anything remotely linked to the broader community.[286] This has consequences when it confronts a calmer more civil

---

[284] J. Collins, 'From Beirut to Bankstown, p. 188.
[285] For example: J. Cowen-Fletcher, *It Takes a Village,* 1994; H. Clinton, *It Takes a Village*, Simon and Schuster, New York, 1996 and finally, R. Palmer, and M. Gasman, "It Takes a Village to Raise a Child": 'The Role of Social Capital in Promoting Academic Success for African American Men at a Black College', *Journal of College Student Development,* Vol. 49, Num 1, January/February 2008, pp. 52-70.
[286] A. Jakubowicz, 'Once Upon a Time in Punchbowl rescues Lebanese honour from shame', *The Conversation,* June 19, 2014.

notion of community, such as Sydney then and now:

> "They come from a very patriarchal culture. They don't go for the greater good. Their families have survived a brutal civil war. They are tribal. They are aggressive. They are in your face. And they are not grateful".[287]

In other words, when respect and honour is your main currency, and your tools of trade for protecting it are disproportionate violence, and this approach to life, community and family is transhipped across the world, then is it little wonder that peaceable integration becomes and continues to be problematic. It has in our view, resulted in a "menacing few" believing they hold a unique unfettered right to do as they please, in protecting what they regard as their familial, clannish or community honour. This is what we have called, Lebanese Muslim ethnic exceptionalism. That is, the criminally violent few within the Lebanese Muslim community believe they have a right, above all others, to defend and protect their honour, territory, fealty and more often than not, their own commercial drug trade. This attitude of being free to do as they please, is like no other community in Sydney, and accordingly warrants the description as 'ethnic exceptionalism'.

Drawing on the least qualified

In normal circumstances, many of the Lebanese immigrants from the mid-70s onwards would not have migrated but for a desire to escape the civil war which had engulfed their country. Many were ill equipped to settle well and integrate comfortably into their new way of life. They were generally unskilled with little education and few prospects. This ingredient combined with settlers who had come from regions whose economy depended on industrial crime, the wholesale drug trade, violence and vendetta, all made for a less than desirable collection of newcomers to Australia.

They came not from the capital Beirut, but from deprived rural areas seeking an escape from economic and war-torn hardship. However, they did not satisfy the then technical definition of a refugee and the requirements for

---

[287] M. Kennedy, referred to in *'A great divide takes some understanding'*, The Sydney Morning Herald, December 17, 2005.

issuing a visa into Australia.[288] The rules needed bending to let this many migrants in who would not satisfy the applicable immigration criteria, and this rule bending became known as the "Lebanese concession".

Cabinet papers released from the time refer to these hybrid "refugees" as *"unskilled, illiterate"* and of *"questionable character"*.[289] Ray Hadley was blunter than anyone else on the record:

> **Hadley**: *"You know what the Maronites say to me,? 'Ray, Mr Fraser got the worst of the worst, he didn't get the best of the best, he got the worst of the worst', but they're not prepared to say it".*

Stephen Stanton, Christian Lebanese barrister, did go on the record in an interview we conducted with him, on the broader issues of what occurred during the Cronulla riots and he was quite forthcoming:

> **Interviewer:** *"And the people that came here were the least salubrious migrant you would have, and with complete disrespect for the rule of law..."*
>
> **Stanton:** *"No argument with me at all".*
>
> **Interviewer:** *"And taught their children the same thing"?*
>
> **Stanton:** *"No argument with me at all".*
>
> **Interviewer:** *"And the children were the ones who turned up"?*
>
> **Stanton:** *"You are completely correct".*
>
> **Interviewer:** [With respect to the mid-1970s migration] *"They were criminals"?*
>
> **Stanton:** *"And not only criminals, they were even worse than criminals...they were participants in a war that knew no bounds in terms of decency".*[290]

It is impossible to take account of this migration programme without some regard to the sheer horrors of that civil war between multiple religious, political and ethnic groups and which lasted from 1975 until 1990. It has

---

[288] G. Henderson, '1970s Lebanese Concession led to an immigration debacle', The Sydney Institute, May 22, 2015.
[289] See interview between Peter Dutton and Ray Hadley, 2GB, Thursday November 25, 2016.
[290] S. Stanton, Transcript of Interview, February 16, 2021.

been estimated that 150,000 died, 100,000 were permanently disabled and as many as 900,000 rendered homeless.[291]

It must have been a terrifying time and hardly the environment from which a deep and enduring respect would flow for the rule of law and civil society in a place remote from where all of this had been endured.

If these accounts of the times, and of the character and quality of the Lebanese migrants who came to our shores in their thousands in the mid to late 1970s, is an accurate portrayal, then it is little wonder that it was seen as unsuccessful. How could it have been otherwise?

However, what is more difficult to embrace is the sheer extent to which these character traits, involving a universal disregard for police, the law and how to behave peaceably in a civil community, were passed onto many 2nd and 3rd generation Muslim Lebanese. It was these 'inheritors' who turned up in force in revenge in late 2005 early 2006.

Stephen Stanton believes that these 'tough as nails' immigrants taught their children and grandchildren to carry a contempt for police and the rule of law and an encouragement of gangs, violence and serious crime. He agreed that this was *"acculturated disrespect for the law"* and referred to the Greenacre Bankstown area in Southwest Sydney as a *"crucible of discontent...that... was inflamed by the riots"*.

Stanton has provided as good an explanation for the intergenerational baton changing as any:

> **Stanton:** *"...it's regrettably a failure on the part of the family units concerned, and ultimately the monitoring of those people who were encouraged to be ethnically exclusive...*[which] *fuelled their right, unbridled in terms of the arrogance, to act whatever way they liked".*

And this in his view was manifested in *"a terrible intolerance of the police force...fuelled by members of the Lebanese community...who were adamant and, more importantly, intrepid"* in doing so.

Interestingly, Stanton believes that the anger and discontent against the mores and expectations of civil society, were already well in place prior

---

[291] J. Wood, 'After 2 Decades, Scars of Lebanon's Civil War Block Path to Dialogue', *New York Times*, July 11, 2012; 'Lebanon (Civil War 1975-1991)', GlobalSecurity.org.

to December 2005, and that far from the events at Cronulla provoking a response, they simply gave a convenient outlet for its angry expression. If that is an accurate explanation of their behaviour, then they weren't provoked to act so violently as they did but were simply given a welcome excuse to do so.

The inter-generational aspect of Lebanese Muslim disrespect for law and order and civil society has in more recent times caught the attention of a Federal Minister for Immigration. Peter Dutton, in 2016, then Minister for Immigration, went so far as to say that the decision in 1976 to allow so many Muslim Lebanese into Australia was a mistake arguing that many 2nd and 3rd generation Lebanese immigrants were disproportionately represented amongst serious criminal law breakers.

> **Dutton:** *"The advice I have is that out of the last 33 people who have been charged with terrorist related offences in this country, 22 of those people are from second and third generation Lebanese-Muslim background".*[292]

Task Force Gain and MEOC

We earlier discussed that the setting up of Task Force Gain by NSW Police in the mid to late 1990s was necessary to focus solely on Lebanese gang violence, commercial drug dealing and serious lawlessness. It successfully locked up about twenty very violent Lebanese Muslim criminals. That Task Force then changed its name to The Middle Eastern Organised Crime Squad (MEOC) with its very public branding of where its attentions would be directed. The squad did outstanding work in dismantling organised crime gangs, but in time with complaints that this was an unacceptable ethnic profiling of police work, the squad at least in name was disbanded. But its work continued.

Lebanese Muslim gangs

It is unlikely that the work of violent Lebanese Muslim gangs and their police counterparts will be over anytime soon. The murderous and terrorising 'activities' of the Hamzy and Alameddine crime gangs in southwest Sydney

---

[292] Stephanie Anderson, 'Peter Dutton suggests Fraser government made mistake by resettling Lebanese refugees', abc.net.au, 22 November 22, 2016.

is simply frightening. And not just against each other.

NSW Police may have felt resurrecting MEOC was not necessary, but now draws on a skilled team of detectives focussed on criminal gangs, in what is known as Strike Force Raptor. Part of their remit is to now deal with what Task Force Gain dealt with over twenty years ago, and now as then, police are focussed on a disproportionately and intergenerationally generated violent crime scenario from Lebanese Muslim crime families.

As with all those years ago, the chillingly violent antics of the more recent iterations of Middle Eastern gangs dominated by Lebanese Muslims will continue until all the worst and most violent of their number are locked up.

29

Conclusion

"Not...racially inspired but...racially hijacked"[293]

Implications of this book

We set out in writing this book with initially two objectives in mind: First, to provide an eyewitness perspective from the two most senior law enforcement participants during the Cronulla Riots; the minister for police and the police commander. Second, to give better meaning and explanation as to why the riots had occurred.

However, after concluding the main part of the book we added a third; to test the trustworthiness and reliability of our perspectives by conducting a number of interviews from 'the field' of MPs, community leaders and police officers all of whom had important and relevant roles and positions at the time of the riots.

In this final chapter, we have endeavoured to provide a brief summary of the importance and implications of these three threads which we have woven together, to provide a better, more considered, constructed and contextual meaning to the Cronulla riots, than any which may have been provided to date. In doing so, we have drawn on our perspectives, the opinions of scholars and commentators, and finally, the thoughts of the interviewees.

And as this book is as much an historical perspective, as it is a sociological and political explanation for human behaviour, both communal and policing, we have provided at the end, a number of recommendations for NSW Police to consider.

---

[293] S. Stanton, Transcript of Interview, February 16, 2021.

An unexpected outcome

The participant interviews we conducted started out as a process to challenge and test our own views, assertions and findings, but became instead an unexpected confirmation of them. As there were only twelve interviews conducted, their views and opinions of events are not statistically generalisable. However, they were nevertheless key people with important roles in the community, a number of whom we simply assumed would have expressed views at variance with our own. To that extent alone, conducting interviews with significant community, political and law enforcement personnel was of great value, but even more so when unexpected and even surprising findings are forthcoming.

From the first interview with Dr Jamal Rifi, through to the last one with retired police Supt. Ron Mason, we realised that we weren't just two ex-public servants, with particular subjective perspectives based on our own personal experiences. The positions we took, it would seem, were well shared. It was a very rewarding and reassuring experience to have expected our views to be challenged, and then the reverse happening in interview after interview. The research we undertook through these interviews, and through own analysis of the events and the academic literature on the matter, have in our submission, provided significant contributions and implications for a better understanding of what became known by the misnomer as, 'The Cronulla Riots'.

The most significant implications which emerged from this research and analysis, requires a serious rethinking of the where, what, and why of the events of late 2005/early 2006. Put in another way: Where did it actually happen, what description should be ascribed to it to define what occurred, and finally, why did it take place?

It wasn't just Cronulla: Redefining place

The geographical locational name of 'Cronulla' as the epicentre of the then ubiquitously named 'Cronulla Riots' is both unfair, inaccurate and in our view, a misnomer. Yes, the initial 'event' did start at North Cronulla beach but many who attended were not Cronulla locals, and more pointedly, the troubles in late 2005/early 2006 were not isolated to Cronulla but emanated from Lakemba and Punchbowl and unfolded at Maroubra and Brighton-le-Sands, as well as Cronulla. In fact, far more violent acts were committed at Maroubra, from young men in convoys from the Canterbury Bankstown area, than anything contemplated at Cronulla.

It was Lakemba and Maroubra, which were the real suburban focal points of tribal attack and defence, rather than just the now infamous Cronulla. However, what we all 'saw' on the TV evening news of the 11th of December, 2005 told us all a very different 'truth' which we now challenge. Pinpointing the troubles to one geographic point, needs in our view, to be reimagined and redefined more accurately for what really occurred, rather than what the selectively reported TV news coverage implied had happened. Lasting collective communal and scholarly memories, formed by digital editing, angled camera shots and a focus on only the Caucasian rioters and little on Lebanese revenge attackers, ought not to be the basis upon which a lasting judgement is formed of what happened.

If it was the 'Paris Riots' of 2005, then why was it not also the 'Sydney Riots' of 2005. Both were mobile with lawlessness, violence and property damage breaking out across various parts of both cities, but one wears the moniker of the whole city, whereas the other, just a small suburban part of it. Identifying the place of all the trouble, violence, law breaking and property damage, as 'Cronulla', is simply untrue, and ought to be so acknowledged by anyone commentating on the issues which arose from it.

A 'riot'?

Former Supt. Ron Mason, perhaps NSW Police's foremost expert on planning and responding to public order events, confirmed during interview our assertion in chapters 15 and 17, that what occurred at Cronulla did not satisfy the requirements of being designated as a 'riot'. As did Chief Bratton then head of the LAPD on visiting Sydney in respect of the 'Macquarie Fields Riots' of January 2005. His words then could have been equally applied just a few months later to Cronulla:

> **Bratton:** [Macquarie Fields] *"doesn't equate with some of my experiences...there was minimal damage, minimal injuries to police and civilians...I had to chuckle. I'm looking and I'm asking, 'What's the problem?', I just don't see it...What you are dealing with here doesn't approach in any way shape or form the state of what we deal with in America".*

Notwithstanding this, we were still surprised to find in our interviews, that participants generally distanced themselves from the word 'riot' as an accurate descriptor of what had occurred at Cronulla. From their perspectives, it should be more accurately described as a 'disturbance', and hardly worthy of the name, 'riot'. Supt. Ron Mason's dismissal of the riot misnomer, as the *"so called 'Cronulla Riots"*, given his experience in dealing with real riots, ought to be enough on its own to warrant a rethink, a rebadge, and a reframing of not only this part of Sydney's past, but more generally, what actually is a 'riot'.

It wasn't racially inspired

The scholarly 'research', social commentary, and general stigmatising of Cronulla, as the place of a 'race riot', racialised behaviour and rank racism, has been so comprehensive as to render any attempt to correct this misnomer as a demanding exercise.

Undeniably there were many racist chants, slogans, tattoos and texts during the 'riot' and revenge of the 'Cronulla Riots'. However, our contention is that to conclude racist language as the defining point of determining that the whole event was racially motivated and little else, is unjustifiably cursory and superficial.

Being offended by what are demonstrably racialised motifs and messaging, ought not to justify an incurious approach to learning what might have been the real motivation for expressing them, rather than asserting a description solely based on the simple fact of their expression. This will remain a challenge for many, including rather surprisingly, many scholars who chose not to dig a little sociologically deeper on the matter.

In Part 5 of this book, 'Explaining the riot', we endeavoured to establish that it was 'differenceism' and not 'racism', which underpinned the cross-tribal conflicts of late 2005/early 2006. That is, people involved were not motivated to harm the 'other' because of colour or creed, but simply because they were perceived as not 'us'. And someone becomes a 'them' when they don't behave like 'us'. Hence the real causal factors being incivility, disrespect, and the cultural clash of seeing the beach as a space for the towel or the soccer ball, but importantly, not both. Race played a part only as a motif to gather the tribe for that 'us' and 'them' struggle, and not as the reason for that gathering.

This is a critically important difference and compels a reimagining of this part of our tawdry history, as something somewhat less and quite different as to how it is actually remembered, defined, and labelled. The 'race card' is easily pulled out, but hard to put back in the deck, and so it will continue to be with the use of the term the 'Cronulla race riot', as the convenient but widely inaccurate description of what actually happened all those years ago.

We have argued that the initial 'event' and response to it, were 'racially badged' not 'racially inspired', as a means of creating a motivating clarion call for the tribal defence against perceived incivility, disrespect, and how the beach space should be used and occupied. Additionally, it then became a cover for those with an already unbridled contempt for the police and the law, to express that contempt in response, both forcefully and violently. The initial event at North Cronulla beach was primarily an excuse for the intensity of the revenge attacks, which were only secondarily caused by the provocation of it.

Our case for rioters and revenge attackers being classed as difference-ists and not race-ists, was earlier set out in detail, as well as an outline of it being underpinned by the work of political sociologist, Karen Stenner. How this troubling period in our history could come and go, never to return, requires a deeper explanation than simply saying, "they were all racist". We believe we have provided a plausible one for readers to consider.

The three misnomers: Cronulla, riot and race. In our view, it wasn't just, or even mainly, at Cronulla; it wasn't a riot, and it wasn't racially caused or inspired. The triple misnomer of the much acclaimed 'Cronulla Race Riot', is wrong on all three counts.

Media influence

Much has been written about the media stirring up local Cronulla sentiment after the 'attack on the lifeguard', so much so apparently, that locals almost couldn't help themselves but to react in defence of 'their beach'. It is always a difficult task to attribute cause and effect to media outbursts, and the Cronulla Riots were no different.

Alan Jones, the then outspoken and opinionated radio host of 2GB's morning radio programme, did his usual stirring up of 'moral panic', which was unhelpful, but not causative. We found that whilst some complaints were upheld regarding his broadcasts, there was no evidence that his audience did anything other than cheer from their radio sets, as they heard what they wanted to hear, and then didn't bother turning up. Most of those who did turn up on the day didn't tune in to listen to Mr Jones' exhortations.

Equally, the Daily Telegraph, in living up to its tabloid reputation did provide much provocative copy but little if any of that, in our view, motivated young men to protest. The important exception here is the extraordinary publication by that newspaper, in the lead up to the initial 'demonstration', of effectively a dare by a leader of the Maroubra Bra boys surfing gang, that Lebanese men would be too scared to turn up and take them on. They did, in great number, causing so much violence and property damage, that the suburb felt terrorised. In our view, it is likely that this story, published twice by this newspaper, caused Maroubra to be targeted by revenge attackers.

We have argued that TV and newspaper coverage of the daytime protest at Cronulla focused solely on strung together isolated incidents of violence, with dramatised newsreader voice-overs, but excluded the actual fact the bulk of the day was uneventful. In our view, this gave a false and out-of-proportion impression that the whole 5000 strong crowd were racist and behaved like that the whole day. Undoubtedly this graphic footage contributed to the anger experienced by Middle Eastern young men who subsequently took part in the revenge attacks, however, the real cause for their violence was the already existing tension. The imagery also contributed to (and continues to do so) the unfair and ongoing stigmatisation of the whole of the Cronulla and Sutherland Shire as a white supremacist enclave every time a racist issue is brought to the fore in Australia.

We conclude that the most significant media contributions to fuelling, igniting, if not causing, both riot and revenge, were the tens of thousands of emotionally violent text messages sent by both sides throughout this period.

Police performance

We believe that what should stand as the record of police performance during the Cronulla Riots was an extraordinarily effective law enforcement response, which used new emergency powers to lock down suburbs, close beaches and roads and confiscate phones, cars, knives, guns, hand-grenade, bats, clubs and a vast array of home-made weapons. That incredible effort drew on over 2,000 uniformed police from every quarter of general duties and specialist policing, including a new combination of Riot Squad personnel becoming mobile with Highway Patrol, thereby quickly restoring order and peace to Sydney, and averting what could have easily been a much worse scenario. We assert and maintain it was a commendable performance by police leaders in extremely difficult circumstances and an outstanding effort by the troops they led.

In our view, this is the account of police performance during the Cronulla Riots, which should stand as a lasting record of NSW Police 'serving and protecting' the community.

Right up to the moment that the Commissioner for Police announced a 'Strike Force' investigation of law enforcement during the riots, police performance and leadership had been universally praised and lauded, as we believe it should have been. We trust the analysis presented in this book, based on factual evidence, consultation with those involved and presenting actual wording of corroborative documents that still exist to this day, provides alternate viewpoints to consider on key issues and a deeper understanding of police performance than presented to date.

During the interview stage of our research, any interviewee referencing police performance expressed appreciation for a job well done. Police were lauded for their community engagement, and for doing what needed to be done to restore peace to the streets of Sydney. This is the record and account we believe should endure.

In our view, NSW Police continuing to leave on the record the Strike Force Neil Report as the only official account of policing performance at Cronulla, is unacceptable. An independent assessment even at this late hour would go a long way to 'setting the record straight'.

Recognising those who matter

We have also discussed at length the treatment of both Sergeant Craig Campbell and Superintendent John Richardson. It should not have been so.

How is it sustainable, that not a single individual Commissioner's commendation was meted out to the scores of policing heroes of Cronulla and beyond. The current NSW Police Commissioner could set this right with a stroke of the pen but will probably choose to do nothing. At least the lead hero, Craig Campbell, ought to be given the award, which was recommended to him, before someone in Police HQ intervened and reneged on giving it. Having the written evidence of this recommendation being deleted from official police records, certainly raises legitimate questions regarding the conduct of NSW Police. At least the now Mr Campbell is entitled to an official response in respect of these questionable dealings in NSW Police administrative affairs.

Recommendations

Our recommendations for action are summarised in the table below:

Number	Subject	Commentary	Recommendation
1	The report	A broader transparent inquiry of police performance during the Cronulla riots needs to be undertaken.	That NSW Police take action to ensure the Strike Force Neil Report of October 2006 does not continue as the last and official word on police performance during the 'Cronulla Riots'. NSW Police to conduct interviews with senior Operation Seta police concerning their perspectives on the 'findings' and publicise the results.
2	Recognition	Commissioner's Commendations ought to flow to Operation Seta police.	That appropriate Commissioner's Commendations be issued to former Sgt Craig Campbell, former Supt John Richardson and others as per original recommendations.
3	No-blame inquiries	The Strike Force Neil Terms of Reference and process missed learning opportunities for NSW Police.	Our recommendation was to be that NSW Police publicly commit to a no-blame internal inquiry process of learning after any major policing event. Pleasingly, we are informed such policy has apparently now been put in place.
4	Complaints	Goodwin and his Senior Counsel on his behalf, made a series of complaints to NSW Police that were inappropriately ignored.	That NSW Police carry out a thorough investigation of those complaints in accordance with published and mandated procedures.

Conclusion

Number	Subject	Commentary	Recommendation
5	A new name	It wasn't just at Cronulla; it wasn't really a riot, and it wasn't racially inspired. It is time to update the badging of these events to a more factually based one.	That the 'Cronulla Race Riots' be now referred to as the 'Sydney Breaches of the Peace'. (Being realists, we doubt this moniker will ever take hold).
6	Further research	Like any organisation, having a commitment to continuous evidence-based improvement, ought to be a strong part of NSW Police culture.	That NSW Police conduct its own research, to confirm or contrast with our findings, and to assess how best to draw on the perspectives of key community stakeholders involved in key public events.

Writing this book has been both rewarding and surprising, and in some ways, the undertaking of the interviews was the most enjoyable part of presenting a new, yet far more historically accurate perspective on the 'Cronulla Riots'.

Whilst only twelve people were interviewed, we believe the gamut of roles, positions, and experiences of all twelve, and their confirmation of our views, gives us great confidence in the trustworthiness and credibility of what we have argued and found in the body of this book.

We would like to thank all the interviewees for their time, patience, and contributions to this book. Addtionally, we would like to acknowledge and express appreciation to the many people who gave their time and skill in reading drafts and providing valuable feedback, as we also do in respect of Anthony Cappello of Connor Court Publishing.

We also thank the many stakeholders who so willingly participated in the peacemaking process post-riots. But above all, we want to thank all the police men and women who stepped up and delivered peace and security to the people of Sydney all those years ago. We thank them for their service.

ABOUT THE AUTHORS

Mark Goodwin

Mark grew up in Sutherland Shire and spent much of his life as a teenager on Cronulla Beach. Detective novels and the imagination they fuelled of living out some of the characters of law enforcement's finest, certainly had an impact on seeking a policing career.

A career as a NSW Police officer spanning three decades until an unexpected early retirement in 2007 was rich, rewarding, challenging and different. From the parade grounds of Redfern Police Academy as a trainee, to the battle for the beach as an Assistant Commissioner of Police, has meant a life of service and commitment to the community.

His twenty years as a detective, first at Bankstown and then within a multitude of major crime squads such as the Drug Squad, Undercover Unit, Armed Hold-Up Squad, Homicide Squad and the Organised Crime Squad, gave him enormous experience in investigating, finding and imprisoning some of Sydney's worst criminals.

For over a decade he was a Hostage Negotiator regularly called upon, at any hour of the day or night, to assist in the resolution of armed offender situations, sieges or suicide interventions. But it was his experience as Crime Manager at Bankstown that brought him directly into contact with serious and violent law breakers from the local Lebanese Muslim community, with police stations being shot at, gang rapes, violent confrontations with police and shootings between rival drug gangs. This experience would directly assist him in commanding the planning and delivering of the huge police response to the revenge attacks in Mid December 2005.

As an Assistant Commissioner of Police, Mark initially oversaw all NSW Police Covert Units and Operations as well as the Water Police, Air Wing and Traffic Services. His performance in this demanding role led to him being appointed Asst. Commissioner commanding over 2,500 front line police in the 'Central Metropolitan Region' of Sydney. Additionally this involved the planning, resourcing and delivering of police operations to all CBD major public events. This experience was also enormously beneficial in planning for the 'Cronulla Riots' and in leading police to quickly restore peace and order back to the streets of Sydney.

Throughout his long career he was given incredible support by his wife Melissa and his three sons; Ryan, Brad and Dylan, the latter two of whom are now serving NSW Police officers, a fitting bookend to where it all began at the Redfern Police Academy all those years ago.

Carl Scully

Carl grew up in Chatswood and attended local schools, before completing an arts/law degree (Hons) at Macquarie University and starting work as a solicitor in Fairfield in March 1983. A plan to seek pre-selection for the federal seat of Prospect, instead became one of seeking a career in state politics after Wran government minister Janice Crosio, shifted to Canberra, leaving Carl with a clear run into politics.

On the 2nd of December 1989, he was preselected as the ALP candidate for the state seat of Smithfield and would serve as its MP from June 1990 until March 2007. A backbencher in opposition from 1990 until April 1995, he was commissioned on his 38th birthday, as a minister in the new Carr Labor Government and would go on to serve nearly twelve years in the New South Wales cabinet in a range of portfolios.

Perhaps the most challenging were roads, transport and police. Building a number of Sydney's motorways, delivering transport for the Sydney Olympics, and oversighting the laudably successful restoration of peace to the streets of Sydney as Police minister, are some of his more rewarding memories of a long period of public service.

Throughout a long and successful career of serving the community, Carl was strongly supported by his wife, Dr Ann Leaf and their two children, James and Sarah, both of whom, completed their own law degrees at UTS Sydney.

www.ingramcontent.com/pod-product-compliance
Lightning Source LLC
Chambersburg PA
CBHW052056300426
44117CB00013B/2147